THE NATURE
OF THE PSYCHE
Its Human Expression

BOOKS BY JANE ROBERTS

HOW TO DEVELOP YOUR ESP POWER (1966)

THE SETH MATERIAL (1970)

SETH SPEAKS: The Eternal Validity of the Soul (1972)

THE EDUCATION OF OVERSOUL SEVEN (1973)

THE NATURE OF PERSONAL REALITY: A Seth Book (1974)

ADVENTURES IN CONSCIOUSNESS: An Introduction to Aspect Psychology (1975)

DIALOGUES OF THE SOUL AND MORTAL SELF IN TIME (1975)

PSYCHIC POLITICS: An Aspect Psychology Book (1976)

THE "UNKNOWN" REALITY: A Seth Book (*In 2 Volumes*, 1977/1979)

THE WORLD VIEW OF PAUL CÉZANNE: A Psychic Interpretation (1977)

THE AFTERDEATH JOURNAL OF AN AMERICAN PHILOSOPHER: The World View of William James (1978)

THE FURTHER EDUCATION OF OVERSOUL SEVEN (1979)

EMIR'S EDUCATION IN THE PROPER USE OF MAGICAL POWERS (1979)

THE NATURE OF THE PSYCHE: Its Human Expression (*A Seth Book*, 1979)

THE NATURE OF THE PSYCHE

Its Human Expression

A Seth Book by
Jane Roberts

Prentice-Hall, Inc., Englewood Cliffs, New Jersey

The Nature of the Psyche: Its Human Expression
by Jane Roberts
Copyright © 1979 by Jane Roberts

Printed in the United States of America
Prentice-Hall International, Inc., London/Prentice-Hall of Australia, Pty. Ltd., Sydney/
Prentice-Hall of Canada, Ltd., Toronto/Prentice-Hall of India Private Ltd., New Delhi/
Prentice-Hall of Japan, Inc., Tokyo/Prentice-Hall of Southeast Asia Pte. Ltd., Singapore/
Whitehall Books Limited, Wellington, New Zealand
10 9 8 7 6 5 4

Library of Congress Cataloging in Publication Data
Roberts, Jane.
    The nature of the psyche, its human expression.
    Includes index.
    1. Psychology.   2. Self-actualization
(Psychology)   I. Seth.   II. Title.
BF121.R59   158   79-1084
ISBN 0-13-610469-X

TO TAM MOSSMAN

Contents

THE NATURE
OF THE PSYCHE
Its Human Expression

Introduction
by Jane Roberts

As I write this Introduction, I've already forgotten those many anonymous nights during which Seth, my trance personality, dictated this book. Only the session notes taken by my husband, Robert Butts, tell me what particular daily events we were engaged in during the time of the book's production. One thing is certain: On session nights I went into trance and, as Seth, dictated these chapters. The triumphs and defeats of any given day have more or less vanished, but those nightly hours are somehow contained in these pages, and to that extent they endure.

Is Seth actually *my* trance personality, though—a native of timeless psychological realms, who sends his messages to our time-tinted world? Or am I *Seth's* trance personality, living in space and time, nearly forgetful of my heritage? Perhaps I'll never really know. My continuing experiences, however, show me that Seth's personality is stamped upon the sessions and his writings, and perhaps also upon my own consciousness, in unique ways.

Unless I "turn into Seth," go the whole way, alter my very psychological alignment—unless Seth smiles and speaks—there is no Seth material. So although only two people are in our living room on session nights, it's also quite fair to say that we aren't alone.

I know very well that there were evenings when I "should" have held our regular Seth session, but didn't, for reasons also forgotten. Perhaps I didn't feel up to par, or sat at my desk, involved in my own writing. Perhaps an unbidden guest dropped by, or holidays intruded. Actually, I was quite concerned with the quick passage of time, and the pressure to prepare manuscripts for publication. During the period that Seth was dictating this book, Rob was typing the two volumes of Seth's previous work, *The "Unknown" Reality,* and adding innumerable notes that correlated Seth's material with that of his earlier books. I knew that on session nights, Rob "lost" his work time on that project, and he still had to type up the latest book session on the following day, while all I had to do was . . . what? Turn into Seth.

Many correspondents write, commenting on the dramatic element of the sessions, and surely the entire affair *is* a richly evocative psychological drama. Most people, however, don't realize the time or work required to keep up with Seth's seemingly endless creativity: the sessions to be typed, the various stages of manuscript preparation, or the simple persistence necessary, so that the sessions continue despite life's normal distractions.

Rob typed Seth's other books, *Seth Speaks: The Eternal Validity of the Soul, The Nature of Personal Reality,* and the two volumes of *The "Unknown" Reality,* added his own notes, and did almost all the work of preparing them for publication. He was still working on *The "Unknown" Reality* when Seth finished this present book. Then almost immediately Seth began another, *The Individual and the Nature of Mass Events.*

I'd been producing my own books during this time, and getting them ready for publication, so surely Seth wasn't taking up any creative slack of my own. Still, I stared at *Psyche* when Seth finished it, wishing that *he* could type, too! I thought back to all of those unremembered trance hours, looking at them from a different standpoint—and almost startled by a simple thought that just hadn't occurred to me in quite that way before: Those trance hours were *productive.* They yielded results in the world of time. That trance consciousness, by whatever name, knew what it was doing. And I wondered: What must I look like to Rob as I leaned forward as Seth, smiling, (*my* glasses off, Seth's eyes darker than mine), joking as Seth, gesturing, waiting while Rob got me (Jane), a beer? I'm sure there is a kind of trance memory, but my ordinary memory records very little of those trance hours.

Yet I can't remember offhand what happened in my normal daily life during those past days, either. So "real" time and trance time have each vanished: And this week I'll go into trance, and again Seth will dictate part of another book that Rob will be typing up for publication a year or so from now. Then, *this* today will also be part of the past. In our terms.

I say: "In our terms," because the sessions themselves seem ever-present, despite all I've just said. They seem to contain an energy that comes alive in Seth's words, so that they belong to the future as well as to the past. Those words were all originally spoken, spontaneously and emphatically, though slowly enough for Rob to take notes. They were enunciated in Seth's own peculiarly accented tones; accompanied by gestures in a living performance that I hope the reader will keep in mind.

Piles of trance hours! Here they are. But if I was in trance, was Seth also? He certainly is alert, active, responsive, concerned about people individually and in general, and about the world. And yet I feel that only a portion of his consciousness is here during sessions—the part expressed through me—so that whatever the nature of Seth's native experience, his performance in our world only hints of a psychological complexity quite beyond our present understanding.

In *Psyche,* Seth addresses himself to the matter of human sexuality for the first time in his published works, discussing it as it relates to the private and mass psyche, and connecting sexuality with its spiritual and biological sources.

As most of our readers know, Seth began calling me Ruburt, and my husband, Rob, Joseph, early in the sessions. He explained that these were our entity names, and I was half amused to have a male one, and to find Seth referring to me as "he" or "him." When I had classes, Seth gave many students their entity names also, and there was much lively discussion over the names' sexual designations.

Now we discover that such references were tailored to our own rather limited ideas of the qualities assigned to the sexes, for in *Psyche* Seth makes it clear that the psyche is not male or female, "but a bank from which sexual affiliations are drawn." He stresses the bisexual nature of humanity and the importance of bisexuality, both spiritually and biologically.

But Seth's bisexuality is a far vaster concept than the ones usually suggested by that term, and he sees it as a basic source from which our sexual definitions arise. What are those definitions? How many are basic, and how many learned? It is to such questions that Seth addresses himself. More: He ties in his discussion of sexuality with the birth of languages and the nature of "the hidden God."

The psyche is not only the repository for sexual affiliation, however, but contains hidden abilities and characteristics which are then triggered into activity by exterior stimuli. In Chapter 3 of *Psyche* Seth says: "Certainly mathematical formulas are not imprinted in the brain, yet they are inherent in the structure of the brain, and implied within its existence."

According to Seth, our own desires, focuses, and intents dictate what inner information we draw from the endless fields available; for he sees all knowledge existing at once, not as dry data or records, but enlivened by the consciousness that perceives it. The minds of the past and future are open to us, or at least their contents are, not in a parasitic relationship but in a lively give-and-take, in which knowledge from each time period enriches every other historical era. Seth gives this pooling of knowledge both a spiritual and biological reality.

The implications of such statements for education are astonishing: Besides teaching rote information, our schools and universities should acquaint us with as many fields as possible; for these act as exterior triggers, bringing forth natural inner knowledge, sparking skills which are waiting for activation by suitable stimuli in the exterior world.

While Seth dictated this book, devoted to the potentials of the psyche and its reception of inner information, my own experiences—as usual—seemed to serve as object lessons backing up his thesis. Seth had barely begun *Psyche,* for instance, when I suddenly became the psychic recipient of a book on art philosophy and techniques. It purported to come from the "world view" of Paul Cézanne, the famous French artist who died at the start of this century.

Seth began discussing world views in his *"Unknown" Reality.* Simply put, a world view is a living psychological picture of an individual life, with its knowledge and experience, which remains responsive and viable long after the physical life itself is over. So, the material I received didn't come from Paul Cézanne per se, but from his world view.

Actually, while getting the book, I felt like a secretary taking mental dictation. But what dictation! For this manuscript not only presented a fascinating picture of a genius at work, but gave specialized knowledge of a field—art—in which I am at best an amateur. Seth himself did the Introduction, first dictating his own material on *Psyche,* then switching over to the Cézanne Introduction during the same sessions.

That book, *The World View of Paul Cézanne,* was published by Prentice-Hall in 1977. No sooner had I finished it, than another, similar experience happened, just as Seth was completing *Psyche. The Afterdeath Journal of an American Philosopher: The World View of William James* came the same way, like mental dictation; only where the Cézanne world view had specialized in art, the James world view was more comprehensive. It commented in depth upon our world since James's death, and covered American history as it was related to spiritualism, psychology, and democracy.

According to Seth any of us can tune in to such "extra" information, but we would receive it in accordance with our own desires and intents. My own interest in art and Rob's appreciation of Cézanne's works helped trigger the Cézanne book, for example; and my own curiosity about William James and Rob's appreciation of *his* work helped bring about the James manuscript.

Seth maintains that inner information often comes into our minds, though it is sifted through our individual psyches and tinted by our own lives so that frequently we never recognize its source. Sometimes this happens in dreams or as inspiration: Inventors, for example, might be receiving a given idea from the future, or an archeologist might make a discovery as the result of receiving information from the past.

Seth maintains that our inner knowledge usually merges so smoothly with our present concerns that we seldom recognize its source, yet it provides the individual and the species with a reliable, constant stream of information through a psychological lifeline to which we are each connected.

He discusses in depth the experience of early man and the different organizations of perception that prevailed, and stresses that the species has always had access to "inner data" so that its source of knowledge was never exclusively dependent upon exterior circumstances. According to Seth, it is from this interior body of knowledge that our systemized, objective, information-storing social processes emerge.

It follows, then, that precognition would be involved in evolutionary alterations, so that the various species would prepare themselves in the present to take on those changes that would be necessary in the future.

And in all of this, as always, Seth stresses probabilities as playing a vital role in the development of the individual and the species, and as representing the basis for free will. He sees the psyche experimenting privately with probable actions in the dream state, and envisions humanity's mass dreams as providing an inner vehicle by which man chooses global events. The psyche *is* private, yet all in all, each psyche contains access to the public psyche.

As Seth makes clear, however, this book is not a dry treatise about *"the* psyche," but is constructed in such a way that it will put each reader in more direct contact with his or her individual psyche. It includes many exercises to acquaint each person with that deeper portion of the self, and invites the reader to search into his or her ideas and experiences on many levels.

Distorted beliefs about sexuality can hold back psychic or spiritual progress, for example, and Seth discusses such issues thoroughly. The questions of lesbianism and homosexuality are also considered, along with their private and social effects.

We were most eager to get this particular material to the public, since many correspondents write requesting Seth's views on sexuality. This desire, coupled with Seth's seemingly endless creativity, led us to a decision: From now, the Seth books will carry far fewer notes. In the two volumes of *The "Unknown" Reality*, Rob tried to correlate Seth's views on various subjects, tracing them backward to his earlier books (and often to unpublished material), showing the context in which the books were written. Now we will include usual session notes, but the reader will have to keep track of the development of the theories or correlate them with previous Seth books at his or her leisure.

At this writing, Seth is nearly halfway through *The Individual and the Nature of Mass Events*, which will show where and how private beliefs become public events. I've finished for publication *Emir's Education in the Proper Use of Magical Powers* (the entire first chapter came in a dream), and *The Further Education of Oversoul Seven*. All of this, Seth's books and my own, surely gives evidence of the psyche's vast creativity, and of its abilities to perceive and use information that comes from the inner, as well as from the exterior environment.

Books are my speciality. For others, this creativity may show itself in family relationships and emotional comprehensions, in the other arts, in the sciences, in sports, or simply in lifting the quality of living to a newer, richer level.

Chapter 1
The Environment
of the Psyche

SESSION 752, JULY 28, 1975
9:25 P.M. MONDAY

(At supper time this evening I told Jane that tonight she was going to start dictating a new book for Seth, the "energy personality essence" for whom she speaks while she's in trance—and that she was going to do the notes also. I'd record the "sessions," adding times, dates, and the barest sort of other material, so that Jane could build up her own notes around those ingredients. My idea here was that as soon as I had a session typed from my original "shorthand," Jane could add whatever she wanted to about her trance states, feelings, or ideas, while the session circumstances were still fresh in her mind.

(I told her that I didn't care if the book was short, medium, or long— or whether it took six months to produce, or a year, or five years: If she held one or two sessions a week, or one a month, *it would still give her a book in the works, and she would have that comforting knowledge. I said that if she preferred no notes, that was all right with me too.*

(Seth finished dictating his last book, The "Unknown" Reality: A Seth Book, *three months ago, in the 744th session for April 23. Jane finally*

admitted earlier today that she's had only seven sessions since then be-
cause she didn't want to make too much extra work for me while I'm busy
with the complicated notes for that book. As soon as I realized why she
was holding off, I decided to put her back to work on the Seth material, even
though she hasn't yet finished her own Psychic Politics.

(Jane said very little when I sprang the idea of a new book on her
during the supper hour. "You took me by surprise," she said at 9:10, as we
sat for the session. "You called my bluff or something. . . ."

("Just the way I planned it," I said.

("You'll have to be lenient with me. If I'm going to do the notes, there
won't be many. And I don't know about a new book tonight. At least, I
don't have an idea in my head."

("You don't need any. Which would you rather do?" I joked. "Start
a new book or give birth to a child?"

("This," she said promptly, meaning the session. "But you have nine
months to get used to having a baby. And I'm not ready for either of the books
Seth has mentioned doing—the Christ book, or the one he talked about last
month, on cultural reality. So what could a new one possibly be about?"

(I laughed as I watched her procrastinate. We talked for a few
moments, then Jane said, somewhat wonderingly: "I think I've got the title.
It's The Nature of the Psyche, *colon:* Its Human Expression. *I'm not*
sure, but I think that's it. . . ."

(So it seemed that we were about to get underway with another
excellent production from Seth, with Jane's considerable—indeed vital—
help. I understood that she might be a little concerned about his starting a new
book on such short notice; but on the other hand, I had no doubt at all that
Seth—and Jane—could do it. And I wanted her to be creatively involved
with a continuing project. I thought it could underlie her daily life like a
foundation.

("As soon as I get it, we'll start," Jane said, and we sat waiting and
sipping red wine. It was 9:23. She lit a cigarette. We fell silent.

("Now I'm getting it," she said. "It's just taking me a few minutes to
put it all together. . . ." Then, beginning at 9:25, and with many pauses:)

Now—

("Good evening, Seth.")

—no Preface. Chapter One: You come into the condition
you call life, and pass out of it. In between you encounter a lifetime. Suspended—or so it certainly seems—between birth and
death, you wonder at the nature of your own being. You search
your experience and study official histories of the past, hoping to
find there clues as to the nature of your own reality.

Your life seems synonymous with your consciousness.

Therefore it appears that your knowledge of yourself grows gradually, as your self-consciousness develops from your birth. It appears, furthermore, that your consciousness will meet a death beyond which your self-consciousness will not survive. You may think longingly and with an almost hopeful nostalgia of the religion of your childhood, and remember a system of belief that ensured you of immortality. Yet most of you, my readers, yearn for some private and intimate assurances, and seek for some inner certainty that your own individuality is not curtly dismissed at death.

(9:35.) Each person knows intuitively that his or her own experiences somehow matter, and that there is a meaning, however obscured, that connects the individual with a greater creative pattern. Each person senses now and then a private purpose, and yet many are filled with frustration because that inner goal is not consciously known or clearly apprehended.

(Pause.) When you were a child you knew you were growing toward an adulthood. You were sustained by the belief in projected abilities—that is, you took it for granted that you were in the process of learning and growing. No matter what happened to you, you lived in a kind of rarefied psychic air, in which your being was charged and glowing. You knew you were in a state of becoming. The world, in those terms, is also in a state of becoming.

In private life and on the world stage, action is occurring all the time. It is easy to look at yourselves or at the world, comma, to see yourself and become so hypnotized by your present state that all change or growth seems impossible, or to see the world in the same manner.

You do not remember your birth, as a rule. Certainly it seems that you do not remember the birth of the world. You had a history, however, before your birth—even as it seems to you that the world had a history before you were born.

(Pause at 9:49.) The sciences still keep secrets from each other. The physical sciences pretend that the centuries exist one after the other, while the physicists realize that time is not only relative to the perceiver, but that all events are simultaneous. The archeologists merrily continue to date the remains of "past" civilizations, never asking themselves what the past means—or saying: "This is the past relative (underlined) to my point of perception."

Astronomers speak of outer space and of galaxies that would dwarf your own. In the world that you recognize there are also wars and rumors of wars, prophets of destruction. Yet in spite of all, the private man or the private woman, unknown, anonymous to the world at large, stubbornly feels within a rousing, determined affirmation that says: "I am important. I have a purpose, even though I do not understand what it is. My life that seems so insignificant and inefficient, is nevertheless of prime importance in some way that I do not recognize." Period.

Though caught up in a life of seeming frustration, obsessed with family problems, uneasy in sickness, defeated it seems for all practical purposes, some portion of each individual rouses against all disasters, all discouragements, and now and then at least glimpses a sense of enduring validity that cannot be denied. It is to that knowing portion of each individual that I address myself. Period.

(10:01. Emphatically:) I am not, on the one hand, an easy author to deal with, because I speak from a different level of consciousness than the one with which you are familiar. On the other hand, my voice is as natural as oak leaves blowing in the wind, for I speak from a level of awareness that is as native to your psyche as now the seasons seem to be to your soul.

I am writing this book through a personality known as Jane Roberts. That is the name given her at her birth. She shares with you the triumphs and travails of physical existence. *(A one-minute pause.)* Like you, she is presented with a life that seems to begin at her birth, and that is suspended from that point of emergence until the moment of death's departure. She has asked the same questions that you ask in your quiet moments.

Her questions were asked with such a vehemence, however, that she broke through the barriers that most of you erect, and so began a journey that is undertaken for herself and for you also— for each of your experiences, however minute or seemingly insignificant, becomes part of the knowledge of your species. Where did you come from and where are you going? What are you? What is the nature of the psyche?

I can only write a portion of this book. You must complete it. For "The Psyche" is meaningless except as it relates to the individual psyche. I speak to you from levels of yourself that you have forgotten, and yet not forgotten. I speak to you through the printed page, and yet my words will rearouse within you the voices that spoke to you in your childhood, and before your birth.

This will not be a dry treatise, studiously informing you about some hypothetical structure called the psyche, but will instead evoke from the depths of your being experiences that you

have forgotten, and bring together from the vast reaches of time
and space the miraculous identity that is yourself.

Take your break.

*(10:17. "Now I've forgotten even the title," Jane said as soon as she
came out of an excellent trance, or dissociated state.*

("Congratulations, hon," I said.

*(Jane laughed. "You tell me to do something and I do it. Now I've got
to go to the john, though—and besides that, I feel like I could go to bed and
sleep for hours. . . ."*

*("Okay, go ahead," I said, bantering. "Cop out if you want to." I
reminded her of the full title of* Psyche, *and made a few suggestions as to how
she could proceed with her own written comments for the book, stressing that
she could handle them any way she liked. I just didn't have time for more
than the barest of session notes. However, I confessed to Jane, I couldn't say
that I really expected her to produce both the book itself, through Seth, and
then do all the work involved in writing the notes too—yet as it turned out, to
some extent she* did *help me annotate this work.*

*(Finally: "I'm just waiting," Jane said. "I feel more stuff coming
now. . . ." Resume at a faster rate at 10:41.)*

Now: The earth has a structure. In those terms (underlined),
so does the psyche. You live in one particular area on the face of
your planet, and you can only see so much of it at any given
time—yet you take it for granted that the ocean exists even when
you cannot feel its spray, or see the tides.

And even if you live in a desert, you take it on faith that
there are indeed great cultivated fields and torrents of rain. It is
true that some of your faith is based on knowledge. Others have
traveled where you have not, and television provides you with
images. Despite this, however, your senses present you with only a
picture of your immediate environment, unless they are cultivated
in certain particular manners that are relatively unusual.

You take it for granted that the earth has a history. In those
terms, your own psyche has a history also. You have taught yourselves to look outward into physical reality, but the inward validity
of your being cannot be found there—only its effects. You can
turn on television and see a drama, but the inward mobility and
experience of your psyche is mysteriously enfolded within all of
those exterior gestures that allow you to turn on the television
switch to begin with, and to make sense of the images presented.
So the motion of your own psyche usually escapes you.

Where is the television drama before it appears on your channel—and where does it go afterwards? How can it exist one moment and be finished the next, and yet be replayed when the conditions are correct? If you understood the mechanics, you would know that the program obviously does not go anywhere. It simply is, while the proper conditions activate it for your attention. In the same way, you are alive whether or not you are playing on an earth "program." You are, whether you are in time or out of it.

Hopefully in this book we will put you in touch with your own being as it exists outside of the context in which you are used to viewing it.

(10:55. A one-minute pause.) As you dwell in one particular city or town or village, you presently "live" in one small area of the psyche's inner planet. You identify that area as your home, as your "I." Mankind has learned to explore the physical environment, but has barely begun the greater inner journeys that will be embarked upon as the inner lands of the psyche are joyously and bravely explored. In those terms, there is a land of the psyche. However, this virgin territory is the heritage of each individual, and no domain is quite like any other. Yet there is indeed an inner commerce that occurs, and as the exterior continents rise from the inner structure of the earth, so the lands of the psyche emerge from an even greater invisible source.

(Louder:) That is the end of dictation for the evening.

("Okay.")

(At 11:14 Seth delivered a message to a scientist who had written us, finally ending the session at 11:43 P.M.)

SESSION 753, AUGUST 4, 1975
9:21 P.M. MONDAY

(With many pauses to start:)
Good evening.

("Good evening, Seth.")

Now: Dictation *(on The Nature of the Psyche: Its Human Expression):* As the earth is composed of many environments, so is the psyche. As there are different continents, islands, mountains, seas, and peninsulas, so the psyche takes various shapes. If you live in one country, you often consider natives in other areas of the world as foreigners, while of course they see you in the same light. In those terms, the psyche contains many other levels of reality. From your point of view these might appear alien, and yet they are as much a part of your psyche as your motherland is a portion of the earth.

Different countries follow different kinds of constitutions, and even within any geographical area there may be various local laws followed by the populace. For example, if you are driving a car you may discover to your chagrin that the local speed limit in one small town is miles slower than in another. In the same manner, different portions of the psyche exist with their own local "laws," their different kinds of "government." They each possess their own characteristic geography.

If you are traveling around the world, you have to make frequent time adjustments. When you travel through the psyche, you will also discover that your own time is automatically squeezed out of shape. If for a moment you try to imagine that you were able to carry your own time with you on such a journey, all packaged neatly in a wristwatch, then you would be quite amazed at what would happen.

(9:34.) As you approached the boundaries of certain psychic lands, the wristwatch would run backwards. As you entered other kingdoms of the psyche your watch would go faster or slower. Now, if time suddenly ran backward you would notice it. If it ran faster or slower enough, you would also notice the differences. If time ran backward very slowly, and according to the conditions, you might not be aware of the difference, because it would take so much "time" to get from the present moment to the one "before" it that you might be struck, instead, simply with the feeling that something was familiar, as if it had happened before.

In other lands of the psyche, however, even stranger events might occur. The watch itself might change shape, or turn heavy as a rock, or as light as a gas, so that you could not read the time at all. Or the hands might never move. Different portions of the psyche are familiar with all of these mentioned occurrences—because the psyche straddles any of the local laws that you recognize as "official," and has within itself the capacity to deal with an infinite number of reality-hyphen-experiences.

Now *(elaborately and quietly):* Obviously your physical body has capacities that few of you use to full advantage. But beyond this, the species itself possesses the possibilities for adaptations that allow it to exist and persist in the physical environment under drastically varying circumstances. Hidden within the corporal biological structure there are latent specializations that would allow the species to continue, and that take into consideration any of the planetary changes that might occur for whatever reasons.

The psyche, however, while being earth-tuned in your experience, also has many other systems of reality "to contend with." Each psyche, then, contains within it the potentials, abilities, and powers that are possible, or capable of actualization under any conditions.

(Pause at 9:51.) The psyche, your psyche, can record and experience time backward, forward, dash—or <u>sideways</u> through systems of alternate presents *(intently)*—or it can maintain its own integrity in a no-time environment. The psyche is the creator of time complexes. Theoretically, the most fleeting moment of your day can be prolonged endlessly. This would not be a static elongation, however, but a vivid delving into that moment, from which <u>all</u> time as you think of it, past and future <u>and</u> all its probabilities, might emerge.

If you are reading this book, you have already become weary with official concepts. You have already begun to sense those greater dimensions of your being. You are ready to step aside from all conventionalized doctrines, and to some extent or another you are impatient to examine and experience the natural flowing nature that is your birthright. That birthright has long been clothed in symbols and mythologies.

Consciousness forms symbols. It is not the other way around. Symbols are great exuberant playthings. You can build with them as you can with children's blocks. You can learn from them, as once you piled alphabet blocks together in a stack at school. Symbols are as natural to your minds as trees are to the earth. There is a difference, however, between a story told to children about forests, and a real child in a real woods. Both the story and the woods are "real." But <u>in your terms</u> the child entering the real woods becomes involved in its life cycle, treads upon leaves that fell yesterday, rests beneath trees far older than his or her memory, and looks up at night to see a moon that will soon disappear. Looking at an illustration of the woods may give a child some excellent imaginative experiences, but they will be of a different kind, and the child knows the difference.

(10:09.) If you mistake the symbols for the reality, however, you will program your experience, and you will insist that each forest look like the pictures in your book. In other words, you will expect your own experiences with various portions of your psyche to be more or less the same. You will take your local laws with you, and you will try to tell psychic time with a wristwatch.

(Long pause, one of many.) We will have to use some of your terms, however, particularly in the beginning. Other terms with which you are familiar, we will squeeze out of all recognition. The reality of your own being cannot be defined by anyone but you, and then your own definition must be understood as a reference point at best. The psychologist, the priest, the physicist, the philosopher or the guru, can explain your own psyche to you only insofar as those specialists can forget that they are specialists, and deal directly with the private psyche from which all specializations come.

Take your break.

(10:21. Jane's trance had lasted for just one hour. "He's really going to town—I can tell," she said. I suggested that she devote the rest of the session to some personal questions she wanted to ask Seth. She agreed, so this break marked the end of book dictation for the evening.)

SESSION 755,   SEPTEMBER 8, 1975
8:59 P.M. MONDAY

(Because of the press of other matters following the 753rd session— my work doing the notes for Seth's "Unknown" Reality, Jane's involvement in writing a new introduction for one of her own books that's coming out in a new paperback edition, and a stream of unexpected visitors—we didn't hold any sessions for several weeks. [The paperback in question is The Coming of Seth, *originally published in hardcover as* How to Develop Your ESP Power.]*

(Then in the 754th session, on August 25, Seth gave an excellent dissertation on what he called "the stamp of identity"—explaining how the individual psychically marks certain exterior aspects of reality and "makes them his or her own," in tune with personal inner symbols. Later in the session Jane felt that Seth was taking her on a guided tour of Jerusalem, way back in the first century A.D. None of this consisted of book work, though, so the session remains in our files along with other material that we hope to publish one day.

(An hour before she went into trance this evening, Jane told me that she could get several channels from Seth, each one concerning a different

subject, and that "we'd better see" which one came through tonight. Then just before the session started, she said it would concern dictation on Seth's new book.)

Now: Good evening.

("Good evening, Seth.")

We will begin with dictation.

When I use the term "psyche," many of you will immediately wonder about my definition.

Any word, simply by being thought, written or spoken, immediately implies a specification. In your daily reality it is very handy to distinguish one thing from another by giving each item a name. When you are dealing with subjective experience, however, definitions can often serve to limit rather than express a given experience. Obviously the psyche is not a thing. It does not have a beginning or ending. It cannot be seen or touched in normal terms. It is useless, therefore, to attempt any description of it through usual vocabulary, for your language primarily allows you to identify physical rather than nonphysical experience.

I am not saying that words cannot be used to <u>describe</u> the psyche, but they cannot define it. It is futile to question: "What is the difference between my psyche and my soul, my entity and my greater being?" for all of these are terms used in an effort to express the greater portions of your own experience that you sense within yourself. Your use of language may make you impatient for definitions, however. Hopefully this book will allow you some intimate awareness, some definite experience, that will acquaint you with the nature of your own psyche, and then you will see that its reality escapes all definitions, defies all categorizing, and shoves aside with exuberant creativity all attempts to wrap it up in a neat package.

When you begin a physical journey, you feel yourself distinct from the land through which you travel. No matter how far you journey—on a motorcycle, in a car or plane, or on foot—*(gesturing to me as Seth, Jane then changed the sentence:)* by bicycle or camel, or truck or vessel, still you are the wanderer, and the land or ocean or desert is the environment through which you roam. When you begin your travels into your own psyche, however, everything changes. You are still the wanderer, the journeyman or journeywoman—but you are <u>also</u> the vehicle and the environment. You form the roads, your method of travel, the hills or mountains or oceans, as well as the hills, farms, and villages of the self, or of the psyche, as you go along.

(9:15.) When in colonial times men and women traveled westward across the continent of North America, many of them took it on faith that the land did indeed continue beyond—for example—towering mountains. When you travel as pioneers through your own reality, you create each blade of grass, each inch of land, each sunset and sunrise, each oasis, friendly cabin or enemy encounter as you go along.

Now if you are looking for simple definitions to explain the psyche, I will be of no help. If you want to experience the splendid creativity of your own being, however, then I will use methods that will arouse your greatest adventuresomeness, your boldest faith in yourself, and I will paint pictures of your psyche that will lead you to experience even its broadest reaches, if you so desire. The psyche, then, is not a known land. It is not simply an alien land, to which or through which you can travel. It is not a completed or nearly complete subjective universe already there for you to explore. It is, instead, an ever-forming state of being, in which your present sense of existence resides. You create it and it creates you.

(Long pause.) It creates in physical terms that you recognize. On the other hand, you create physical time for your psyche, for without you there would be no experience of the seasons, their coming and their passing.

There would be no experience of what Ruburt *(Seth's "entity" name for Jane)* calls "the dear privacy of the moment," so if one portion of your being wants to rise above the solitary march of the moments, other parts of your psyche rush, delighted, into that particular time-focus that is your own. As you now desire to understand the timeless, infinite dimensions of your own greater existence, so "even now" multitudinous elements of that non-earthly identity just as eagerly explore the dimensions of earth-being and creaturehood.

(9:30.) Earlier I mentioned some odd effects that might occur if you tried to take your watch or other timepiece into other levels of reality. Now, when you try to interpret your selfhood in other kinds of existence, the same surprises or distortions or alterations can seem to occur. When you attempt to understand your psyche, and define it in terms of time, then it seems that the idea of reincarnation makes sense. You think: "Of course. My psyche lives many lives physically, one after the other. If my present experience is dictated by that in my childhood, then surely my current life is a result of earlier ones." And so you try to define

the psyche in terms of time, and in so doing you limit your understanding and even your experience of it.

(Long pause.) Let us try another analogy: You are an artist in the throes of inspiration. There is before you a canvas, and you are working in all areas of it at once. In your terms each part of the canvas could be a time period—say, a given century. You are trying to keep some kind of overall balance and purpose in mind, so when you make one brushstroke in any particular portion of this canvas, all the relationships within the entire area can change. No brushstroke is ever really wiped out, however, in this mysterious canvas of our analogy, but remains, further altering all the relationships at its particular level.

These magical brushstrokes, however, are not simple representations on a flat surface, but alive, carrying within themselves all of the artist's intent, but focused through the characteristics of each individual stroke.

If the artist paints a doorway, all of the sensed perspectives within it open, and add further dimensions of reality. Since this is our analogy, we can stretch it as far as we like—far further than any artist could stretch his canvas *(leaning forward humorously)*. Therefore, there is no need to limit ourselves. The canvas itself can change size and shape as the artist works. The people in the artist's painting are not simple representations either—to stare back at him with forever-fixed glassy eyes, or ostentatious smiles *(again humorously)*, dressed in their best Sunday clothes. Instead, they can confront the artist and talk back. They can turn sideways in the painting and look at their companions, observe their environment, and even look out of the dimensions of the painting itself and question the artist.

Now the psyche in our analogy is both the painting and the artist, for the artist finds that all of the elements within the painting are portions of himself. More, as he looks about, our artist discovers that he is literally surrounded by other paintings that he is also producing. As he looks closer, he discovers that there is a still-greater masterpiece in which he appears as an artist creating the very same paintings that he begins to recognize.

Take your break.

(9:55. Jane was really charged up from the day's events: She'd received the first six copies of her poetry book, Dialogues of the Soul and Mortal Self in Time, *which was just off the press at Prentice-Hall, and during break we discussed that book.*

(Resume at 10:05.)

Our artist then realizes that all of the people he painted are also painting their own pictures, and moving about in their own realities in a way that even he cannot perceive.

In a flash of insight it occurs to him that he also has been painted—that there is another artist behind him from whom his own creativity springs, and he also begins to look out of the frame.

Now: If you are confused, that is fine—for it means that already we have broken through conventional ideas. Anything that I say following this analogy will seem comparatively simple, for by now it must appear at least that you have little hope of discovering your own greater dimensions.

(Pause.) Again, rather than trying to define the psyche, I will try to incite your imagination so that you can leap beyond what you have been told you are, to some kind of direct experience. To some extent this book itself provides its own demonstration. I call Jane Roberts "Ruburt" *(and, hence, "he" and "him")* simply because the name designates another portion of her reality, while she identifies herself as Jane. She writes her own books and carries on as each of you do in life's ordinary context. She has her own unique likes and dislikes, characteristics and abilities; her own time and space slot as each of you do. She is one living portrait of the psyche, independent in her own context, and in the environment as given.

Now I come from another portion of reality's picture, from another dimension of the psyche in which your existence can be observed, as you might look upon a normal painting.

In those terms, I am outside of your "frame" of reference. My perspective cannot be contained in your own painting of reality. I write my books, but because my primary focus is in a reality that "is larger than your own," I cannot appear as myself fully within your reference.

(10:20.) So Ruburt's subjective perspective opens up because of his desire and interest, and discloses my own. He opens up a door in himself that leads to other levels of his being, but a being that cannot be completely expressed in your world. That existence is mine, expressed in my experience at another level of reality, so I must write my books through Ruburt. Doors in the psyche are different from simple openings that lead from one room to another, so my books only show a glimpse of my own existence. You all have such psychological doors, however, that lead into dimensionally greater areas of the psyche, so to some

extent or another I speak for those other aspects of yourselves that
do not appear in your daily context.

Beyond what I recognize as my own existence, there are
others. To some extent I share in their experience—to a far greater
extent, for example, than Ruburt shares in mine.

(10:29.) You had better give him some beer and cigarettes,
and we will continue.

("All right.")

On some relatively few occasions, for example, Ruburt has
been able to contact what he calls "Seth Two." That level of reality,
however, is even further divorced from your own. It represents an
even greater extension of the psyche, in your terms. *(Long pause.)*
There is a much closer relationship, in that I recognize my own
identity as a distinct portion of Seth Two's existence, where
Ruburt feels little correspondence. In a manner of speaking, Seth
Two's reality includes my own, <u>yet I am aware of my contribution</u>
to "his" experience.

In the same way, each of my readers has a connection with
the same level of psychic reality. In greater terms, all of this is
happening at once. Ruburt is contributing and forming a certain
portion of my experience, even as I am contributing to his. Your
identities are not something already completed. Your most minute
action, thought, and dream adds to the reality of your psyche, no
matter how grand or austere the psyche may appear to you when
you think of it as a hypothetical term.

End of dictation.

(10:37. "Okay," I said.)

Rest your fingers a moment, and we will continue.

*(10:39. Seth did continue with personal material for both of us.
Ordinarily he'd have ended the session after that. This evening, however,
Jane felt so much energy that Seth returned for some more book dictation—the
first time a session has worked out that way as far as I can remember.*

(Anyhow, Seth finished his personal material this way:

(11:30.) Now: Since I imagine you are not ready for a
continuation of our first chapter, I will—

("I'm all right for another half hour or so," I said.)

Then take your break.

(11:31. But no break ensued. Seth continued speaking:)

Dictation: Ruburt has specialized in a study of consciousness
and the psyche. Most of my readers are very interested, yet they
have other pressing concerns that prevent them from embarking
upon such an extended study.

You all have physical reality to deal with. This applies equally to Ruburt and Joseph *(Seth's entity name for me.)* Thus far, my books have included Joseph's extended notes. They have set the scene, so to speak. My books have gone beyond those boundaries, however. In your terms, only so much can be done in time. Joseph is even now involved in typing my previous manuscript *(The "Unknown" Reality.)* It was written in such a way that it tied the personal experience of Ruburt and Joseph in with a greater theoretical framework, so that one could not be separated from the other.

In this new book, therefore, I will sometimes provide my own "scene setting." The psyche's production, in other words, has escaped practical, physical bounds, so that from my level of reality I can no longer expect Joseph to do more than record the sessions. I will ask you, my readers, to bear with me then. In my own way, I will try to provide suitable references so that you know what is going on physically in your time, as this book is written.

Largely, the writing of this book occurs in a "no-time, or out-of-time context." Physically, however, Ruburt and Joseph take many hours in its production. They have moved to a new house. Ruburt, as usual, is smoking as I speak. His foot rests upon a coffee table, as he moves back and forth in his rocking chair. It is nearing midnight as I speak *(at 11:42)*. Earlier, a great thunderstorm raged, its reverberations seeming to crack the sky. Now it is quiet, with only the drone of Ruburt's new refrigerator sounding like the deep purr of some mechanical animal.

As you read this book, you are also immersed in such intimate physical experiences. Do not consider them as separated from the greater reality of your being, but as a part of it. You do not exist outside of your psyche's being, but within it. Some of you may have just put children to bed as you read these lines. Some of you may be sitting at a table. Some of you may have just gone to the bathroom. These mundane activities may seem quite divorced from what I am telling you, yet in each simple gesture, and in the most necessary of physical acts, there is the great magical un-knowing elegance in which you reside—and in the most ordinary of your motions, there are clues and hints as to the nature of the psyche and its human expression.

(Loudly and humorously:) End of Chapter One, and end of session.

("Thank you, Seth. Good night. . . .")

Chapter 2
Your Dreaming Psyche Is Awake

(It was 11:50. Jane had been in an excellent trance state. After we talked for a few minutes, she added: "My God, I've got Chapter Two. No, it's too late! I don't have the heading for Chapter One yet, but I've got it for the next one. . . ." She looked bleary, her eyes dark. I told her she appeared to be too tired to continue.

("No, I'm not," she retorted. Her denial was both funny and dogged, for I could see that she was tired. But she went on: "Now let me get a couple of paragraphs on the chapter . . . The heading is: 'Your Dreaming Psyche Is Awake.' " Then Seth came through at once:)

You have hypnotized yourselves so that it seems to you that there are great divisions between your waking and your sleeping experience. Yet each of you will fall sleep tonight, and you will have experiences that you forget only because you have been told that you cannot remember them. Many of the other dimensions of your own reality appear clearly when you are sleeping, however. When you sleep, you forget all definitions that you have placed upon yourself and your own existence through training. In sleep you use images and languages in their pure form.

In the dream state, languages and images are wedded in a way that seems alien only because you have forgotten their great alliance. Initially, language was meant to express and release, not to define and limit. So when you dream, images and language merge often, so that each becomes an expression of the other and each fulfills the other. The inner connections between each are practically used.

When you awaken, you try to squeeze the psyche's language into terms of definition. You imagine that language and images are two different things, so you try to "put them together." In dreams, however, you use the true ancient language of your being.

That will be enough for now. End of session. As Ruburt would say: "Peace and cheers."

("Thank you, Seth. Good night.")

(The session ended at 11:59 P.M.—and once again, Jane was full of energy.

(Jane has decided that she'll let my ordinary session notes—brief as they are—suffice for Psyche, and that she'll add few, if any, of her own. She does plan to write an introduction, though.

(Before Seth finished dictating Chapter Two, Jane got from him mentally the heading for Chapter One, and inserted it into this manuscript.)

SESSION 756, SEPTEMBER 22, 1975
9:17 P.M. MONDAY

(Shortly before the session, Jane told me she thought we'd get material on the new book, as well as some other information we were interested in.

(We've had several guests since the last session was held. I've been busy putting my own notes for Seth's "Unknown" Reality in order, and have also allowed myself some painting time each day. Jane is involved in writing notes of her own—she's had three dream visits to what certainly seemed to be probable realities, and is describing those in her own records.)

Good evening.

("Good evening, Seth.")

Now: We will begin with dictation—the continuation of Chapter Two.

(Pause.) Your "dreaming" psyche seems to be dreaming only because you do not recognize that particular state of awareness as your own. The "dreaming" psyche is actually as awake as you are in your normal waking life. The organization of wakefulness is different, however. You come into dreaming from a different angle, so to speak.

The "off-center" quality sensed in dream activity, comma, the different viewpoints, the perspective alterations, all can add to a chaotic picture when the dream state is viewed from the waking one.

Centuries ago, in your terms, words and images had a closer relationship—now somewhat tarnished—and this older relationship appears in the dream fabric. We will use English here as an example. The great descriptive nature of names, for instance, can give you an indication of the unity of image and word as they appear in your dreams. Once, a man who tailored clothes was named "Tailor." A man who was a robber was called "Robber." If you were the son of a man with a certain name, then "son of" was simply added, so you had "Robberson." Each reader can think of many such examples.

Now, names are not as descriptive. You may have a dream, however, in which you see a tailor's shop. The tailor may be dancing or dying or getting married. Later, in waking life, you may discover that a friend of yours, a Mr. Taylor *(spelled),* has a party, or dies, or gets married, whatever the case may be; yet you might never connect the dream with the later event because you did not understand the way that words and images can be united in your dreams.

(9:32.) Your waking life is the result of the most precise kind of organization, held competently and with amazing clarity. While each person views that reality from a slightly different focus, still it occurs within certain ranges or frequencies. You bring it into clear focus in almost the same way that you adjust your television picture, only in this case not only sound and images are synchronized, but phenomena of far greater complexity. Following this analogy, everyone sees a slightly different picture of reality, and follows his or her own program—yet all of the "sets" are the same.

When you dream, however, you are to some extent experiencing reality from a different "set" entirely. Now, when you try to adjust your dreaming set in the same way that you would the waking one, you end up with static and blurred images. The set itself, however, is quite as effective as the one you use when you are awake, and it has a far greater range. It can bring in many programs. When you watch your ordinary television program, perhaps on a Saturday afternoon, you view the program as an observer. Let me give you an example.

Ruburt and Joseph often watch old *Star Trek* reruns

(humorously) as they eat their evening meal. They sit quite comfortably on their living room couch, with dinner on the coffee
table, surrounded by all of the dear, homey paraphernalia that is
familiar to your society.

As they sit thus comfortably ensconced *(leaning forward with a
smile),* they observe dramas in which planets explode, and other-
world intelligences rise to challenge or to help the dauntless
captain of the good ship *Enterprise* and the fearless "Spock"—but
none of this threatens our friends, Ruburt and Joseph. They drink
their coffee and eat their dessert.

Now: Your normal waking reality can be compared to a
kind of television drama in which you participate directly in all of
the dramas presented. You create them to begin with. You form
your private and joint adventures, and bring them into experience
by using your physical apparatus—your body—in a particular
way, tuned in to a large programming area in which, however,
there are many different stations. In your terms, these stations
come alive. You are the drama that you experience, and all of your
activities seem to revolve about you. You are also the perceiver.

In the dream state, it is as if you have a still-different television set that is, however, connected with your own. Using it, you
can perceive events not only from your own viewpoint, but from
other focuses. Using that set, you can leap from station to station,
so to speak—not simply perceiving, but experiencing what is
happening in other times and places.

(9:51.) Events, then, are organized in a different fashion.
Not only can you experience dramas in which you are intimately
involved, as in waking life, but your range of activities is multiplied
so that you can view events "from outside" your own usual
context. You can look down at a drama on the one hand, for
example, and participate in it as well.

When you are dealing with normal waking reality, you are
operating at one level of the many that are native to your psyche.
When you are dreaming, from your viewpoint you are entering
other levels of reality quite as native to your psyche, but usually
you are still experiencing those events through your current
"waking station" The dreams that you remember are colored or
altered or even censored to a certain extent. There is no inherent
psychological or biological necessity for this. Your ideas and
beliefs, however, about the nature of reality, and sanity, have
resulted in such a schism.

Let us return to our friends, Ruburt and Joseph, watching *Star Trek* as each of you watch your own favorite programs.

Ruburt and Joseph know that *Star Trek* is not "real." Planets can explode on the television screen, and Ruburt will not spill one drop of coffee. The cozy living room is quite safe from the imaginary catastrophes that are occurring just a few feet from the couch. Yet in a way the program reflects certain beliefs of your society in general, and so it is like a specialized mass waking dream—real but not real. For a moment, though, let us change the program to your favorite cops-and-robbers show. A woman is shot down in the street. Now this drama becomes "more real," more immediately probable, less comfortable. So watching such a program, you may feel slightly threatened yourself, yet still largely unconcerned.

Some of my friends may not watch such programs at all, but instead look at wholesome sagas, or religious dramas. A preacher may stand golden-faced, earnest-eyed, extolling the merits of goodness and damning the legions of the devil—and to some of my readers that devil, unseen, never appearing, may nevertheless seem quite real.

You form certain focuses, then, You will blithely ignore certain televised dangers as sheer good adventure, while others may strike you to the heart as "too real." So in your waking and dreaming experiences, you will make the same kind of distinctions. You will be touched or untouched by waking or dreaming events according to the significance you place upon them.

If you do not like a television program, you can switch to another with a mere flick of the wrist. If you do not like your own physical experience, you can also change to another, more beneficial station—but only if you recognize the fact that you are the producer.

(10:15.) In the dream state, many people have learned to escape from a bad dream by waking up, or altering the focus of consciousness. Ruburt and Joseph do not feel threatened, again, by *Star Trek. (Long pause.)* The program does not make them feel less safe. When you are in the middle of a frightening physical experience, however, or caught in the throes of a nightmare, then you wish you knew how to "change the station."

Take your break.

(10:20 to 10:44.)

Dictation, briefly.

You can often get carried away by a television drama, so that for a moment you forget that it is "not real," and in your concentration upon it you can momentarily ignore the greater reality about you.

Sometimes you are deliciously frightened by a horror program, for example. You may feel compelled to see how it comes out, and find yourself unable to go to bed until the horrendous situation is resolved. All the time you know that salvation is nearby: You can always switch off the program. If someone watching a gory midnight special suddenly screams or shouts or leaps up from the chair, how comical this seems, because the action is appropriate not to the "real" situation, but geared instead to a pseudodrama. The yelling and screaming will have absolutely no effect upon the program's actors, and will alter the drama not one whit. The appropriate action would be to turn the station off.

In this case, the frightened perceiver knows full well that the terrible events on the screen will not suddenly explode into the living room. When you become caught in frightening physical events, however, it is equally foolhardy to yell or shout or stamp your feet, because that is not where the action is (smiling). Again, you have only to change your station. But often you become so engrossed in your life situation that you do not realize the inappropriateness of your response.

In this case you are yourself the programmer, and the true action is not where it appears to be—in the exterior events—but instead in the psyche, where you are writing and performing the drama. In the dream state, you are writing and performing many such dramas.

End of dictation.

(10:57. Seth now delivered several pages of material on other subjects for Jane and me. The session finally ended at 11:42 P.M.)

SESSION 758,   OCTOBER 6, 1975
9:14 P.M. MONDAY

(Session 757 was devoted to other matters that Jane and I were interested in.)

Good evening.

("Good evening, Seth.")

(Whispering humorously:) Dictation.

Using an analogy again, the brain is quite capable of operating on innumerable "frequencies," each presenting its own picture of reality to the individual, each playing upon the physical senses in a certain manner, organizing available data in its own specialized way, and each dealing somewhat differently with the body itself and with the contents of the mind.

Generally speaking, you use one particular frequency in waking life. Therefore it seems there is no other reality than the one you recognize—and no greater data available than those with which you are normally familiar.

Events seem to happen to you. Often it seems that you have no more control over the drama of your own life than you have over the outcome of a television program. Sometimes, however, your own dreams or inspirations startle you by giving you information that is usually not available in the recognized order of events. It becomes very difficult to explain such occurrences in the light of the plots and scenes provided by your usual mental programming. You are so conditioned that even when you sleep you try to monitor your experiences, and to interpret dream events according to the habitual frequency that you have learned to accept as the only criterion of reality. Quite literally, however, when you are dreaming you are tuning in to different frequencies, and biologically your body responds to those on many levels.

For that matter, the body is naturally well-equipped to handle "projection of consciousness," or out-of-body travel, whatever you prefer to call it. Your biological makeup includes mechanisms that allow a certain portion of your consciousness to leave your body and return. These mechanisms are a part of the nature of animals as well. The body is equipped to perceive many other kinds of experiences that are not officially recognized as native to human experience. To one extent or another, then, you learn to constantly monitor your behavior, so that it conforms to the established criteria set up for sane or rational experience.

You are social creatures, as the animals are. Despite many of your cherished, erroneous beliefs, your nations exist as the result of cooperation, not competition, as do all social groupings. To be ostracized is no laughing matter. The comfort of social discourse represents one of the great building blocks of families and civilizations. The set criteria of reality, therefore, operate as organizing, psychic, and physical frameworks. There is still more flexibility within those frameworks, however, than is recognized. You still try to carry your own cultural versions of reality into the dream state, for example, but the natural heritage of both body and mind escapes such repression—and despite yourselves, in your dreams you come in touch with a greater picture of reality that will not be shunted aside.

(9:39.) There is nothing inherent in the waking state that causes it to be so limited. The boundaries set are your own. The body naturally heals itself, for example. Many give lip service to such a belief. In actuality, however, most of you believe—and experience—a far different picture, in which the body must be protected at all costs from a natural leaning toward disease and poor health. Viruses must be warded off, as if you had no protection against them. The natural healing that often occurs in the dream state is undone in the waking state, in which any such cure is seen as "miraculous" and against "the rules."

(Pause.) Yet in your dreams, you often see quite correctly the reasons for your physical difficulties, and begin a therapy that you could consciously take advantage of. Waking, however, you forget—or you do not trust what you remember.

On occasion, definite physical cures happen in the dream state, even though you may think that you are intellectual and knowing when you are awake, and ignorant or half-insane in your dreams. If you were that "dumb" in the waking state, then you would be in far better health.

In such dreams you tune in to other frequencies that are, indeed, closer to your biological integrity, but there is no reason why you cannot do so in the waking state. When such seeming miracles occur, it is because you have transcended your usual official beliefs about your body and its health, and disease, and so allowed nature to take its course. Often in the dream state you become truly awake, and grab ahold of your spirithood and creaturehood with both hands, so to speak, understanding that each has a far greater reality then you have been led to suppose.

More often, however, there are instead only blurred glimpses and tantalizing views of a more expansive kind of experience. To make matters more confusing you may automatically try to interpret the dream events according to your usual picture of reality, and swich channels, so to speak, as you waken.

(9:57.) Suppose that you turned on your television set to watch a program, for example, and found that through some malfunction a massive bleed-through had occurred so that several programs were scrambled, and yet appeared at once, seemingly without rhyme or reason. No theme would be apparent. Some of the characters might be familiar, and others, not. A man dressed as an astronaut might be riding a horse, chasing the Indians, while

an Indian chief piloted an aircraft. If all of this was transposed over the program that you expected, you would indeed think that nothing made any sense.

Each character, however, or portion of a scene, would represent in fragmented form another quite valid program [or reality, in brackets]. In the dream state, then, you are sometimes aware of too many stations When you try to make them fit into your recognized picture of reality, they may seem chaotic. There are ways to bring the picture into focus: There are ways to tune into those other quite-natural frequencies, so that they present you with a more expansive view both of the world as you define it, and of its greater aspects. Period. The psyche is not encased, in your case *(amused),* within a frame too fragile to express it. Only your <u>beliefs</u> about the psyche and about the body limit your experience to its present degree.

Take your break.

(10:09 to 10:25.)

Dictation. *(Seth-Jane leaned forward, whispering and smiling, as if telling a joke.)*

In dreams you are so "dumb" that you believe there is a commerce between the living and the dead. You are so "irrational" as to imagine that you sometimes speak to parents who are dead. You are so "unrealistic" that it seems to you that you visit old houses, long ago torn down, or that you travel in exotic foreign cities that you have actually never visited.

In dreams you are so "insane" that you do not feel yourself locked in a closet of time and space, but feel instead as if all infinity but waited your beckoning.

If you were as knowledgeable and crafty when you were awake, then you would put all religions and sciences out of business, for you would understand the greater reality of your psyche. You would know "where the action is."

The physicists have their hands on the doorknob. If they paid more attention to their dreams, they would know what questions to ask.

(Long pause at 10:33.) The psyche is a gestalt of aware energy in which your own identity resides, inviolate, yet ever-changing as you fulfill your potentials.

(Long pause.) Your dead relatives survive. They often appear to you in the dream state. You usually interpret their visitations, however, in terms of your own station of reality. You see them as they <u>were</u>, confined to their relationship with you, and you usually

do not perceive or remember other aspects of their existences that would not make sense in terms of your own beliefs.

So, often such dreams are like programmed dramas, in that you clothe such visitations in familiar props. The same sort of thing frequently occurs when you experience extraordinary flashes of inspiration, or perceive other unofficial data. Quickly you try to make sense of such material in usual terms. An out-of-body experience into another level of reality becomes a visit to heaven, for example; or the heretofore-unrecognized voice of your own greater identity becomes the voice of God, or a spaceman or prophet.

Your dreaming experience, however, gives you a guideline that will help you understand the nature of your own psyche, and the deeper reality in which it has its being. Again: The dreaming psyche is awake.

End of dictation. Give us a moment, or take a brief break as you prefer.

(10:44. "Go ahead," I said, and Seth delivered material on several other subjects. By now we saw that he was dividing his sessions often into two sections—book dictation, then discussions either on other topics, or private material for us.

(The session ended at 11:34 P.M.)

SESSION 759,   OCTOBER 27, 1975
9:31 P.M. MONDAY

("I have the feeling the session will be on the book," Jane said, just before going into trance.

(I nodded, but I'd had a particularly interesting dream experience last night, and I also hoped that Seth might discuss that. As you'll see, he managed to do both, winding a discussion of my dream into his own material about the psyche.)

Good evening.

("Good evening, Seth.")

Dictation. Again: Your dreaming psyche is awake.

It deals with a different kind of experience than the one with which you are physically familiar, although that experience is also a part of the psyche. Daily life is a focus taken on the part of that portion of the psyche you call you, and there are many other such focuses. The psyche is never destroyed. Nor is that unique individuality of your own ever minimized. The psyche's experiences straddle your ideas of time, however. It seems to you quite definitely that you come alive and die. At your particular focus of consciousness, no arguments will suffice to convince you otherwise, for you are everywhere presented with the physical evidence of "fact." Period.

You may believe in an afterlife to some extent or another, or you may or may not be convinced by the general theory of reincarnation. But certainly most of you are united in the seemingly irrefutable belief that you are definitely alive now, and not dead. Dead people do not read books. Period.

(Amused:) On the other hand, dead people do not usually write books either—now do they?

In a strange manner I am telling you that your "life" is simply the only portion of your existence of which you are presently aware. In greater terms, you are alive and dead at the same time, even as I am. My focus, however, is in an area that you do not perceive. Again: Existences are like notes played along certain frequencies. You are tuned in to an earth song, following this analogy, but you are only following your own melody, and usually you are unaware of the greater orchestration in which you also take part.

Sometimes in dreams you do tune in to a greater picture, but again, certain things appear to be facts, and against these so-called facts even definite experiences can appear ludicrous or chaotic.

Last night our friend, Joseph, had a dream experience that intrigued him, and yet seemed highly distorted. He found himself greeting a large number of people. He believed them to be family members, though he only recognized some. His parents, known to be dead, were there. A brother and a sister-in-law, who are alive, were also present. The brother was definitely himself, yet somehow altered in appearance, his features having an Oriental cast. The entire dream was very pleasant, and seemed to be like a home-coming.

(9:50.) Joseph wondered, however, at this mixture of the living and the dead. It would be easy to think that the dream foresaw Joseph's own death, and that of his brother and sister-in-law. You follow your own time sequences, however. The psyche is not so limited. To it, your death has already occurred, from your standpoint. Yet it is also true that from its standpoint, your birth has not yet happened. You have a greater experience, then, of your recognized time and existence frameworks.

There, you can meet with relatives long dead, or with children not yet born. There, you can meet other portions of your own personhood that exist simultaneously with your own.

In that framework the so-called living and the so-called dead can mix freely. In such circumstances you are literally becoming aware of other perspectives of existence. You are turning corners of being and discovering multidimensional depths of the psyche.

Artists use perspective on a flat surface to try to capture there the feelings and experiences of depth that are, in themselves, alien to the flat canvas, or paper or board. The artist may vividly evoke the image of a disappearing road that appears to be broad in the picture's foreground, only to turn smaller and smaller until it seems to vanish in some distant hidden point. No physical person will walk that road, however. An ant crawling upon such a canvas would hasten across just another flat surface, and be quite unaware of the inviting avenue and any painted fields or mountains.

Now in the dream state, you suddenly become aware on occasion of greater perspective. This perspective cannot "work" at your usual level of consciousness, any more than the artist's perspective will work for the ant's—though there is much you could learn from an ant's consciousness *(intently)*. Say that I smiled.

(10:07.) Your own waking consciousness deals specifically with certain kinds of distinctions. These help form the very structure of physical existence. They highlight your lives, providing them also with a kind of frame. Quite simply, you want to experience a certain kind of reality, so you put boundaries about events, that allow you to concentrate upon them. When an artist paints a picture, he uses discrimination. He or she chooses one area of concentration. Everything within the painting fits; so in your physical lives, you do the same thing.

The artist knows that many pictures can be painted, and holds in mind paintings already produced and those in the planning stage as well. So the psyche holds equally lives in progress, lived or not yet lived, and deals with a greater perspective from which your ordinary perspective emerges.

I often speak of you and the psyche as if they were separate, yet of course this is not the case. You are that portion of the psyche that you presently recognize. Many people say: "I want to know myself," or "I want to find myself," when the truth is that few really want to take the time or effort. *(Pause.)* There is one place to begin, however: Try becoming better acquainted with the self you are now. Stop telling yourself that you do not know yourself.

There is little use in trying to discover other levels of your own reality if you insist upon applying the laws of physical life to your own larger experience. Then you will always be in a quandary, and no facts will fit. You cannot, however, insist that the laws of your vaster existence, as you discover them, supersede the physical conditions of known life—for then no facts would apply either. You will expect to live forever in the same physical body, or think that you can levitate with your body at will. You can indeed levitate, but not with your physical body, practically speaking in operational terms. You accepted a body, and that body will die. It has limitations, but these also serve to highlight certain kinds of experience. The body in which our friend, Joseph, viewed his relatives *(in the dream mentioned earlier)* was not operationally physical. It was quite real, however, and at another level of reality it was operational, suited to its environment.

Take your break.

(10:27 to 10:50.)

Now, in many ways you simply have a brief attention span.

The "true facts" are that you exist in this life and outside it simultaneously. You are "between lives" and "in lives" at once. The deeper dimensions of reality are such that your thoughts and actions not only affect the life you know, but also reach into all of those other simultaneous existences. What you think now is unconsciously perceived by some hypothetical 14th-century self. The psyche is open-ended. No system is closed, psychological systems least of all. Your life is a dreaming experience to other portions of your greater reality which focus elsewhere.

Their experiences are also a part of your dream heritage.

You may ask how real are those other existences, but if so, you must ask in whose terms. Existence has a physical version. In that framework you are born and die, and in a definite sequence. Death is a physical reality. It is real, however, only in physical terms. If you accept those terms as the only criterion of reality, then surely it appears that death is an end to your consciousness.

If, however, you learn to know yourself better in daily life, to become more fully aware even of your earthly life, then you will indeed receive other information that hints of a deeper, more supportive reality, in which physical existence rests. You will find yourself having experiences that do not fit recognized facts. These can add up to an alternate set of facts, pointing toward a different kind of reality, and give evidence for an inner existence that takes precedence over the physical assumptions. A certain kind of discretion and understanding is necessary, however. Basically the inner reality is the creative source of the physical one. Yet to some extent, the physical rules are also inviolate—at their level.

(11:07.) You can learn to vastly enrich your own experience. Theoretically, you can even become aware of other existences to some degree. You can travel in the dream state into levels of reality separated from your own. You can learn to use and experience time in new fashions. You can obtain knowledge from other portions of your own being, and tap the psyche's resources. You can improve the world in which you live, and the quality of life. But while you are physical, you will still experience birth and death, dawn and dusk, and the privacy of the moments, for this is the experience you have chosen.

Even within that context, however, there are surprises and enchantments waiting, if you simply learn to expand your awareness, exploring not only the dream state, but your waking reality in more adventuresome ways. Your dreaming psyche is awake. Many of you have allowed your normal waking consciousness to become blurred—inactive, relatively speaking, so that you are only half aware of the life that you have. You are your psyche's living expression, its human manifestation. *(Pause.)* Yet you allow yourselves often to become blind to brilliant aspects of your own existence.

In Joseph's dream, his brother's features had an Oriental cast. Joseph knew that his brother lived as himself, and also as an Oriental, unknown to Joseph in his present life. If Joseph had seen two people—one his brother and one an Oriental—he would not have recognized the stranger, so in the dream his brother's known appearance dominated, while the Oriental affiliation is merely suggested. In your own lives you will use such psychic shorthand, or utilize symbols in which you try to explain the greater dimensions of one reality in terms of the known one.

Again, the dimensions of the psyche must be experienced, to whatever degree. They cannot be simply defined. In the following chapter, then, I will suggest some exercises that will allow you direct experience with portions of your own reality that may have escaped you thus far.

(Louder, and smiling:) End of Chapter Two.

Chapter 3

Association, the Emotions, and a Different Frame of Reference

Take a brief break and we will continue.

(11:25 to 11:32.

(With humorous emphasis:) Chapter Three: "Association, the Emotions, and a Different Frame of Reference." That is the heading.

You normally organize your experience in terms of time. Your usual stream of consciousness is also highly associative, however. Certain events in the present will remind you of past ones, for example, and sometimes your memory of the past will color present events.

Association or no, physically you will remember events in time, with present moments neatly following past ones. The psyche deals largely with associative processes, however, as it organizes events through association. Time as such has little meaning in that framework. Associations are tied together, so to speak, by emotional experience. In a large manner, the emotions defy time.

End of dictation.

(11:39.) Give us a moment . . . That is just enough to let Ruburt know we are on our next chapter.

(Now Seth delivered some material on other subjects, ending the session at 11:52 P.M.)

SESSION 762, DECEMBER 15, 1975
9:10 P.M. MONDAY

(Sessions 760–61 were devoted to separate topics that Seth has been developing apart from his regular book dictation for Psyche.

("I feel half massive, but half relaxed, too," Jane said as we waited for the session to begin. "I feel an odd sense of frustration—or maybe just impatience is a better way to put it . . . I think all of this psychic stuff that I'm half aware of has to be organized and expressed in our world—Seth, Cézanne, this book—so that we can make sense of the whole thing."

(Her reference to the French painter, Paul Cézanne, involves an experience that she began just the other day. Since Seth discusses this himself in the session, I'll let him carry on from here.)

Good evening.

("Good evening, Seth.")

Dictation—Continuation of Chapter Three.

When you are in touch with your psyche, you experience direct knowledge. Direct knowledge is comprehension. When you are dreaming, you are experiencing direct knowledge about yourself or about the world. You are comprehending your own being in a different way. When you are reading a book, you are experiencing indirect knowledge that may or may not lead to comprehension. Comprehension itself exists whether or not you have the words—or even the thoughts—to express it. You may comprehend the meaning of a dream without understanding it at all in verbal terms. Your ordinary thoughts may falter, or slip and slide around your inner comprehension without ever really coming close to expressing it.

Dreams deal with associations and with emotional validities that often do not seem to make sense in the usual world. I said before that no one can really give you a definition of the psyche. It must be experienced. Since its activities, wisdom and perception rise largely from another kind of reference, then you must often learn to interpret your encounter with the psyche to your usual self. One of the largest difficulties here is the issue of organization. In regular life, you organize your experience very neatly and push it into accepted patterns or channels, into preconceived ideas and beliefs. You tailor it to fit time sequences. Again: The psyche's organization follows no such learned predisposition. Its products can often appear chaotic simply because they splash over your accepted ideas about what experience is.

(9:25.) In *Seth Speaks* I tried to describe certain extensions of your own reality in terms that my readers could understand. In *The Nature of Personal Reality* I tried to extend the practical boundaries of individual existence as it is usually experienced. I tried to give the reader hints that would increase practical, spiritual, and physical enjoyment and fulfillment in daily life. Those books were dictated by me in a more or less straight narrative style. In *"Unknown" Reality* I went further, showing how the experiences of the psyche splash outward into the daylight, so to speak. Hopefully in that book, through my dictation and through Ruburt's and Joseph's experiences, the reader could see the greater dimensions that touch ordinary living, and sense the psyche's magic. That book required much more work on Joseph's part, and that additional effort itself was a demonstration that the psyche's events are very difficult to pin down in time.

Seemingly its action goes out in all directions. It may be easier to say, for example: "This or that event began at such a time, and ended later at such-and-such a time." As Joseph did his notes, however, it became apparent that some events could hardly be so pinpointed, and indeed seemed to have no beginning or end.

Because you tie your experience so directly to time, you rarely allow yourselves any experiences, except in dreams, that seem to defy it. Your ideas about the psyche therefore limit your experience of it. Ruburt is far more lenient than most of my readers in that regard. Still, he often expects his own rather unorthodox experiences to appear in the kind of orderly garb with which you are all familiar.

In our last book session, I gave the title for this chapter, mentioning the emotions and association; and the fact that the psyche must be directly experienced. I have not dictated a book session per se again until this evening. In the meantime, Ruburt has been experiencing dimensions of the psyche new to him.

(9:43. Our cat, Willy, woke up and insisted upon climbing into Jane's lap as she sat in trance. I finally had to deposit him in the writing room and close the door.)

It did not occur to him that those experiences had anything to do with this book, or that in acting so spontaneously he was following any kind of inner order. He wanted these pages to follow neatly one by one. Each of his experiences, however, demonstrates the ways in which the psyche's direct experiences defy your prosaic concepts of time, reality, and the orderly sequence of events. They also served to point up the differences between knowledge and comprehension, and emphasize the importance of desire and of the emotions.

In a way, of course, my own experience is divorced from that of my readers. As this information—the Seth material—is sifted through Ruburt's experience, you are able to see how it applies to the existence that is "presently" yours.

Ruburt's experiences of late are particularly important, in that by implication they run counter to many accepted core beliefs that are generally held. We will use these latest episodes as an opportunity to discuss the presence of knowledge that appears to be "supernormal"—available, but usually untouched. We will further describe the triggers that can make such information practical, or bring it into practical range.

First of all, there are several points I want to make.

You are born with the inclination toward language. Language is implied in your physical structure. You are born with the inclination to learn and to explore. When you are conceived, there is already a complete pattern for your grown physical body—a pattern that is definite enough to give you the recognizable kind of adult form, while variable enough to allow for literally infinite variations (very intently).

It would be idiotic of you to say that you were forced to become an adult, however. For one thing, at any given time you could end the process—and many do. In other words, because the pattern for development exists in your terms, this does not mean that each such development is not unique.

In your terms again, then, at any one earth time many such patterns exist. In greater respects however, all time is simultaneous, and so all such physical patterns exist at once.

(10:02.) Rest your fingers. Get Ruburt some cigarettes. I will keep him in trance. Do you want to rest?

("No."

(A minute later:) In the psychic areas, all patterns for knowledge, cultures, civilizations, personal and mass accomplishments, sciences, religions, technologies and arts, exist in the same fashion.

The private psyche, the part of you that you do not recognize, is aware of those patterns even as it is aware of private physical biological patterns about which it forms your image.

Certain leanings, inclinations, and probabilities are present then in your biological structure, to be triggered or not according to your purposes and intents. You may personally have the ability to be a fine athlete, for example. Yet your inclinations and intents may carry you in a different direction, so that the necessary triggers are not activated. Each individual is gifted in a variety of ways. His or her own desires and beliefs activate certain abilities and ignore others.

(10:11.) The [human] species has built into it all of the knowledge, information, and "data" that it can possibly need under any and all conditions. This heritage must be triggered psychically, however, as a physical mechanism such as a muscle is triggered through desire or intent.

This does not mean that you learn what in larger terms you already know; as for example, if you learn a skill. Without the triggering desire, the skill would not be developed; but even when you do learn a skill, you use it in your own unique way. Still, the knowledge of mathematics and the arts is as much within you as your genes are within you. You usually believe that all such information must come from outside of your self, however. Certainly mathematical formulas are not imprinted in the brain, yet they are inherent in the structure of the brain *(intently),* and implied within its existence. Your own focus determines the information that is available to you. I will here give you an example.

Ruburt paints as a hobby. Sometimes he paints for fairly long periods of time, then forgets about it. Joseph is an artist. Ruburt has been wondering about the contents of the mind, curious as to what information was available to it. The Christmas holidays were approaching. He asked Joseph what he would like for a gift, and Joseph more or less replied: "A book on Cézanne."

Ruburt's love for Joseph, his own purposes, and his growing questions, along with his interest in painting in general, triggered exactly the kind of stimulus that broke through conventional beliefs about time and knowledge. Ruburt tuned in to Cézanne's "world view." He did not contact Cézanne per se, but Cézanne's comprehension of painting as an art.

Ruburt is not technically facile enough even to follow Cézanne's directions. Joseph is facile enough, but he would not want to follow the vision of another. The information, however, is extremely valuable, and knowledge on any kind of subject is available in just such a manner—but it is attained through desire and through intent.

This does not mean that <u>any</u> person, spontaneously, with no instruction, can suddenly become a great artist or writer or scientist. It does mean, however, that the species possesses within itself those inclinations which will flower. It means also that you are limiting the range of your knowledge by not taking advantage of such methods. It does not mean that in your terms all knowledge already exists, either, for knowledge automatically becomes individualized as you receive it, and hence, new.

Take your break or end the session, as you prefer.

("We'll take the break."

(10:30. Seth did an excellent job of describing the conditions that resulted in Jane's "Cézanne experience." Specifically, though, this is what happened: Quite suddenly in the predawn hours of December 11 she began to write an automatic script that purported to come from the artist Paul Cézanne, who lived from 1839 to 1906. She has no idea whether or not the manuscript will continue "to come." Already, though, I am struck by the insights on art and life as they are presented.

(Resume in the same manner at 10:42.)

Your desire automatically attracts the kind of information you require, though you may or may not be aware of it.

If you are gifted, and want to be a musician, for example, then you may literally learn while you are asleep, tuning in to the world views of other musicians, both alive and dead in your terms. When you are awake, you will receive inner hints, nudges or inspirations. You may still need to practice, but your practice will be largely in joy, and will not take as long as it might others. The reception of such information facilitates skill, and operates basically outside of time's sequences.

Ruburt's Cézanne material therefore comes very quickly, taking a bare portion of the day. Yet its quality is such that professional art critics could learn from it, though some of their productions might take much longer periods of time, and result from an extensive conscious knowledge of art, which Ruburt almost entirely lacks. The productions of the psyche by their nature, therefore, burst aside many most cherished beliefs.

It seems almost heresy to suppose that such knowledge is available, for then what use is education? Yet education should serve to introduce a student to as many fields of endeavor as possible, so that he or she might recognize those that serve as natural triggers, opening skills or furthering development. The student will, then, pick and choose. The Cézanne material was from the past, yet future knowledge is quite as accessible. There are, of course, probable futures from the standpoint of your past. Future information is theoretically available there, just as the body's "future" pattern of development was at your birth—and that certainly was practical.

    End of session. A fond good evening.

    ("Thank you, Seth.")

    Unless you have questions. . . .

    (At 10:55 I did ask Seth a question, which he discussed until 11:24 P.M.)

SESSION 763,   JANUARY 5, 1976
9:28 P.M. MONDAY

    (While we were out for a drive in the country yesterday, Jane abruptly wondered aloud if Seth ever dreamed. If he did, what was his dream state like? Tonight at 9:00 she told me she thought he'd answer her questions by weaving them into the book session.

    (We took our Christmas tree down today, after enjoying it through the holidays. Jane called them "the Cézanne days" since she's still getting Cézanne material.)

    Now: Dictation.

    ("Good evening, Seth.")

    There are, then, other ways of receiving information than those you take for granted.

    There are other kinds of knowledge, also. These deal with organizations with which you are generally not familiar. It is not merely a matter of learning new methods to acquire knowledge, then, but a situation in which old methods must be momentarily set aside—along with the type of knowledge that is associated with them.

    It is not a matter, either, of there simply being one other category of knowledge, for there are numerous other such categories, many of them biologically within your reach. Various so-called esoteric traditions provide certain methods that allow an individual to set aside accepted modes of perception, and offer patterns that may be used as containers for these other kinds of knowledge. Even these containers must necessarily shape the information received, however. *(Pause.)* Some such methods are very advantageous, yet they have also become too rigid and autocratic, allowing little room for deviation. Dogmas are then set up about them so that only a certain body of data is considered acceptable. The systems no longer have the flexibility that first gave them birth.

The kind of knowledge upon which you depend needs verbalization. It is very difficult for you to consider the accumulation of any kind of knowledge without the use of language as you understand it. Even your remembered dreams are often verbalized constructs. You may also use images, but these are familiar images, born of the educated and hence prejudiced physical perceptions. Those remembered dreams have meaning and are very valuable, but they are already organized for you to some extent, and put into a shape that you can somewhat recognize.

(9:41.) Beneath those levels, however, you comprehend events in an entirely different fashion. These whole comprehensions are then packaged even in the dream state, and translated into usual sense terms.

Any information or knowledge must have a pattern if you are going to understand it at all. Ruburt's own painting, his knowledge of his psychic abilities, his love of Joseph—all served to form a pattern which then attracted the Cézanne material. He received this "automatically," writing down the words that came almost too quickly for him to follow. His craft or art of writing brought the material to clear focus. The information itself, however, had nothing to do with words, but with an overall comprehension of the nature of painting, a direct knowing. Ruburt used his own abilities as a container, then. This direct kind of knowledge is available, again, on any subject, to anyone who provides a suitable pattern through desire, love, intent or belief.

Ruburt wondered later if I dreamed. My own usual state of consciousness is far different from yours. I do not alternate between waking and sleeping as you do. Still, I have states of consciousness that could be compared to your dream state, in that I am myself not as involved in them as I am in others. If I said to you, "I control my dream state," you might have an idea of what I mean. Yet I do not control my dreams—I fulfill them. What you could call my dreaming state is involved with the levels I spoke of that exist beneath your remembered dreams.

(Pause.) I said earlier that there were many kinds of knowledge. Think of them instead as states of knowledge. Perception of any of these takes a consciousness attuned to each. In my "waking" condition, I operate at many levels of consciousness at once, and deal therefore with different systems of knowledge. In my "dream"

condition, or rather conditions, I form links of consciousness that combine these various systems, creatively forming them into new versions. "Waking" again, I become consciously aware of those activities, and use them to add to the dimensions of my usual state, creatively expanding my experience of reality. What I learn is transmitted automatically to others like me, and their knowledge is transmitted to me.

(Pause at 10:05.) We are each consciously aware of these transmissions. In the terms usually familiar to you, you think of "the conscious mind." In those terms, there are many conscious minds. You are so prejudiced, however, that you ignore infor-mation that you have been taught cannot be conscious. All of your experience, therefore, is organized according to your beliefs.

It is much more natural to remember your dreams than not to remember them. It is presently in the vogue to say that the conscious mind, as you consider it, deals with survival. It deals with survival only insofar as it promotes survival in your particular kind of society. In those terms, if you remembered your dreams, and if you benefited consciously from that knowledge, even your physical survival would be better assured.

One level of dream life deals particularly with the biological condition of the body, giving you not just hints of health diffi-culties, but the reasons for them and the ways to circumvent them. Information about the probable future is also given to help you make conscious choices. You have taught yourselves that you cannot be conscious in your dreams, however, because you inter-pret the word "conscious" so that it indicates only your own prejudiced concept. As a result, you do not have any culturally acceptable patterns that allow you to use your dreams competently.

Trance states, daydreaming, hypnotism—these give you some hint of the various differences that can occur from the standpoint of waking consciousness. In each, reality appears in another fashion, and for that matter, different rules apply. In the dream state far greater variations occur. The key to the dream state, however, lies in the waking one as far as you are concerned. You must change your ideas about dreaming, alter your concepts about it, before you can begin to explore it. Otherwise your own waking prejudice will close the door.

Take your break.

(10:24 to 10:35.)

As it is, you express very little of your entire personhood.

My remark has nothing to do with your accepted concepts

of the unconscious portions of the self. Your ideas of the unconscious are so linked to your limited ideas of personhood as to be meaningless in this discussion. It is as if you used only one finger of one hand, and then said: "This is the proper expression of my personhood." It is not just that there are other functions of the mind, unused, but that in those terms you have other minds. You have one brain, it is true, but you allow it to use only one station, or to identify itself with only one mind of many.

It seems evident to you that one person has one mind. You identify with the mind you use. If you had another, then it would seem as if you must be someone else. A mind is a psychic pattern through which you interpret and form reality. You have physical limbs that you can see. You have minds that are invisible. Each one can organize reality in a different fashion. Each one deals with its own kind of knowledge.

These minds all work together to keep you alive through the physical structure of the brain. When you use all of these minds, then and only then do you become fully aware of your surroundings: You perceive reality more clearly than you do now, more sharply, brilliantly, and concisely. At the same time, however, you comprehend it directly. You comprehend what it is apart from your physical perception of it. You accept as yourself those other states of consciousness native to your other minds. You achieve true personhood.

In terms of history, some ancient races achieved such goals, but in your terms, so long ago that you cannot find evidence of their knowledge.

(Long pause.) Throughout the centuries various individuals have come close, yet had no vehicle of expression that would have enabled the members of the species to understand. They possessed methods, but the methods presupposed or necessitated a knowledge that others did not possess.

(10:54.) End of dictation. Give us a moment.

(Seth immediately began a short discussion of a dream Jane had last night. She hardly remembered it, but wrote in her notebook this morning that she knew it involved a new, rather odd kind of perception that she couldn't verbalize at all. Since this fits in with Seth's chapter here, I'm including his comments:)

Ruburt's nearly forgotten dream last night represents a breakthrough, in that he was at least consciously aware of receiving knowledge in yet another different fashion.

He could not verbalize it, nor did he have a suitable pattern to contain it. He received it, however. His painting of late is no coincidence, for he is dealing with nonverbal information, organizing data in another way, and thus activating other "portions" of the mind.

The Cézanne material, the dream and the painting, are all aspects of another kind of perception. Your joint library experiments* helped set the stage, as you added your encouragement. All of this will help Ruburt toward a nonverbal comprehension that will, on another level, reorganize some of his beliefs.

This type of perception cannot be described until he forms suitable verbal patterns that can come only with further experience. In this, I am a touchstone. He accelerates mentally to a certain degree, and that puts him in touch with me—an additional energy source. He activates certain portions of the brain that connect it to another mind, that people do not as yet realize they possess.

(Louder and humorously:) Now, end of session and a fond good evening.

("Thank you very much, Seth. Good night.")

(11:05 P.M.)

SESSION 764, JANUARY 26, 1976
9:12 P.M. MONDAY

Now: Good evening.

("Good evening, Seth.")

Dictation: You experience yourself in a certain way topside, so to speak, and so in order to take advantage of information at other levels of awareness, you must learn to experience those other organizational systems with which you are usually unfamiliar.

Often the seeming meaninglessness of dreams is the result of your own ignorance of dream symbolism and organization. For example: You may also misinterpret "revelatory" material because you try to structure it in reference to your ordinary conscious organizations. Many valuable and quite practical insights that could be utilized go astray, therefore. I am going to suggest, then, some simple exercises that will allow you to directly experience the "feel of your being" in a different way.

First of all, the various kinds of organizations used by the psyche can be compared at one level, at least, with different arts.

---

*Jane describes her psychic "library" in her book *Psychic Politics.*

Music is not better than the visual arts, for example. A sculpture cannot be compared with a musical note. I am not saying, then, that one mode of organization is better than another. You have simply specialized in one of the many arts of consciousness, and that one can be vastly enriched by knowledge and practice of the others.

(9:20.) First of all, these other organizations do not deal primarily with time at all, but with the emotions and associative processes. When you understand how your own associations work, then you will be in a much better position to interpret your own dreams, for example, and finally to make an art of them.

There are several approaches to these exercises. The idea will be to experience emotions and events as much as possible outside of time sequences.

As I have mentioned many times, cellular comprehension deals with probabilities and encompasses future and past, so at that level of activity time as you understand it does not exist. You are not consciously aware of such data, however. The psyche—at the other end of the scale, so to speak—is also free of time. Often, however, your own stream of consciousness leads you to think of events outside of their usual order. You may receive a letter from your Aunt Bessie, for example. In a matter of moments it may trigger you to think of events in your childhood, so that many mental images fly through your mind. You might wonder if your aunt will take an anticipated journey to Europe next year, and that thought might give birth to images of an imagined future. All of these thoughts and images will be colored by the emotions that are connected to the letter, and to all of the events with which you and your aunt have been involved.

The next time you find yourself in the middle of a like experience, with associations flowing freely, then become more aware of what you are doing. Try to sense the mobility involved. You will see that the events will not necessarily be structured according to usual time, but according to emotional content.

Thoughts of your own next birthday, for instance, may instantly lead you to think of past ones, or a series of birthday pictures may come to mind of your own twelfth birthday, your third, your seventh, in an order uniquely your own. That order will be determined by emotional associations—the same kind followed by the dreaming self.

What did you wear to work three days ago? What did you have for breakfast a week ago? Who sat next to you in kindergarten? What frightened you last? Are you afraid of sleep? Did your parents beat you? What did you do just after lunch yesterday? What color shoes did you wear three days ago? You remember only significant events or details. Your emotions trigger your memories, and they organize your associations. Your emotions are generated through your beliefs. They attach themselves so that certain beliefs and emotions seem almost synonymous.

(9:40.) The next time an opportunity arises, and you recognize the presence of a fairly strong emotion in yourself, then let your associations flow. Events and images will spring to mind in an out-of-time context. Some such remembered events will make sense to you. You will clearly see the connection between the emotion and event, but others will not be so obvious. Experience the events as clearly as you can. When you are finished, purposefully alter the sequence. Remember an event, and then follow it with the memory of one that actually came earlier. Pretend that the future one came before the past one.

Now for another exercise. Imagine a very large painting, in which the most important events of your life are clearly depicted. First of all, see them as a series of scenes, arranged in small squares, to be viewed as you would, say, a comic-book page. The events must be of significance to you. If school graduation meant nothing, for example, do not paint it in. Have the pictures begin at the upper left-hand corner, ending finally at the lower right-hand corner. Then completely switch the sequence, so that the earliest events are at the lower right-hand corner.

When you have done this, ask yourself which scene evokes the strongest emotional response. Tell yourself that it will become larger and larger, then mentally watch its size change. Certain dynamics are involved here, so that such a scene will also attract elements from other scenes. Allow those other scenes to break up, then. The main picture will attract elements from all of the others, until you end up with an entirely different picture—one made up of many of the smaller scenes, but united in an entirely new fashion. You must do this exercise, however, for simply reading about it will not give you the experience that comes from the actual exercise. Do it many times.

(9:54.) Now: Consciously construct a dream. Tell yourself you are going to do so, and begin with the first thought or image that comes to mind. When you are finished with your daydream, then use free association to interpret it to yourself.

Some of you will meet with some resistance in these exercises. You will enjoy reading about them, but you will find all kinds of excuses that prevent you from trying them yourself. If you

are honest, many of you will sense a reluctance, for certain qualities of consciousness are brought into play that run counter to
your usual conscious experience.

You might feel as if you are crossing your wires, so to speak,
or stretching vaguely sensed psychic muscles. The purpose is not
so much the perfect execution of such exercises as it is to involve
you in a different mode of experience and of awareness that comes
into being as you perform in the ways suggested. You have been
taught not to mix, say, waking and dreaming conditions, not to
daydream. You have been taught to focus all of your attention
clearly, ambitiously, energetically in a particular way—so daydreaming, or mixing and matching modes of consciousness, appears passive in a derogatory fashion, or nonactive, or idle.
(Louder:) "The devil finds work for idle hands"—an old Christian
dictum.

Unfortunately, certain aspects of Christianity were stressed
over others, and that dictum was based upon the belief in a wicked
self that needed to be disciplined and diverted into constructive
activity. The belief in such an unsavory self stops many people
from any exploration of the inner self—and, therefore, from any
direct experience that will give them counter-evidence. If you are
afraid of yourself, if you are afraid of your own memories, you will
block your associative processes, fearing for example that they will
bring to light matters best forgotten—and usually sexual matters.

(10:08.) Sexuality is the only strong area of energy with
which some people are connected, so it becomes the focal point
for all of their beliefs about the self in general. In doing some of
these exercises, you might come across images of masturbation,
homosexual or lesbian encounters, or simply old sexual fantasies,
and immediately backtrack because your beliefs may tell you that
these are evil.

You will not remember, or want to remember, your own
dreams for the same reason. Many people, therefore, tell themselves that they are very impatient to discover the nature and
extent of the psyche, and cannot understand why they meet with
so little success. At the same time, such beliefs convince them that
the self is evil. These beliefs must be weeded out. If you cannot
honestly encounter the dimensions of your creaturehood, you
surely cannot explore the greater dimensions of the psyche. This
blocking of associations, however, is a very important element that
impedes many people. The psyche's organizations are broader,

and in their way more rational than most of your conscious beliefs about the self.

Many individuals are afraid that they will be swept away by inner explorations, that insanity will overtake them, when instead the physical stance of the body and personality is firmly rooted in these alternate organizations. There is nothing wrong with the conscious mind. You have simply put a lid on it, allowing it to be only so conscious, and no more. You have said: "Here it is safe to be conscious, and here it is not."

Many of you believe that it is safe to make a nuclear bomb, but that it is insane to use your dreams as another method of manipulating daily life; or that it is all right to be consciously aware of your viruses, wars, and disasters, but that it is not all right to be consciously aware of other portions of the self that could solve such problems.

The idea, then, is not to annihilate normal consciousness, but quite literally to expand it by bringing into its focus other levels of reality that it can indeed intrinsically perceive and utilize.

I will suggest many exercises throughout this book. Some of them will necessitate variations of normal consciousness. I may ask you to forget physical stimuli, or suggest that you amplify them, but I am nowhere stating that your mode of consciousness is wrong. It is limited, not by nature, but by your own beliefs and practice. You have not carried it far enough.

Take your break.

(10:27 to 10:43.)

Some night as you fall to sleep, try telling yourself that you will pretend you are awake while you sleep.

Suggest that instead of falling asleep, you will come into another kind of wakefulness. Try to imagine that you are awake when you sleep. On other occasions when you go to bed, lie down and settle yourself, but as you fall asleep imagine that you are awakening the next morning. I will not tell you what to look for. The doing of these exercises is important—not the results in usual terms.

I said that there were different kinds of knowledge; so will these exercises bring you in contact with knowledge in another way. Done over a period of time, they will open up alternate modes of perception, so that you can view your experience from more than one standpoint. This means that your experience will itself change in quality. Sometimes when you are awake, and it is convenient, imagine that your present experience of the moment is a dream, and is highly symbolic. Then try to interpret it as such.

Who are the people? What do they represent? If that experience were a dream, what would it mean? And into what kind of waking life would you rise in the morning?

The qualities of consciousness cannot be elucidated. These exercises will bring you in contact with other kinds of knowing, and acquaint you with different feelings of consciousness that are not familiar. Your consciousness itself will then have a different feel as the exercises are done. Certain questions that you may have asked may be answered in such a state, but not in ways that you can anticipate, nor can you necessarily translate the answers into known terms. The different modes of consciousness with which I hope to acquaint you are not alien, however. They are quite native, again, in dream states, and are always present as alternatives beneath usual awareness.

(10:58.) Sometime as you walk down a street, pretend that you are seeing the same scene from the sky in an airplane, yourself included. On another occasion, as you sit inside your house imagine that you are outside on the lawn or street. All of these exercises should be followed by a return to the present: You focus your attention outward in the present moment as clearly as possible, letting the sounds and sights of the physical situation come into your attention.

The other exercises, in fact, will result in a clearer picture of the world, for they will facilitate the very motion of your perceptions, allowing you to perceive nuances in the physical situation that before would have escaped your notice. We will be dealing with practical direct experience. It will do you no good if you are simply intellectually aware of what I say, but practically ignorant. Period. Therefore the exercises will be important because they will offer you evidence of your own greater perceptive abilities.

Continue to rely upon known channels of information, but implement these and begin to explore the unrecognized ones also available. What information do you have, for example, presently unknown to yourself? Try your hand at predicting future events. In the beginning, it does not matter whether or not your predictions are "true." You will be stretching your consciousness into areas usually unused. Do not put any great stake in your predictions, for if you do you will be very disappointed if they do not work out, and end the entire procedure.

If you continue, you will indeed discover that you are aware of some future events, when such knowledge is not available in usual terms. If you persist, then over a period of time you will discover that you do very well in certain areas, while in others you may fail miserably. There will be associative patterns that you follow successfully, leading toward "correct" precognitions. You will also discover that the emotions are highly involved in such procedures: You will perceive information that is significant to you for some reason. That significance will act like a magnet, attracting those data to you.

Now, in the normal course of events you attract experience in the same fashion. You anticipate events. You are aware of them before they happen, whether or not you ever succeed in conscious predictions. You form your life, however, through the intimate interworkings of your own conscious goals and beliefs.

(11:17.) While your future can on occasion be correctly perceived ahead of time by a gifted psychic, the future is too plastic for any kind of systematized framework. Free will is always involved. Yet many people are frightened of remembering dreams because they fear that a dream of disaster will necessarily be followed by such an event. The mobility of consciousness provides far greater freedom. In fact, such a dream can instead be used to circumnavigate such a probability.

Only if you understand your own freedom in such areas will you allow yourselves to explore alternate states of consciousness, or the environment of dreams. Such exercises are not to be used to supersede the world you know, but to supplement it, to complete it, and to allow you to perceive its true dimensions.

There is no need to divorce the waking and dreaming states in the particular fashion that currently operates—for they are complementary states, not opposite ones. A good deal of life's normal dimensions are dependent upon your dream experience. Your entire familiarity with the world of symbols arises directly from the dreaming self.

In certain terms, language itself has its roots in the dreaming condition—and man dreamed [that] he spoke long before language was born *(intently)*.

He dreamed of flying, and that impetus led to the physical inventions that made mechanical flight possible. I am not speaking symbolically here, but quite literally. From the beginning, I said that the self was not confined to the body. This means that the consciousness has other methods of perceiving information, that even in physical life experience is not confined to what is sensed in usual terms. This remains fine theory, however, unless you allow yourself enough freedom to experiment with other modes of perception.

End of dictation. End of session—unless you have questions.

("No, not unless you want to comment on some questions Jane had in mind.")

Take a brief break then, and give us a moment. Rest your hand. . . .

(Book work ended at 11:35 P.M., after which Seth commented on some other matters Jane was interested in.)

Chapter 4

The Psyche in Relationship to Sexual Elements. The He and She—the She and He

SESSION 765, FEBRUARY 2, 1976
9:23 P.M. MONDAY

Good evening.

("Good evening, Seth.")

Dictation: Chapter Four: "The Psyche in Relationship to Sexual Elements. The He and She," dash—"the She and He." That was the heading.

Now: Distorted ideas about sexuality prevent many people from attaining any close connection with the inner experience that continually stirs beneath ordinary consciousness. It is a good idea, then, to look at the psyche and its relationship to sexual identity.

The psyche is not male or female. In your system of beliefs, however, it is often identified as feminine, along with the artistic productions that emerge from its creativity. In that context, the day hours and waking consciousness are thought of as masculine, along with the sun—while the nighttime, the moon, and the dreaming consciousness are considered feminine or passive. In the same manner, aggression is usually understood to be violent

55

assertive action, male-oriented, while female elements are identified in terms of the nurturing principle.

Physically speaking, you would have no males or females unless first you had individuals. You are each individuals first of all, then. After this, you are individuals of a specific sex, biologically speaking. The particular kind of focus that you have is responsible for the great significance you place upon male and female. Your hand and your foot have different functions. If you wanted to focus upon the differences in their behavior, you could build an entire culture based upon their diverse capabilities, functions and characteristics. Hands and feet are obviously equipment belonging to both sexes, however. Still, on another level the analogy is quite valid.

The psyche is male and female, female and male; but when I say this I realize that you put your own definitions upon those terms to begin with.

(Pause at 9:38.) Biologically, the sexual orientation is the method chosen for continuation of the species. Otherwise, however, no specific psychological characteristics of any kind are attached to that biological functioning. I am quite aware that in your experience definite physical and psychological differences do exist. Those that do are the result of programming, and are not inherent—even biologically—in the species itself.

The vitality of the species in fact was assured because it did not overspecialize in terms of sexuality. There was no fixed mating period, for example. Instead, the species could reproduce freely so that in the event of a catastrophe of any kind, it would not be so tied into rigid patterns that it might result in extinction.

(Long pause, one of many.) The challenges and problems of the species were different from those of others. It needed additional safeguards. The more flexible mating pattern was one. With this came a greater diversity in individual characteristics and behavior, so that no individual was bound to a strictly biological role. If that were true, the species never would have been concerned beyond the issues of physical survival, and such is not the case. The species could have survived quite well physically without philosophy, the arts, politics, religion, or even structured language. It could have followed completely different paths, those tied strictly to biological orientation.

There would have been no question of men performing so-called feminine tasks, or of women performing so-called masculine tasks, for there no leeway for that kind of individual action would have existed.

For that matter, there is far greater leeway in the behavior of animals than you understand, for you interpret animal behavior according to your own beliefs. You interpret the past history of your species in the same manner. It seems to you that the female always tended to the offspring, for example, nursing them, that she was forced to remain close to home while the male fought off enemies or hunted for food. The ranging male, therefore, appears to have been much more curious and aggressive. There was instead a different kind of situation. Children do not come in litters. The family of the caveman was a far more "democratic" group than you suppose—men and women working side by side, children learning to hunt with both parents, women stopping to nurse a child along the way, the species standing apart from others because it was not ritualized in sexual behavior.

(10:00.) Except for the fact that males could not bear children, the abilities of the sexes were interchangeable. The male was usually heavier, a handy physical advantage in some areas— but the woman was lighter and could run faster.

Women were also somewhat lighter because they would bear the additional weight of a child. Even then, of course, there were variances, for many women are larger than small men. But the women could hunt as well as the men. If compassion, kindness, and gentleness were feminine characteristics only, then no male could be kind or compassionate because such feelings would not be biologically possible.

If your individuality was programmed by your biological sex, then it would be literally impossible for you to perform any action that was not sexually programmed. A woman cannot father a child, nor can a male bear one. Since you are otherwise free to perform other kinds of activity that you think of as sexually oriented, in those areas the orientation is cultural.

You imagine, however, that the male is aggressive, active, logical-minded, inventive, outwardly oriented, a builder of civilizations. You identify the ego as male. The unconscious therefore seems to be female, and the feminine characteristics are usually given as passive, intuitive, nurturing, creative, uninventive, concerned with preserving the status quo, disliking change. At the same time, you consider the intuitive elements rather frightening, as if they can explode to disrupt known patterns, dash—in unknown ways.

Males who are creatively gifted find themselves in some dilemma, for their rich, sensed creativity comes into direct conflict with their ideas of virility. Women who possess characteristics that are thought to be masculine have the same problem on the other side.

In your terms the psyche is a repository of characteristics that operate in union, composed of female and male elements. The human psyche contains such patterns that can be put together in multitudinous ways. You have categorized human abilities so that it seems that you are men or women, or women and men primarily, and persons secondarily. Your personhood exists first, however. Your individuality gives meaning to your sex, and not the other way around.

Take your break.

(10:23 to 10:38.)

Now: In direct opposition to current theories about the past, there was far less sexual specialization, say, in the time of the caveman than now.

The family was a very cooperative unit. The basis of early society was cooperation, not competition. Families grouped together. There were children of various ages in such a band all the time. When women were near birth, they performed those chores that could be done in the cave dwellings, or nearby, and also watched other young children; while the women who were not pregnant were off with the males, hunting or gathering food.

If a mother died, the father took over her responsibilities, the qualities of love and affection being quite as alive in him as in the female. After a woman bore, she nursed the child, taking it with her on food-gathering excursions, or sometimes letting other women in the group nurse the child. Often after childbirth, women immediately joined the hunting expeditions, and the fathers made clothing from animals' hides at home. This allowed the male to rest after prolonged hunting activity, and meant that no adult member of a family became overexhausted. The work, then, was interchangeable.

(Slowly:) Children began food gathering and hunting as soon as they were able to—females as well as males—led by the older children, going further away as they progressed in strength. Qualities of inventiveness, curiosity, ingenuity, could not be delegated to one sex alone. The species could not have survived such a division.

(10:52.) You are so used to thinking in terms of mechanics, that it seems to you that uneducated people did not understand the connection between the sexual act of intercourse and childbirth. You are so used to one kind of explanation for childbirth, so

familiar with one specific framework, that alternate explanations appear to be the height of nonsense. So it is fashionable to believe that early man did not understand the connection between intercourse and birth.

Even the animals, however, understand without words or language the importance of their sexual behavior. Early man was hardly more ignorant. The male knew what he was doing even without textbooks that outlined the entire procedure. The female understood the connections between the child born and the sexual act.

(Intently:) It is the height of idiocy to imagine that because of the time taken in pregnancy, the female could not understand the child's origin in intercourse. The body's knowledge did not need a complicated language. For that matter, your literal interpretation of childbirth is by some standards a highly limited one. In your terms, it is technically correct.

But a child born to two parents is also an offspring of the earth, its tissues as surely a part of earth as any tree or flower, or burst of ocean spray. A human child, true; but an offspring in which the entire history of the earth is involved—a new creation arising not just from two parents, but from the entire gestalt of nature, from which the parents themselves once emerged; a private yet public affair in which the physical elements of earth become individualized; in which psyche and earth cooperate in a birth that is human, and in other terms, divine.

Now: Historically speaking, early man in his way understood those connections far better than you do, and used language as he developed it to express first of all this miracle of birth. For he saw that he constantly replenished his kind, and that all other species were replenished in the same manner.

There was always more land. No matter how fast he ran or how far he traveled, early man could not run out of land, or trees, or forests, or food supplies. If he came to a desert, he still knew that fertile lands were somewhere available, even if it was a matter of finding them. But the world itself seemed to have no end. It was literally a limitless world in a way most difficult for you to understand; for to you, the world has shrunk.

(11:16.) This unlimited world constantly replenished itself. Children came from women's wombs. Man was acquainted with death, and many children were stillborn, or were naturally aborted. This also, however, was in the natural order of things, and was done far more easily then than now. All flower seeds do not fall on

fertile ground and bring forth other flowers. The seeds that do not grow go [back] into the ground, forming the basis for other life. Biologically speaking, fetuses grow and develop—I am going slowly here because I am being tricky—and when innate consciousness merges with proper form, the conditions are right for the birth of a healthy child. When the conditions are not right, the child does not develop properly. Nature aborts it. The physical elements return to the earth to become the basis for other life.

Only those children perfectly attuned to their environment in time and space survived. This does not mean that the consciousness of a child was annihilated, for example, if it was naturally aborted. It did not develop.

While there was no mating period, still there was a close biological relationship between the species and the earth, so that women naturally conceived when situations of climate, food supplies, and other elements were beneficial.

Biologically, the species knew ahead of time when droughts would appear, for example, and it automatically altered its rate of conception to compensate. Left alone, animal species do the same thing. In broad terms, early man was struck by the fact that all things seemed to reproduce themselves, and it was this fact that first caught his attention. Later he used what you think of as myths to explain this abundance. Yet those myths contained a kind of knowledge that escapes your literal, specific interpretations of sexual events. Such knowledge resides in the psyche, however. If you have any direct experience with your own psyche, then you will most likely find yourself encountering some kinds of events that will not easily fit with your own ideas about your sexual nature.

Take your break.

(11:35 to 11:49.

(This was the end of book work. Seth came through with a few pages of material for me, and ended the session at 12:15 A.M.)

SESSION 768, MARCH 22, 1976
9:43 P.M. MONDAY

(The last two sessions are highly interesting, but weren't devoted to book dictation. Both contain information about suicide, and were given after we heard about the self-inflicted death of a young friend of ours. We hope to see them published eventually.

(Tonight, though, Seth began work on Psyche *right where he left off well over a month ago.)*

Good evening.

("Good evening, Seth.")

Dictation: The continuation of our sexual fireside chat. *(Humorously:)* The remark is an aside—and not necessarily part of the book, though it may be if you prefer.

Your beliefs about sexuality, and hence your experience with it, makes you consider it in a very limiting light. The psyche's own knowledge, of course, is far more expansive. Alterations of consciousness, or attempts on the part of the individual to explore the inner self, may then easily display glimpses of a kind of sexuality that can appear to be deviant or unnatural.

Even when social scientists or biologists explore human sexuality, they do so from the framework of sexuality as it <u>appears</u> in your world. There are quite natural sexual variations, even involving reproduction, that are not now apparent in human behavior in any culture. These variations appear in your world on only fairly microscopic levels, or in the behavior of other species than your own.

New paragraph: When racial conditions require it, it is quite possible for an individual to both father and mother a child.* In such cases, what you would call complete spontaneous sexual reverses or transformations would occur. Such processes are quite possible at microscopic levels, and inherent in the cellular structure. Even in your world, currently speaking, some individuals known as women could father their own children.

Some individuals known as men could give birth to a child fathered by the same person—<u>could</u> (underlined). The abilities are there.

The male-female, female-male orientation is not nearly as separate as it appears to be in your present experience. It is not nearly as tied to psychological characteristics as you suppose. Nor is it <u>inherently</u> focused in the particular age period in which it now shows itself. Puberty arrives, so to speak, but the time of its arrival varies according to the needs of the species, its conditions and beliefs. You are an individual for life. You operate as a reproducing individual, generally speaking, for only a portion of that time.

(Pause at 10:01.) During that period, many elements come into play and are meant to make the process attractive to the

---

*In these passages Seth refers to phenomena similar to parthenogenesis: the reproduction of an unfertilized ovum, seed, or spore, as in some polyzoans, insects, algae, and so forth. There's also artificial parthenogenesis, brought about by the development of an ovum that's mechanically or chemically stimulated.

individuals involved, and to their tribes, societies, or civilizations. A relatively strong "sexual" identification is important under those circumstances—but *(louder)* an overidentification with them, before or afterward, can lead to stereotyped behavior, in which the greater needs and abilities of the individual are not allowed fulfillment.

All of this becomes very complicated because of your value judgments, which oftentimes seem to lack—if you will forgive me—all natural common sense. You cannot separate biology from your own belief systems. The interplay is too vital. If each act of intercourse were meant to produce a child, you would have overrun the planet before you began. Sexual activity is therefore also meant as enjoyment, as an expression of pure exuberance. A woman will often feel her most sexually active in the midst of the menstrual period, precisely when conception is least apt to occur. All kinds of taboos against sexual relations have been applied here, particularly in so-called native cultures. In those cultures, such taboos make good sense. Such peoples, building up the human stock, intuitively knew that the population would be increased if relations were restricted to periods when conception was most likely to occur. The blood was an obvious sign that the woman at her period was relatively "barren." Her abundance was gone. It seemed to their minds that she was indeed "cursed" during that time *(emphatically)*.

I have spoken before about the growth of what you call ego-consciousness—which, let me reiterate, has its own unique rewards. That psychological orientation will lead the species to another, equally unique kind of consciousness.

When the process began, however, the deep power of nature had to be "controlled" so that the growing consciousness could see itself as apart from this natural source. Yet children, so necessary to the species, continued to spring from women's wombs. Therefore the natural source was most flagrant, observable, and undeniable. For that reason the species—and not the male alone—placed so many taboos about female behavior and sexuality. In "subduing" its own female elements, the species tried to gain some psychological distance from the great natural source from which it was, for its own reasons, trying to emerge.

(Pause at 10:25.) Do you want a break?

("No.")

In the world of your present experience, sexual differences

are less apparent as you reach old age. Some women display what you think of as masculine characteristics, growing hair about their faces, speaking with heavier voices, or becoming angular; while some men speak with lighter, gentler tones than ever before, and their faces grow smoother, and the contours of their bodies soften.

Before puberty there is the same kind of seeming ambiguity. You stress the importance of sexual identification, for it seems to you that a young child must know that it will grow up to be a man or woman, in the most precise of terms—*(louder:)* toeing the line in the least particular.

The slightest deviation is looked upon with dismay, so that personal identity and worth are completely tied into identification with femaleness or maleness. Completely different characteristics, abilities, and performances are expected from those in each category. A male who does not feel himself fully male, therefore, does not trust his identity as a person. A woman doubtful of her complete femininity in the same manner does not trust the integrity of her personhood.

A lesbian or homosexual is on very shifting psychological ground, because the same interests and abilities that they feel most personally theirs are precisely those that mark them as sexual eccentrics.

These are simple enough examples, but the man who possesses interests considered feminine by your culture, who naturally wants to enter fields of interest considered womanly, experiences drastic conflicts between his sense of personhood and identity— and his sexuality as it is culturally defined. The same, of course, applies to women.

Because of your exaggerated focus, you therefore become relatively blind to other aspects of "sexuality." First of all, sexuality per se does not necessarily lead to intercourse. It can lead to acts that do not produce children. What you think of as lesbian or homosexual activity is quite natural sexual expression, biologically and psychologically. In more "ideal" environments such activity would flourish to some extent, particularly before and after prime reproductive years.

For those literal-minded readers, this does not mean that such activity would predominate at such times. It does mean that not all sexual activity is meant to end in childbirth—which is a biological impossibility, and would represent planetary catastrophe. So the species is blessed, if you will *(louder)* with many avenues for sexual expression. The strong focus that now predominates does inhibit the formation of certain kinds of friendships that would not necessarily at all result in sexual activity.

Lesbianism and homosexuality, as they are currently experienced, also represent exaggerated versions of natural inclinations, even as your experienced version of heterosexuality is exaggerated.

Take your break or end the session as you prefer.

("We'll take the break."

(10:50. After break, Seth returned with some excellent material for Jane and me. Included in it was a discussion of his relationship with us, and the place of his books in our lives. End at 12:05 A.M.)

SESSION 769, MARCH 29, 1976
9:20 P.M. MONDAY

(Jane finished typing her book, Psychic Politics, *and has been receiving more material on the manuscript she now calls* The World View of Paul Cézanne. *She's been getting up about dawn, and has throughout the winter, to write and to enjoy the beginning of the days.*

(Before tonight's session, she and I discussed the importance of Seth's material on human sexuality and hoped he would expand it.)

Now: Good evening.

("Good evening, Seth.")

Dictation. The so-called battle of the sexes, with its ramifications, is not "natural"—nor, in that context, is fighting between members of the same sex. Even in the animal kingdom, for example, males do not fight to the death over the females when they are in their natural state.

I will clear up my meaning of the word "natural" later. However, when you examine animal behavior even in its most natural-seeming environment, for instance, you are not observing the basic behavior patterns of such creatures, because those relatively isolated areas exist in your world. Quite simply, you cannot have one or two or twenty officially-designated natural regions in which you observe animal activity, and expect to find anything more than the current adaptation of those creatures—an adaptation that is superimposed upon their "natural" reactions.

The balance of resources, animal travel patterns, migrations, weather conditions—all of these must be taken into consideration. Such isolated observation areas merely present you with a distorted picture of natural behavior, because the animals are also imprisoned within them. Civilization binds them round.

Other animals are kept out. The hunted and the prey are highly regulated. All areas of animal behavior alter to fit the circumstances as much as possible, and this includes sexual activity. To some extent the animals have been conditioned to the changing world. Now man is obviously part of nature, so you may say: "But those changes wrought by him are natural." When he studies such animal behavior, however, and sometimes uses the sexual patterns of the animals to make certain points about human sexuality, then man does not take this into consideration, but speaks as if the present observed animal behavior is the indication of a prime or basic nature inherent in their biology.

(9:35.) It is not natural, then, for men to fight over women. This is a purely cultural, learned behavior. In terms of history as you understand it, the species could not withstand such misapplied energy, nor could it have withstood such constant antagonism.

Each species is involved in a cooperative venture, upon which ultimately all earthly existence rests. You project your present beliefs backward into history, and you misinterpret many of the conditions that you observe in the natural world. This cooperation that I speak of is based on love, and that love has a biological as well as a spiritual basis. Your beliefs, for example, cause you to deny the existence of emotions in animals, and any instances of love among them are assigned to "blind" instinct.

To some extent the churches as well as the scientists are responsible, but priests and scientists are not some foreign people, thrust upon you. They represent various aspects of yourselves. The species developed its own kind of consciousness, as it found it necessary to isolate itself to some degree from its environment and the other creatures within it. As a result, the religions preached that only man had a soul and was dignified by emotional feelings. In its way science went along very nicely by postulating man in a mechanistic world, with each creature run by an impeccable machine of instinct, blind alike to pain or desire.

The love and cooperation that forms the basis of all life, however, shows itself in many ways. Sexuality represents one aspect, and an important one. In larger terms, it is as natural for a man to love a man, and for a woman to love a woman, as it is to show love for the opposite sex. For that matter, it is more natural to be bisexual. Such is the "natural" nature of the species.

Instead, you have put love into very definite categories, so that its existence is right only under the most limited conditions. Love goes underground, but springs up in distorted forms and exaggerated tendencies. You have followed this course for different reasons at different times. Neither sex is to blame. Instead your sexual situation is simply another reflection of the state of your consciousness. As a species, presently at least in the Western world, you equate sex and love. You imagine that sexual expression is the only one natural to love. Love, in other words, must it seems express itself exclusively through the exploration *(humorously and deeper)*, in one way or another, of the beloved's sexual portions.

This is hardly the only limitation placed upon love's expression, however. There are innumerable books written with instructions, each proclaiming the said methods to be the proper ones. Certain kinds of orgasm are "the best." Love's expression is furthermore permitted only between members of the opposite sex. Generally speaking, these individuals must be more or less of the same age. There are other taboos, involving racial restrictions, or cultural, social, and economic ones. If this were not enough, large segments of the population believe that sex is wrong to begin with—a spiritual debasement, allowed by God only so that the species can continue.

(Pause at 10:02.) Since love and sex are equated, obvious conflicts arise. Mother love is the only category that is considered wholesome, and therefore nonsexual under most conditions. A father can feel very guilty about his love for his children, for he has been conditioned to believe that love is expressed only through sex, or else it is unmanly, while sex with one's children is taboo.

Creativity rides the tides of love. When love is denied its natural expression, creativity suffers. Your beliefs lead you to suppose that a natural bisexuality would result in the death of the family, the destruction of morals, rampant sexual crimes, and the loss of sexual identity. I would say, however, that my last sentence adequately describes your present situation *(with dry humor)*. The acceptance of the species' natural bisexuality would ultimately help solve not only those problems but many others, including the large instances of violence, and acts of murder. In your terms, however, and in your circumstances, there is not apt to be any easy transition.

The parent-child relationship has its own unique emotional structure, which survives even those distortions you have placed upon it, and its ancient integrity would not be weakened, but strengthened, if greater stress were laid upon your bisexual nature.

Children would fare far better if the ancient parental qualities were not so forcibly focused upon the mother. This in itself leads to more dependence upon the mother than is healthy, and forms an artificial allegiance between mother and child against the father.

Take your break.

(10:16 to 10:38.)

Now: Heterosexual love is one important expression of bisexuality, and sexually represents the reproductive abilities. Heterosexuality, however, rests <u>upon</u> the bisexual basis, and *(intently)* without man's bisexual nature, the larger frameworks of the family—the clan, tribe, government, civilization—would be impossible.

Basically, then, man's inherent bisexuality provides the basis for the cooperation that makes physical survival, and any kind of cultural interaction, possible. If the "battle of the sexes" were as prevalent as supposed, and as natural and ferocious, then there literally would be no cooperation between males and females for any purpose. There would be none between men or between women either, for they would be in a constant state of battle against each other.

In the natural biological flow of a person's life, there are periods of varying intensities, in which love and its expression fluctuates, and tends toward different courses. There are also individual variations that are of great importance. These natural rhythms are seldom observed, however. Tendencies toward lesbianism or homosexuality in children are quite natural. They are so feared, however, that often just-as-natural leanings toward heterosexuality are blocked. Instead, the young person is stereotyped.

Individual inclinations toward creativity often emerge in a strong fashion in adolescence. If those drives in either sex do not conform in expression to those expected of the male or female, then such young persons become confused. The creative expression seems to be in direct contradiction to the sexual standards expected.

I am not saying that lesbianism and homosexuality are merely stages leading to heterosexuality. I <u>am</u> saying that lesbianism, homosexuality, and heterosexuality <u>are</u> valid expressions of man's bisexual nature.

(Slowly at 10:54:) I am also stressing the fact that love and sexuality are not necessarily the same thing. Sex is love's

expression, but it is only <u>one</u> of love's expressions. Sometimes it is quite "natural" to express love in another way. Because of the connotations of the word "sex," however, it may seem to some of you that I am advocating a promiscuous sexual relationship with "no holes barred" *(smile)*. You may delete that.

Instead, I am saying that deeper bonds of biological and spiritual love lie at the basis of all personal and cultural relationships, a love that transcends <u>your ideas</u> of sexuality. Heterosexual love, as it is understood at least, gives you a family of parents and children—an important unit, about which other groups form. If only stereotyped ideas of female-male relationships operated, however, there would be no bond or stimulus great enough to forge one family to another. The antagonism between males would be too great. Competition between females would be too severe. Wars would wipe out struggling tribes before any traditions were formed.

In the social world as in the microscopic one, cooperation again is paramount. Only a basic bisexuality could give the species the leeway necessary, and prevent stereotyped behavior of a kind that would hamper creativity and social commerce. That basic sexual nature allows you the fulfillment of individual abilities, so that the species does not fall into extinction. Man's recognition of his bisexual nature is, therefore, a must in his future.

There are, again, obvious differences between the sexes. They are insignificant, and appear large only because you concentrate so upon them. The great human qualities of love, strength, compassion, intellect and imagination do not belong to one sex or the other.

(11:13.) Only an understanding of this inherent bisexual nature will release those qualities in each individual, regardless of sex. Those same abilities are natural characteristics of people in each race, of course, yet you have consistently made the same kind of distinctions in racial terms as you have in sexual ones, so that certain races appear as feminine or masculine to you. You project your sexual beliefs outward upon the nations, then, and often the terminology of the nations and of wars is the same as that used to describe sex.

You speak, for example, of domination and submission, of the master and the slave, of the rape of a nation—terms used in war and sex alike.

Male and female are each members of the human race—or species if you prefer—so these divisions were made in the species itself, by itself. They are the result of distinctions arising, again, as the species experimented with its line of consciousness, and brought into being the appearance of separation between itself and the rest of the natural world.

Take a break.

(11:24 to 11:33.)

Now. *(With dry humor again:)* Before my comments for Ruburt: I thought my risqué remark about "no holes barred" was quite in keeping with the content of such material. It is difficult to be prissy when discussing such a topic—but if you feel that others might be offended, do as you wish.

(After giving some material for Jane, Seth ended the session at 12:09 A.M.

(Until she told me following the session, I didn't realize that Jane was slightly discomfited by Seth's remark about holes. I certainly wasn't. I thought that her reaction itself was humorous; apparently Seth did too. In any case, we obviously didn't delete the passage.

(Both of us were very glad to have Seth deliver this material on sex, as we've received many letters from men and women who were confused about their sexual identities, and often overwhelmed by feelings of guilt because of an orientation toward lesbianism or homosexuality.)

SESSION 770, APRIL 5, 1976
9:41 P.M. MONDAY

(Without further greeting, humorously:) Sexation.

("Good.")

Your identity is simply not dependent upon your psychological or biological sexuality.

Your sexual characteristics represent a portion of your personhood. They provide vital areas of expression, and focal points about which to group experience. Your sexual qualities <u>are a part of your nature</u>, but they do not define it.

Your beliefs so structure your experience individually and *en masse,* however, that evidential material contrary to those ideas shows itself but seldom, or in distorted or exaggerated form. It is quite natural, biologically and psychologically, to operate in certain fashions that are not acceptable in your society, and that seem to run counter to your picture of mankind's history. In terms of your definitions, then, it is quite natural for some people to behave as males sexually and as females psychologically. It is quite "natural" for others to operate in a reverse fashion.

Again, this may seem difficult to understand, because you assign psychological characteristics to sexual affiliation, whichever it is. There will always be people who naturally seek the experience of parenthood. All of them will not necessarily be heterosexual at any given time.

The larger pattern of human personhood demands a bisexual affiliation that allows leeway in sexual encounters, a leeway that provides a framework in which individuals can express' feelings, abilities, and characteristics that follow the natural inclines of the personal psyche rather than sexual stereotypes. I am not speaking here of anything so simple as merely allowing women more freedom, or relieving men from the conventional bread-winner's role. I am certainly not talking about "open marriage" as it is currently understood, but of far greater issues. Before we can consider these, however, there are several points I would like to make.

(9:58.) There are biological possibilities, seldom activated in your present circumstances, that have some bearing upon the subject at hand.

Puberty comes at a certain time, triggered by deep mechanisms that are related to the state of the natural world, the condition of the species, and those cultural beliefs that in a certain sense you transpose upon the natural world. In other respects, your cultural environment is of course natural. The time that puberty comes varies, then, and afterwards it is possible to parent a child. A time then comes when the period is over. During what is called the sexually active time; the larger dimensions of person-hood become strictly narrowed into sexually stereotyped roles—and all aspects of identity that do not fit are ignored or denied. The fact is that few people fit those roles. They are largely the result of the interpretations of religion as conventionally understood. And the scientists, for all their seeming independence, often simply found new intellectually acceptable reasons for unconsciously held emotional beliefs.

Biologically there is a period very rarely experienced, as jokingly suggested in the "sick jokes" about senility and second childhood. This particular latent biological ability shows itself only upon the rarest instances—because, for one thing, it represents a feat now scarcely desirable. Physically, however, the body is quite able to completely regenerate itself as it approaches old age. Indeed, a quite legitimate second puberty is possible, in which the male's seed is youthfully strong and vital, and the woman's womb is pliable and able to bear. There are, I believe, Biblical tales of such births resulting.

In times of overpopulation, this mechanism is hardly desirable, but it is a part of the species held in abeyance now, representing nature's capabilities. In some areas of your world, isolated peoples live on past a hundred years, vital and strong, because they are untouched by your beliefs, and because they live in sympathy and accord with the world as they know and understand it. Occasionally such second puberties happen then, with resulting childbirth, as a small group attempts to maintain its own biological stance.

(10:18.) Usually the second puberty follows the same sexual orientation as the first, but not always—for it is quite possible for the new affiliation to be the opposite of the first. This is even rarer—but so does the species protect itself.

Through medical techniques some of your old people are kept alive long enough so that this process begins, appearing in distorted form, sometimes psychologically apparent but biologically frustrated. The second puberty is dead-ended, then. It has nowhere to go. It is not now biologically pertinent or needed.

Left alone, some of these people would die with a feeling of satisfaction. Kept alive through medical techniques, the physical mechanism continues its struggles to revitalize the body and bring about this second puberty—that naturally would only come about under different conditions, with the mind far more alert and the will unimpaired. Now, to some extent (underlined) there is a connection between this innate, rarely observed second puberty and the development of cancer, in which growth is specifically apparent in an exaggerated manner.

(Long pause.) Give us a moment . . . In almost all such cases involving cancer, spiritual and psychic growth is being denied, or the individual feels that he or she can no longer grow properly in personal, psychic, terms. This attempt to grow then activates body mechanisms that result in the overgrowth of certain cells. The individual insists upon growing or upon death, and forces an artificial situation in which growth itself becomes physically disastrous.

This is because a blockage occurs. The individual wants to grow in terms of personhood, but is afraid of doing so. There are always individual variations that must be taken into consideration, but often such a person feels a martyr to his or her sex, imprisoned by it and unable to escape. This can obviously apply to cancers affecting sexual areas, but is often in the background of any such condition. Energy is being blocked because of problems that began—in your terms—with sexual questions in puberty. Energy is experienced as sexual.

Now, old people who are considered senile or unmanageable are sometimes experiencing new bursts of sexual activity for which no outlet is given. Beside this, they have lost their conventional sexual roles, in which they earlier expressed their energy.

There are often hormonal changes occurring that go unnoticed. Many express a nervous, erratic type of behavior as they are aroused—some not only sexually but intellectually. The new adolescence never comes. The new puberty dies a slow death, for your society has no framework in which to understand it. And indeed it shows itself in a distorted fashion that can appear most grotesque.

Take your break.

(10:39 to 11:02.)

Now: Love is a biological necessity, a force operating to one degree or another in all biological life. Without love there is no physical commitment to life—no psychic hold.

Love exists whether or not it is sexually expressed, though it is natural for love to seek expression. Love implies loyalty. It implies commitment. This applies to lesbian and homosexual relationships as well as to heterosexual ones. In your society, however, identity is so related to sexual stereotypes that few people know themselves well enough to understand the nature of love, and to make any such commitments.

A transitory period is currently taking place, in which women seem to seek the promiscuous sexual freedom more generally granted to men. It is believed that males are naturally promiscuous, aroused by sexual stimuli almost completely divorced from any complementary "deeper" response. The male, then, is thought to want sex whether or not he has any love response to the woman in question—or sometimes to desire her precisely because he does not love her. In such cases, sex becomes not an expression of love, but an expression of derision or scorn.

So women, accepting these ideas often, seek for a situation in which they too can feel free to express their sexual desires openly, whether or not any love is involved. Yet loyalty is love's partner, and the primates display such evidence in varying degrees. The male in particular has been taught to separate love and sex, so that a schizophrenic condition results that tears apart his psyche—in operational terms—as he lives his life.

The expression of sexuality is considered male, while the expression of love is not considered manly. To some extent or another, then, the male feels forced to divide the expression of his love from the expression of his sexuality. It would be disastrous for women to follow the same course.

This great division has led to your major wars. This does not mean that men were alone responsible for wars. It does mean that the male so divorced himself from the common fountain of love and sex that the repressed energy came forth in those aggressive acts of cultural rape and death, instead of birth.

When you look at the animal kingdom, you suppose that the male chooses blindly, led by "dumb" instinct, so that in overall terms one female will do as well as any other. When you discover that a certain chemical or scent will attract a certain male insect, for example, you take it for granted that that element is alone responsible for drawing the male to the female. You take it for granted, in other words, that individual differences do not apply in such cases so remote from your own reality.

You simply are not able to understand the nature of such consciousnesses, and so you interpret their behavior according to your beliefs. This would be sad enough if you did not often use such distorted data to further define the nature of male and female behavior.

In so distorting your ideas of sex, you further limit the great capacities of human loyalty, which is always connected with love and love's expression. Lesbian and homosexual relationships then are at best tenuous, overwrought with confused emotions, very seldom able to maintain a stability that allows for individual growth. Heterosexual relationships also break down, for the identity of each partner becomes based upon sexual roles that may or may not apply to the individuals involved.

Since you feel that sex is the only proper method of love's expression, and yet also believe that sex and love are divided, you are in a quandary. These sexual beliefs are also far more important in national relationships than you realize, for you attempt to take what you think of as a masculine stance as a nation. So, for example, does Russia. India takes a feminine stance—in terms of your beliefs, now.

Take a brief break.

(11:35. "I'm still half in trance," Jane said, "but I think book dictation's over. . . ." I got her a beer. Then, at 11:37:)

One small note: A male with growths of any kind—kidney stones or ulcers, for example—has tendencies he considers feminine, and therefore "dependent," of which he is ashamed. In a mock biological ceremony, he gives birth to the extent that he produces within his body material that was not there before. In ulcers the stomach becomes the womb—bloodied, giving birth to sores—his interpretation of a male's "grotesque" attempt to express feminine characteristics.

End of dictation.

(11:41. Seth now delivered five minutes of material for Jane, and closed the session at 11:46 P.M.

("I'm not up to it tonight," Jane said, "but there's lots of material he could give on the ulcer thing right now. It's all there. Maybe I should take a short break and see if he'll come back, instead of ending the session. . . ."

(She was tired, yet exhilarated too—I could tell. We decided to end the session, though.)

Chapter 5

The Psyche, Love, Sexual Expression, and Creativity

SESSION 771, APRIL 14, 1976
9:05 P.M. WEDNESDAY

Now—

("Good evening, Seth.")

—good evening.

Your ideas about sexuality and your beliefs about the nature of the psyche often paint a picture of very contradictory elements. The psyche and its relationship to sexuality affects your ideas of health and illness, creativity, and all of the ordinary areas of individual life. In this chapter, therefore, we will consider some of the implications that result.

Chapter heading: "The Psyche, Love, Sexual Expression *(louder and humorously)*, and Creativity."

Give us a moment... In your terms, again, the psyche contains what you would consider male and female characteristics, while not being male or female itself.

In those terms and in that regard, the psyche is a bank from which sexual affiliations are drawn. Basically, however, there are

75

no clear, set, human, psychological characteristics that belong to one sex or the other. Again, this would lead to a pattern too rigid for the development of the species, and give you too-specialized behavior patterns that would not allow you to cope as a species— particularly with the many varieties of social groupings possible.

Your psychological tests show you only the current picture of males and females, brought up from infancy with particular sexual beliefs. These beliefs program the child from infancy, of course, so that it behaves in certain fashions in adulthood. The male seems to perform better at mathematical tasks, and so-called logical mental activity, while the female performs better in a social context, in value development and personal relationships. The male shows up better in the sciences, while the female is considered intuitional.

(9:20.) It should be obvious to many of my readers that this is learned behavior. You cannot teach a boy to be "the strong silent male type," and then expect him to excel either verbally or in social relationships. You cannot expect a girl to show "strong, logical thought development" when she is taught that a woman is intuitional—that the intuitions are opposed to logic, and that she must be feminine, or nonlogical, at all costs. This is fairly obvious.

The child is not born a sponge, however, empty but ready to soak up knowledge. It is already soaked in knowledge. Some will come to the surface, so to speak, and be used consciously. Some will not. I am saying here that to some extent the child in the womb is aware of the mother's beliefs and information, and that to some extent (underlined) it is "programmed" to behave in a certain fashion, or to grow in a certain fashion as a result.

Basically the species is relatively so freewheeling, with so many potentials, that it is necessary that the mother's beliefs provide a kind of framework in the beginning, allowing the child to focus its abilities in desired directions. It knows ahead of time then the biological, spiritual, and social environment into which it is born. It is somewhat prepared to grow in a certain direction—a direction that is applicable and suited to its conditions.

Beliefs about the infant's sexual nature are of course a part of its advance programming. We are not speaking here of forced growth patterns, or of psychic or biological directions, impressed upon it so that any later divergence from them causes inevitable stress or pain. The fact remains that the child receives patterns of behavior, gently nudging it to grow in certain directions. In normal learning, of course, both parents urge the child to behave in certain fashions. Beside this, however, certain general, learned patterns are biologically transmitted to the child through the genes. Certain kinds of knowledge are transmitted through the genes besides that generally known, having to do with cellular formations and so forth.

(Pause at 9:35.) Give us a moment . . . Survival of the human species, as it has developed, is a matter of belief far more than is understood—for certain beliefs are now built in. They become biologically pertinent and transmitted. I mean something else here besides, for example, a telepathic transmission: the translation of beliefs into physical codes that then become biological cues. [As a result], it then becomes easier for a boy to act in a given manner biologically than in another.

If women have felt that their biological survival depended upon the cultivation of certain attributes over others, for instance, then this information becomes chromosome data, as vital to the development of the new organism as any other physical data involving cellular structure.

The mother also provides the same kind of information to a a male offspring. The father contributes his share in each case. Over the generations, then, certain characteristics appear to be quite naturally male or female, and these will vary to some extent according to the civilizations and world conditions. Each individual is highly unique, however, so these models for behavior will vary. They can indeed be changed in a generation, for the experience of each person alters the original information. This provides leeway that is important.

The child, also, uses such information as a guide only; as a premise upon which it bases early behavior. As the mind develops, the child immediately begins to question the early assumptions. This questioning of basic premises is one of the greatest divisions between you and the animal world.

The psyche then contains, again in your terms, female and male characteristics. These are put together, so to speak, in the human personality with great leeway and in many proportions.

New paragraph: As simply put as possible, love is the force out of which being comes, and we will consider this statement much more thoroughly later in this book. Love seeks expression and creativity. Sexual expression is one way that love seeks creativity. It is hardly the only way, however. Love finds expression through the arts, religion, play, and helpful actions toward others. Period. It cannot be confined to sexual expression only, nor can rules be given as to how often normal adults should sexually express themselves.

Many men, labeled homosexual by themselves and others, want to be fathers. Their beliefs and those of your society lead them to imagine that they must always be heterosexual or homosexual. Many feel a desire toward women that is also inhibited. Your male or female orientation limits you in ways that you do not understand. For example, in many cases the gentle "homosexual" father has a better innate idea of manliness than a heterosexual male who believes that men must be cruel, insensitive, and competitive. These are both stereotyped images, however.

Love can be expressed quite legitimately through the arts. This does not mean that such a person is repressing sexuality in any given case, and stealing its energy for creative production— though, of course, this may be the case. Many natural artists in any field normally express love through such creative endeavors, rather than through sexual actions.

(10:05.) This does not mean that such persons never have sexual encounters that are enjoyable, and even of an enduring nature. It means that the thrust of their love is, overall, expressed through the production of art, through which it seeks a statement that speaks in other than corporal terms.

A great artist in any field or in any time instinctively feels a private personhood that is greater than the particular sexual identity. As long as you equate identity with your sexuality, you will limit the potentials of the individual and of the species. Each person will generally find it easier to operate as male or female, lesbian or homosexual, but each person is primarily bisexual. Bisexuality implies parenthood as much as it implies lesbian or homosexual relationships. Again, here, sexual encounters are a natural part of love's expression, but they are not the limit of love's expression.

Many quite fine nonsexual relationships are denied, because of the connotations placed upon lesbianism or homosexuality. Many heterosexual relationships are also denied to persons labeled as not being heterosexual, by themselves or society. People so labeled often feel propelled out of sheer confusion to express their love only through sexual acts. They feel forced to imitate what they think the natural male or female is like, and on occasion end up with ludicrous caricatures. These caricatures infuriate those so imitated—because they carry such hints of truth, and point out so cleverly the exaggerations of maleness or femaleness that many heterosexuals have clamped upon in their own natures.

Take your break.

(10:29 to 10:37.)

Now: In some historical periods it was desirable in practical terms that a man have many wives, so that if he died in battle his seed might be planted in many wombs—particularly in times when diseases struck men and women down often in young adulthood.

When physical conditions are adverse, such social traditions have often emerged. In times of overpopulation, so-called homosexual and lesbian tendencies come to the surface—but also there is the tendency to express love in other than physical ways, and the emergence of large social issues and challenges into which men and women can throw their energies. There are "lost" portions of the Bible having to do with sexuality, and with Christ's beliefs concerning it, that were considered blasphemous and did not come down to you through history.

Again, it is natural to express love through sexual acts— natural and good. It is not natural to express love only through sexual acts, however. Many of Freud's sexual ideas did not reflect man's natural condition. The complexes and neuroses outlined and defined are products of your traditions and beliefs. You will naturally find some evidence for them in observed behavior. Many of the traditions do come from the Greeks, from the great Greek play-writers, who quite beautifully and tragically presented the quality of the psyche as it showed itself in the light of Grecian traditions.

The boy does not seek, naturally, to "dethrone" the father. He seeks to emulate him; he seeks to be himself as fully as it seems to him that his father was himself. He hopes to go beyond himself and his own capabilities for himself and for his father.

As a child he once thought that his father was immortal, in human terms—that he could do no wrong. The son tries to vindicate the father by doing no wrong himself, and perhaps by succeeding where it seems the father might have failed. It is much more natural for the male to try to vindicate the father than it is to destroy him, or envy him in negative terms.

(10:54.) The child is simply the male child. He is not jealous of the father with the mother, in the way that is often supposed. The male child does not possess an identity so focused upon its

maleness. I am not saying that children do not have a sexual nature from birth. They simply do not focus upon their maleness or femaleness in the way that is supposed.

To the male child, the penis is something that belongs to him personally in the same way that an arm or leg does, or that his mouth or anus does. He does not consider it a weapon *(humorously)*. He is not jealous of his father's love for the mother, for he understands quite well that her love for him is just as strong. He does not wish to possess his mother sexually in the way that adults currently suppose. He does not understand those terms. He may at times be jealous of her attention, but this is not a sexual jealousy in conventionally understood terms. Your beliefs blind you to the sexual nature of children. They do enjoy their bodies. They are sexually aroused. The psychological connotations, however, are not those assigned to them by adults.

The beliefs involving the son's inherent rivalry with the father, and his need to overthrow him, follow instead patterns of culture and tradition, economic and social, rather than biological or psychological. Those ideas serve as handy explanations for behavior that is not inherent or biologically pertinent.

(11:05. This marked the end of dictation. After giving a page of material for Jane and me, Seth ended the session at 11:18 P.M.)

SESSION 772, APRIL 19, 1976
9:18 P.M. MONDAY

Dictation.
("Good.")
In a manner of speaking, humanity deals with different predominant themes at different times. There may be minor interweaving ones, but the nature of personality, religion, politics, the family, and the arts—all of these are considered in the light of the predominating theme.

In usual historic terms, humanity has been experimenting with its own unique kind of consciousness, and as I have mentioned many times, this necessitated an arbitrary division between the subject and the perceiver—nature and man—and brought about a situation in which the species came to consider itself apart from the rest of existence.

What you think of as (underlined) male ego-oriented characteristics are simply those human attributes that the species encouraged, brought into the foreground, and stressed. Using those actually as guidelines, you have so far viewed your world and formed your cultures. There are some exceptions of note, but here I am speaking historically of the Western world with its Roman and Greek heritage. Your gods became masculine then; competitive. You saw the species pitted against nature, and man pitted against man. You consider the Greek tragedies great because they echo so firmly your own beliefs. Man is seen in opposition in the most immediate fashion with his own father. Family relationships become a mirror of those beliefs, which are then of course taken as statements of fact concerning the human condition. You thus have a very polarized male-female concept.

Those characteristics that you consider female are, then, those that did not predominate because they represented the source of nature from which the species sought release. To some extent this was a true, creative, sexual drama—again, of high pretense, for in its own way the consciousness of the species was playing for high stakes, and the drama had to be believable.

(Pause at 9:34.) It was seeking for a multiplication of consciousness, forming new offshoots from its own source. It had to pretend to dislike and disown that source in the same way that an adolescent may momentarily turn aside from its parents in order to encourage independence. Before the so-called flowering of Greek and Roman cultures, consciousness had not as yet made that specialization. There were gods and goddesses galore, and deities in whose natures the feminine and masculine characteristics merged. There were deities part human and part animal. The species, then, had not yet taken up the theme that has been predominant in Western culture.

These changes first occurred in man's stories of the deities. As the species divorced itself from nature, so the animal gods began to vanish. Man first changed his myths, and then altered the reality that reflected them.

Before then there were various kinds of divisions of labor, but great leeway in sexual expression. Children were a necessary part of the family, for a family was a band of people who belonged together, cooperating in the search for food and shelter.

Homosexual or lesbian relationships, as you term them, existed quite freely, and simultaneously. These were considered pertinent with or without sexual expression, and served as strong bonds of sisterhood and brotherhood.

When you view the animal kingdom, you also do so through your specialized sexual beliefs, studying the behavior of the male and female, looking for patterns of aggressiveness, territorial jealousy, passivity, mothering instincts, or whatever. These specialities of interest make you blind to many larger dimensions of animal behavior. To some degree, the so-called mothering instinct belongs to male and female alike in any species that can be so designated. Animals have close friendships, with or without sexual expression, with members of the same sex. Love and devotion are not the prerogatives of one sex or one species.

Take your break.

(9:52 to 10:19.)

As a result, you see in nature only what you want to see, and you provide yourselves with a pattern or model of nature that conforms with your beliefs.

Love and devotion are <u>largely</u> seen as female characteristics. Societies and organizations of church and state are seen as male. It is not so much that the male and the female be considered equal as it is that the male and female elements in each person should be released and expressed. Immediately, many of you may be annoyed or alarmed, thinking that of course I mean sexual expression. That is a portion of such expression. But I am speaking of releasing within each individual the great human characteristics and abilities that are often denied expression because they are assigned to the opposite sex.

In your present framework, because of the male-female specialization—the male orientation, the implication that the ego is male while the psyche is female—you force upon yourselves great divisions in which operationally the intellect seems separate from the intuitions, and you set up a situation in which opposites seem to apply where there are none. When you think of a scientist, the majority of you will think of a male, an intellectual, an "objective" thinker who takes great pains not to be emotional, or to identify with the subject being examined or studied.

There seems to be a division between science and religion, for even organized religion has an intuitive basis. The male scientist is often ashamed of using his intuitions, for not only do they appear to be unscientific, but female as well. It is what others will think about his masculinity that such a man is concerned with. To be "illogical" is a scientific "crime"—not so much because it is an unscientific attribute, but because it is considered a <u>feminine</u> one. Science has followed the male orientation and become its epitome. Up until the present, science has consistently tried to do without the so-called feminine qualities. It has divorced knowledge from emotion, understanding from identification, and stressed sexuality over personhood.

To an extent, some people in the sciences manage to blend the so-called female and male characteristics. When they do so, seeming oppositions and contradictions disappear. To whatever degree, more than their contemporaries, they do not allow sexual roles to blind them psychologically. Therefore they are more apt to combine reason and emotion, intuitions and intellect, and in so doing invent theories that reconcile previous contradictions. They unify, expand, and create, rather than diversify.

Einstein was such a person in the sciences. While he was tainted to some extent by conventional sexual beliefs, he still felt his own personhood in such a way that he gladly took advantage of characteristics considered feminine. As a youngster particularly, he rebelled against male-oriented learning and orientation. This rebellion was psychological—that is, he maintained an acceptable male orientation in terms of sexual activity, but he would not restrain his mind and soul with such nonsense. The world felt the result of his great intuitive abilities, and of his devotion.

(10:47.) Because of the world situation, and the overall male orientation of science, the results of his work were largely put to the uses of manipulation and control.

Generally, reason and intellect are then considered male qualities, and the frameworks for civilization, science, and an organized world. The intuitions and the impulses are considered erratic, untrustworthy, feminine, and to be controlled. The world exists because of spontaneous order. Civilization began because of the impulse of people to be together. It grew spontaneously and came into order. You only see the outside of many processes because your objectified viewpoint does not allow you the identification that would show you more. It seems to you then that all systems sometime break down—become less orderly or fall into chaos.

You apply this belief to physical systems and psychological ones. In terms of sex, you insist upon a picture that shows you a growth into a sexual identity, a clear focus, and then in old age a falling away of clear sexual identification into "sexual disorder." It does not occur to you that the original premise or focus, the identification of identity with sexual nature, is "unnatural." It is you, then, who form the entire framework from which your judgment is made. In many cases the person is truer to his or her own identity in childhood or old age, when greater individual freedom is allowed, and sexual roles are more flexible.

Any deep exploration of the self will lead you into areas that will confound conventional beliefs about sexuality. You will discover an identity, a psychological and psychic identity, that is in your terms male and female, one in which those abilities of each sex are magnified, released, and expressed. They may not be so released in normal life, but you will meet the greater dimensions of your own reality, and at least in the dream state catch a glimpse of the self that transcends a one-sex orientation.

Such an encounter with the psyche is often met by great artists or writers, or by mystics. This kind of realization is necessary if you are to ever transcend the framework of seeming opposites in which your world is involved.

The overly specific sexual orientation, then, reflects a basic division in consciousness. It not only separates a man from his own intuitions and emotions to some extent, or a woman from her own intellect, but it effectively provides a civilization in which mind and heart, fact and revelation, appear completely divorced. To some degree each person is at war with the psyche, for all of an individual's human characteristics must be denied unless they fit in with those considered normal to the sexual identity.

Take your break.

(11:12 to 11:33.)

To one degree or another in ordinary life, you end up with sexual caricatures in practical existence.

You do not understand what true womanhood or true manhood is. You are forced instead to concentrate upon a shallow kind of diversity. As a result, the reflection of sexual schism taints all of your activities, but most of all it limits your psychological reality.

Since you value sexual performance in the most limited of terms, and use that largely as a focus of identity, then both your old and young suffer consequences that are not so much the result of age as of sexual prejudice. It is interesting to note that both the old and the young also find themselves outside of your organizational frameworks. The young are more freewheeling in their thoughts before they accept sexual roles, and the old are more freewheeling in theirs because they have discarded their sexual roles. I did not say that old or young had no sexual expression— but that both groups did not identify their identities with their sexual roles. There are of course exceptions. If the man or the woman is taught that identity is a matter of sexual performance, however, and that that performance must cease at a certain age, then the sense of identity can also begin to disintegrate. If children feel that identity is dependent upon such performance, then they will begin to perform as quickly as possible. They will squeeze their identity into sexual clothes, and the society will suffer because the great creative thrusts of growing intellect and intuitions will be divided at puberty, precisely when they are needed.

Ideally, the adult male or female would rejoice in sexual expression and find an overall orientation, but would also bask in a greater psychological and psychic identity that experienced and expressed all of the great human capabilities of mind and heart, which splash over any artificial divisions.

End of dictation. Give us a moment . . .

(11:49. After delivering a page or so of material for Jane, Seth wound up the session at 12:12 A.M.)

SESSION 773, APRIL 26, 1976
9:28 P.M. MONDAY

Now: Dictation.

You have put sexual labels, then, on the intellect and the emotions, so that they seem like opposites to you.

You have tried to divide mental and emotional characteristics between the two sexes, forcing a stereotyped behavior. Again, the male who was intuitive or artistically gifted in certain ways often therefore considered himself homosexual, whether or not he was, because his emotional and mental characteristics seem to fit the female rather than the male sex.

The woman who had interests beyond those acceptable as feminine was often in the same position. Because the intellect and the emotions were considered so separately, however, attempts to express intuitive abilities often resulted in, and often do result in, "unreasonable" behavior.

In certain circles now it is fashionable to deny the intellectual capacities in favor of feeling, sentiment, or intuitive actions. Intellectual concerns then become suspect, and recourse to reason is considered a failing. Instead, of course, intellectual and intuitive behavior should be beautifully blended. In the same way you have attempted to force the expression of love into a purely—or exclusively—sexual orientation. An affectionate caress or kiss between members of the same sex is generally not considered proper. The taboos include most aspects of the sense of touch in connection with the human body.

Touching is considered so basically sexual that the most innocuous touching of any portion of the body by another person is considered potentially dangerous. On the one hand you are too specific in your use of the term "sexuality"; yet in another way, and in that context, you feel that any kind of affection must naturally lead to sexual expression, if given its way. Your beliefs make this sexual eventuality appear as a fact of experience.

This also forces you to guard your emotional life very closely. As a result, any show of love is to some extent inhibited unless it can legitimately find expression sexually. In many instances love itself seems wrong because it must imply sexual expression at times when such expression is not possible, or even desired. Some people have a great capacity for love, devotion, and loyalty, which would naturally seek expression in many diverse ways—through strong enduring friendships, devotion to causes in which they believe, through vocations in which they help others. They may not be particularly sexually oriented. This need not mean that they are inhibiting their sexuality. It is pathetic and ludicrous for them to believe that they must have intercourse frequently in their youth, or to set up standards of normality against which they must measure their sexual experience.

(9:51.) In fact, Western society has attempted to force all expression of love and devotion into sexual activity, or otherwise ban it entirely. Sexual performance is considered the one safe way of using the great potential of human emotions. When it seems to you that society is becoming licentious, in many ways it is most restrained and inhibited.

It means that all options except sexual freedom have been denied. The great force of love and devotion is withdrawn from personal areas of individual creativity through purposeful work. It is being withdrawn from expression through government or law. It is being denied expression through meaningful personal relationships, and forced into a narrow expression through a sexuality that then will indeed become meaningless.

It has been said by some women working toward "equal rights" that the species has only used half of its potential by suppressing the abilities of women. In larger terms, however, each individual suffers whenever identity is defined primarily as a matter of sexual orientation.

Generally speaking, there will be a specific overall sexual

orientation of a biological nature, but the mental and emotional human characteristics are simply not meted out according to sex. Such identification cuts the individual in half, so that each person uses but half of his or her potential. This causes a schism in all of your cultural activities.

(10:05.) Give us a moment... On the one hand many of you have been taught that sexual expression is wrong, evil, or debasing. You have also been told that if you do not express your sexuality, you are displaying unnatural repression, and further-more you are led to think that you must above all force yourself to enjoy this ambiguous sexual nature. The old idea that good women do not enjoy sex has hardly disappeared. Yet women are taught that natural expressions of love, playful caresses, are inap-propriate unless an immediate follow-through to a sexual climax is given. Men are taught to count their worth according to the strength of the sexual drive and its conquests. They are taught to inhibit the expression of love as a weakness, and yet to perform sexually as often as possible. In such a sexual climate there is little wonder that you become confused.

Take your break.

(10:13. "I didn't feel particularly with it tonight," Jane said, after I remarked that break came a bit early. Resume at 10:44.)

The sexual schism begins when the male child is taught to identify exclusively with the father image, and the female child with the mother image—for here you have a guilt insidiously incorporated into the growth process.

Children of either sex identify quite naturally with both parents, and any enforced method of exclusively directing the child to such a single identification is limiting. Under such con-ditions, feelings of guilt immediately begin to arise whenever such a child feels natural affiliations toward the other parent.

The stronger those natural inclinations are, the more the child is directed to ignore them in your society, since certain characteristics, again, are considered exclusively male or female. The child is also coerced into ignoring or denying those portions of the personality that correspond with the sex it is being taught it cannot identify with. This squeezing of personality into a sexual mold begins early, then. Continuing guilt is generated because the child knows unerringly that its own reality transcends such simple orientation.

The more able the child is to force such an artificial identi-fication, the greater its feelings of inner rebellion. The lack of a "suitable" father or mother image has "saved" more children than it has hurt. The psyche, with its great gifts, always feels thwarted and attempts to take countering measures. Your schools further continue the process, however, so that the areas of curiosity and learning become separated for males and females. The "she" within the male does indeed represent portions of his personality that are being unexpressed—not because of any natural predominance of mental or emotional characteristics over others, but because of artificial specializations. The same applies to the "male" within the female. You have accepted this version of personhood, again, in line with your ideas about the nature of consciousness. Those ideas are changing, and as they do the species must accept its true personhood. As this happens, your understanding will allow you to glimpse the nature of the reality of the gods you have recognized through the ages. You will no longer need to clothe them in limited sexual guises.

Your religious concepts will change considerably, and the images associated with them. Religion and government have had an uneasy alliance. Males ruled both (they still do), and yet those leading religious organizations at least recognized their intuitive base. They constantly tried to manipulate religion's substructure in the same acceptable male ways that government leaders always use to inhibit and use the emotions.

(Long pause at 11:07.) Heresy was considered female and subversive because it could threaten to destroy the frameworks set about the acceptable expression of religious fervor. The female elements in the Church were always considered suspect, and in the early times of Christianity there was some concern lest the Virgin become a goddess. There were offshoots of Christianity that did not survive, in which this was the case. Parallel developments in religion and government always echo the state of consciousness and its purposes. "Pagan" practices, giving far more leeway to sexual identification and expression, continued well into the 16th century, and the so-called occult underground heretical teachings tried to encourage the development of personal intuition.

Any true psychic development of personality, however, is bound to lead to an understanding of the nature of the psyche that is far too large for any such confusion of basic identity with sexuality. The concept of reincarnation itself clearly shows the change of sexual orientation, and the existence of a self that is apart from its sexual orientation, even while it is also expressed through a given sexual stance. To a good extent, sexual beliefs are responsible for the blocking-out of reincarnational awareness. Such "memory" would necessarily acquaint you with experiences most difficult to correlate with your current sexual roles. Those other-sex existences are present to the psyche unconsciously. They are a portion of your personality. In so specifically identifying with your sex, therefore, you also inhibit memories that might limit or destroy that identification.

Take your break.

(11:28 to 11:57.)

The Church did not restrain the sexuality of its priests or the expression of sexuality in previous centuries as much as it tried to divorce the expression of love and devotion from sexuality.

A high percentage of priests of the Middle ages, for example, had illegitimate children. These were considered products of the weak and lustful flesh—bad enough, but considering man's fallen state, understandable lapses. Such situations were overlooked, if not condoned, as long as a priest's love and devotion still belonged to the Church and were not "squandered" upon the mother of such offspring.

The nuns were kept in subservient positions. Yet the nunneries also served as refuges for many women, who managed to educate themselves even under those conditions.

A good number of nuns were of course carrying the seed of those priests, and bearing children who acted as servants in monasteries, sometimes, as well as in convents. There were numerous rebellions on the part of nuns in various convents, however, for these women found themselves operating rather efficiently though in segregated surroundings. They began to question the entire framework of the Church and their position within it. Some left in groups, particularly in France and Spain, forming their own communities.

The Church, however, never really found a suitable method of dealing with its women, or with the intuitive elements of its own beliefs. Its fear of a goddess emerging was renewed each time another apparition of the Virgin appeared in one corner or another of the world.

There were also some women who passed as monks, living lives of a solitary nature and carrying on for years. No works bear their feminine names, for they used male ones. It goes without saying that lesbian and homosexual relationships flourished in such surroundings. The Church closed its eyes as long as the relationships were sexual in nature. Only when love and devotion were diverted from the Church was there real concern. Intellect and emotions became further divided then. This resulted of course in an overemphasis upon dogma—rules and the ritualization that had to be colorful and rich because it would be the one outlet allowed in which creativity could be handled. The Church believed that sexual experience belonged to the so-called lower or animal instincts, and so did usual human love. On the other hand, spiritual love and devotion could not be muddied by sexual expression, and so any normal strong relationship became a threat to the expression of piety.

End of dictation. End of session, and a hearty good evening. *("Thank you very much, Seth. It's been interesting. Good night."* *12:17 A.M.)*

SESSION 774,   MAY 3, 1976
9:24 P.M. MONDAY

(Since Seth began these sessions on human sexuality, it seems that we've received even more inquiries about the subject through the mail than we did earlier. We only regret that it's taking us so long to get this information to the public.

(The warmer weather now allows us to eat lunch at the picnic table we've installed in one half of our double garage. Jane writes there often— with the garage doors open—so that she can enjoy the view of the hills at the back of the house.)

Good evening.

("Good evening, Seth.")

Dictation: You are obsessed with sexual behavior when you proclaim it evil or distasteful or debasing, hide it, and pretend that it is primarily "animalistic." You are also obsessed with sexual behavior when you proclaim its merits in an exaggerated fashion from the marketplace. You are obsessed with sexual behavior when you put tight, unrealistic bans upon its expression, and also when you set up just as unrealistic standards of active performance to which the normal person is expected to comply.

Sexual freedom, then, does not involve an enforced promiscuity in which young people, for example, are made to feel unnatural if their encounters with the other sex do not lead to bed.

You begin to program sexual activity when you divorce it from love and devotion. It is very easy then for church or state to claim and attract your uncentered loyalty and love, leaving you with the expression of a sexuality stripped of its deepest meanings.

I am not saying here that any given sexual performance is "wrong," or meaningless, or debased, if it is not accompanied by the sentiments of love and devotion. Over a period of time, however, the expression of sex will follow the inclinations of the heart. These inclinations will color sexual expression, then. To that degree, it is "unnatural" to have sexual desire for someone whom you dislike or look down upon. The sexual ideas of domination and submission have no part in the natural life of your species, or that of the animals. Again, you interpret animal behavior according to your own beliefs.

Dominance and submission have often been used in religious literature in periods when love and devotion were separated from sexuality. They became unified only through religious visions or experiences, for only God's love was seen as "good enough" to justify a sexuality otherwise felt to be animalistic. Instead, the words "domination" and "submission" have to do with areas of consciousness and its development. Because of interpretations mentioned earlier in this book, you adopted a prominent line of consciousness that to a certain extent was bent upon dominating nature. You considered this male in essence. The female principle then became connected with the earth and all those elements of its life over which you as a species hoped to gain power.

(9:47.) God, therefore, became male. The love and devotion that might otherwise be connected with the facets of nature and the female principle had to be "snatched away from" any natural attraction to sexuality. In such a way, religion, echoing your state of consciousness, was able to harness the powers of love and use them for purposes of domination. They became state-oriented. A man's love and devotion was a political gain. Fervor was as important as a government's treasury, for a state could count upon the devotion of its lieutenants in the same way that many fanatics will work without money for a cause.

(Long pause.) Give us a moment . . . *(A one-minute pause at 9:56.)*

Some people are naturally solitary. They want to live lone lives, and are content. Most, however, have a need for enduring, close relationships. These provide both a psychic and social framework for personal growth, understanding, and development. It is an easy enough matter to shout to the skies: "I love my fellow men," when on the other hand you form no strong, enduring relationship with others. It is easy to claim an equal love for all members of the species, but love itself requires an understanding that at your level of activity is based upon intimate experience. You cannot love someone you do not know—not unless you water down the definition of love so much that it becomes meaningless.

To love someone, you must appreciate how that person differs from yourself and from others. You must hold that person in mind so that to some extent love is a kind of meditation—a loving focus upon another individual. Once you experience that kind of love you can translate it into other terms. The love itself spreads out, expands, so that you can then see others in love's light.

Love is naturally creative and explorative—that is, you want to creatively explore the aspects of the beloved one. Even characteristics that would otherwise appear as faults attain a certain loving significance. They are accepted—seen, and yet they make no difference. Because these are still attributes of the beloved one, even the seeming faults are redeemed. The beloved attains prominence over all others.

The span of a god's love can perhaps equally hold within its vision the existences of all individuals at one time in an infinite loving glance that beholds each person, seeing each with all his or her peculiar characteristics and tendencies. Such a god's glance would delight in each person's difference from each other person. This would not be a blanket love, a soupy porridge of a glance in which individuality melted, but a love based on a full understanding of each individual. The emotion of love brings you closest to an understanding of the nature of All That Is. Love incites dedication, commitment. It specifies. You cannot, therefore, honestly insist that you love humanity and all people equally if you do not love one other person. If you do not love yourself, it is quite difficult to love another.

Take your break.

(10:22 to 10:41.)

Again, all love is not sexually oriented. Yet love naturally seeks expression, and one such expression is through sexual activities.

When love and sexuality are artificially divided, however, or considered as antagonistic to each other, then all kinds of problems arise. Permanent relationships become most difficult to achieve under such conditions, and often love finds little expression, while one of its most natural channels is closed off. Many children give their greatest expression of love to toys, dolls, or imaginary playmates, because so many stereotyped patterns have already limited other expressions. Their feelings toward parents become ambiguous as a result of the identification procedures thrust upon them. Love, sexuality, and play, curiosity and explorative characteristics, merge in the child in a natural manner. Yet it soon learns that areas of exploration are limited even as far as its own body is concerned. The child is not free to contemplate its own parts. The body is early forbidden territory, so that the child feels it is wrong to love itself in any fashion.

Ideas of love, then, become highly distorted, and its expression also. You do not fight wars for the sake of the brotherhood of man, for example. People who are acquainted with undistorted versions of love in their relationships would find such a concept impossible. Men brought up to be ashamed of the "feminine" sides of their nature cannot be expected to love women. They will see in women instead the despised, feared, and yet charged aspects of their own reality, and behave accordingly in their relationships.

Women taught to be frightened of the "masculine" sides of their nature cannot be expected to love men, either, and the same kind of behavior results.

The so-called war of the sexes originates in the artificial divisions that you have placed about the nature of the self. The psyche's reality is beyond such misunderstandings. Its native language usually escapes you. It is closely connected with what can be loosely called the language of love.

End of chapter.

Chapter 6
"The Language of Love." Images and the Birth of Words

(10:59.) Next chapter heading: " 'The Language of Love.' Images and the Birth of Words."

It is almost commonplace to say that those who are in love can converse without words. Dramas and stories of all kinds have been written about the inner kind of communication that seems to take place between mother and children, sister and brother, or lover and beloved.

Love itself seems to quicken the physical senses, so that even the most minute gestures attain additional significance and meaning. Myths and tales are formed in which those who love communicate, though one is dead while the other lives. The experience of love also deepens the joy of the moment, even while it seems to emphasize the briefness of mortality. Though love's expression brilliantly illuminates its instant, at the same time that momentary brilliance contains within it an intensity that defies time, and is somehow eternal.

In your world you identify as yourself only, and yet love can expand that identification to such an extent that the intimate awareness of another individual is often a significant portion of your own consciousness. You look outward at the world not only through your eyes, but also, to some extent at least, through the eyes of another. It is true to say, then, that a portion of you figuratively walks with this other person as he or she goes about separate from you in space.

All of this also applies to the animals to varying degrees. Even in animal groups, individuals are not only concerned with personal survival, but with the survival of "family" members. Each individual in an animal group is aware of the others' situations. The expression of love is not confined to your own species, therefore, nor is tenderness, loyalty, or concern. Love indeed <u>does</u> have its own language—a basic nonverbal one with deep biological connotations. It is the initial basic language from which all others spring, for all languages' purposes rise from those qualities natural to love's expression—the desire to communicate, create, explore, and to join with the beloved.

(Long pause at 11:22.) Give us a moment . . . Speaking historically in your terms, man first identified with nature, and loved it, for he saw it as an extension of himself even while he felt himself a part of its expression. In exploring it he explored himself also. He did not identify as himself alone, but because of his love, he identified also with all those portions of nature with which he came into contact. This love was biologically ingrained in him, and is even now biologically pertinent.

Physically and psychically the species is connected with all of nature. Man did not live in fear, as is now supposed, nor in some idealized natural heaven. He lived at an intense peak of psychic and biological experience, and enjoyed a sense of creative excitement that in those terms only existed when the species was new.

This is difficult to explain, for these concepts themselves exist beyond verbalization. Some <u>seeming</u> (underlined) contradictions are bound to occur. In comparison with those times, however, children are now born ancient, for even biologically they carry within themselves the memories of their ancestors. In those pristine eras, however, the species itself arose, <u>in those terms</u>, newly from the womb of timelessness into time.

(Long pause.) New paragraph: In deeper terms their existence still continues, with offshoots in all directions. The world that you know is one development in time, the one that you recognize. The species actually took many other routes unknown

to you, unrecorded in your history. Fresh creativity still emerges at
that "point." *(Long pause, one of many.)* In the reckoning that you
accept, the species in its infancy obviously experienced selfhood in
different terms from your own. Because this experience is so alien
to your present concepts, and because it predated language as you
understand it, it is most difficult to describe.

(11:39.) Generally you experience the self as isolated from
nature, and primarily enclosed within your skin. Early man did
not feel like an empty shell, and yet selfhood existed for him as
much outside of the body as within it. There was a constant interaction. It is easy to say to you that such people could identify, say,
with the trees, but an entirely different thing to try to explain what
it would be like for a mother to become so a part of the tree
underneath which her children played that she could keep track of
them from the tree's viewpoint, though she was herself far away.

Take your break.

(11:46 to 11:59.)

Consciousness is far more mobile than you realize. Operationally, you have focused yours primarily with the body. You
cannot experience subjective behavior "from outside," so this
natural mobility of consciousness, which for example the animals
have retained, is psychologically invisible to you.

You like to think in terms of units and definitions, so even
when you consider your own consciousness you think of it as "a
thing," or a unit—an invisible something that might be held in
invisible hands perhaps. Instead consciousness is a particular
quality of being. Each portion of "it" contains the whole, so theoretically as far as you are concerned, you can leave your body and
be in it simultaneously. You are rarely aware of such experiences
because you do not believe them possible, and it seems that even
consciousness, particularly when individualized, must be in one
place or another.

I am certainly putting this in the most simple of terms, but a
bird may have a nest, though it leaves it frequently and never
confuses itself with its nesting place. In a manner of speaking that
is what you have done, though the body is more animate than
the nest.

In those early times, then, consciousness was more mobile.
Identity was more democratic. In a strange fashion this does not
mean that individuality was weaker. Instead it was strong enough
to accept within its confines many divergent kinds of experience. A
person, then, looking out into the world of trees, waters and rock,

wildlife and vegetation, literally felt that he or she was looking at the larger, materialized, subjective areas of personal selfhood.

To explore that exterior world was to explore the inner one. Such a person, however, walking through the forest, also felt that he or she was also a portion of the inner life of each rock or tree, materialized. Yet there was no contradiction of identities.

(12:19.) A man might merge his own consciousness with a running stream, traveling in such a way for miles to explore the layout of the land. To do this he became part water in a kind of identification you can barely understand—but so did the water then become part of the man.

You can imagine atoms and molecules forming objects with little difficulty. In the same way, however, portions of identified consciousness can also mix and merge, forming alliances.

End of dictation. End of session.

("Okay. Very nice.")

A fond good evening to you both.

("Thank you. Good night." 12:26 A.M.)

SESSION 776, MAY 17, 1976
9:14 P.M. MONDAY

(Our last session, the 775th, was not book dictation. Instead, Seth devoted it to "strings of consciousness"—explaining why Jane "picked up" the "William James" material, which is discussed in her book, Psychic Politics. Every once in a while she feels as if more material "from James" is available, though none has been forthcoming.)

Good evening.

("Good evening, Seth.")

Dictation. There are channels of interrelatedness, connecting all physical matter—channels through which consciousness flows.

In those terms of which I am speaking, man's identification with nature allowed him to utilize those inner channels. He could send his own consciousness swimming, so to speak, through many currents, in which other kinds of consciousness merged. I said that the language of love was the one basic language, and I mean that quite literally. Man loved nature, identified with its many parts, and added to his own sense of being by joining into its power and identifying with its force.

It is not so much that he personified the elements of nature as that he threw his personality into its elements and rode them, so to speak. As mentioned, love incites the desire to know, explore,

and communicate with the beloved; so language began as man
tried to express his love for the natural world.

Initially language had nothing to do with words, and indeed
verbal language emerged only when man had lost a portion of his
love, forgotten some of his identification with nature, so that he no
longer understood its voice to be his also. In those early days man
possessed a gargantuan arena for the expression of his emotions.
He did not symbolically rage with the storms, for example, but
quite consciously identified with them to such a degree that he
and his tribesmen merged with the wind and lightning, and
became a part of the storms' forces. They felt, and knew as well,
that the storms would refresh the land, whatever their fury.

Because of such identification with nature, the death experience, as you understand it, was in no way considered an end. The
mobility of consciousness was a fact of experience. The self was
not considered to be stuck within the skin. The body was considered more or less like a friendly home or cave, kindly giving the
self refuge but not confining it.

(Pause at 9:35, one of many.) The language of love did not
initially (underlined) involve images, either. Images in the mind,
as they are understood, emerged in their present form only when
man had, again, lost a portion of his love and identification, and
forgotten how to identify with an image from its insides, and so
began to view it from outside.

I would like to emphasize the difficulty of explaining such a
language verbally. In a way the language of love followed molecular roots—a sort of biological alphabet, though "alphabet" is far
too limiting a term.

(A one-minute pause.) Each natural element had its own key
system that interlocked with others, forming channels through
which consciousness could flow from one kind of life to another.
Man understood himself to be a separate entity, but one that was
connected to all of nature. The emotional reaches of his subjective
life, then, leapt far beyond what you think of as private experience.
Each person participating fully in a storm, for example, still
participated in his or her own individual way. Yet the grandeur of
the emotions was allowed full sway, and the seasons of the earth
and the world were jointly felt.

The language or the method of communication can best be
described perhaps as direct cognition. Direct cognition is dependent upon a lover's kind of identification, where what is known is
known. At that stage no words or even images were needed. The

wind outside and the breath were <u>felt</u> to be one and the same, so that the wind was the earth breathing out the breath that rose from the mouths of the living, spreading out through the earth's body. Part of a man went out with breath—therefore, man's consciousness could go wherever the wind traveled. A man's consciousness, traveling with the wind, became part of all places.

(Long pause.) A person's identity was private, in that man always knew who he was. He was so sure of his identity that he did not feel the need to protect it, so that he could expand his awareness in a way now quite foreign to you.

(Long pause at 10:00.) Give us a moment . . .

Take the English sentence: "I observe the tree." If that original language had words, the equivalent would be: "As a tree, I observe myself."

(Long pause at 10:03.) Or: "Taking on my tree nature, I rest in my shade." Or even: "From my man nature, I rest in the shade of my tree nature." A man did not so much stand at the shore looking down at the water, as he immersed his consciousness within it. Man's initial curiosity did not involve seeing, feeling, or touching the object's nature as much as it involved a joyful psychic exploration in which he plunged his consciousness, rather than, say, his foot into the stream—though he did both.

If that language I speak of had been verbal, man never would have said: "The water flows through the valley." Instead, the sentence would have read something like this: "Running over the rocks, my water self flows together with others in slippery union." <u>That</u> translation is not the best, either. Man did not designate his own as the only kind of consciousness by any means. He graciously thanked the tree that gave him shade, for example, and he understood that the tree retained its own identity even when it allowed his awareness to join with it.

In your terms, the use of language began as man lost this kind of identification. I must stress again that the identification was not symbolic, but practical, daily expression. Nature spoke for man, and man for nature.

(Long pause at 10:18.) In a manner of speaking, the noun and the verb were one. The noun did not disappear, but expressed itself as the verb.

(Long pause at 10:20.) In a kind of emotional magnification unknown to you, each person's private emotions were given an expression and release through nature's changes—a release that was understood, and taken for granted. In the most profound of

terms, weather conditions and the emotions are still highly related. The inner conditions cause the exterior climatic changes, though of course it now seems to you that it is the other way around.

(Long pause at 10:26.) You are robbed, then, or you rob yourselves, of one of the most basic kinds of expression, since you can no longer identify yourselves with the forces of nature. Man wanted to pursue a certain kind of consciousness, however. In your terms, over a period of time he pulled his awareness in, so to speak; he no longer identified as he did before, and began to view objects through the object of his own body. He no longer merged his awareness, so that he learned to look at a tree as one object, where before he would have joined with it, and perhaps viewed his own standing body from the tree's vantage point. It was then that mental images became important in usual terms—for he had understood these before, but in a different way, from the inside out.

Now he began to draw and sketch, and to learn how to build images in the mind that were connected to real exterior objects in the presently accepted manner. Now he walked, not simply for pleasure, but to gain the information he wanted, to cross distances that before his consciousness had freely traveled. So he needed primitive maps and signs. Instead of using whole images he used partial ones, fragments of circles or lines, to represent natural objects.

He had always made sounds that communicated emotions, intent, and sheer exuberance. When he became involved with sketched or drawn images, he began to imitate their form with the shape of his lips. The "O" was perfect, and represents one of his initial, deliberate sounds of verbalized language.

Take your break.

(10:41 to 11:08.)

Now: Regardless of the language you speak, the sounds that you can make are dependent upon your physical structure, so that human language is composed of a certain limited number of sounds. Your physical construction is the result of inner molecular configurations, and the sounds you make are related to these.

I said before that early man felt a certain emotional magnification, that he felt, for example, the wind's voice as his own. In a manner of speaking your languages, while expressing your individual intents and communications, also represent a kind of amplification arising from your molecular configurations. The wind makes certain sounds that are dependent upon the characteristics of the earth. The breath makes certain sounds that are

dependent upon the characteristics of the body. There is a connection between alphabets and the molecular structure that com-
poses your tissue. Alphabets then are natural keys also. Such
natural keys have a molecular history. You form these keys into
certain sound patterns that have particular meanings.

(11:19.) This provides you with a certain kind of communication, but it also allows a molecular expression that is
natural at that level, and then used by you for your own purposes.
I am not saying that molecules speak. I am saying that they are
expressed through your speech, however—and that your speech
represents an amplification of their existence. Through your words
their reality is amplified, in the same way that man's emotions
once found amplification through the physical elements.

Certain sounds are verbal replicas of molecular construc-
tions, put together by you to form sentences in the same way, for
example, that molecules are put together to form cells and tissue.

(Long pause at 11:26.) There are "inner sounds" that act like
layers between tissues, that "coat" molecules, and these serve as a
basis for exterior sound principles. These are also connected to
rhythms in the body itself.

To some extent punctuation is sound that you do not hear,
a pause that implies the presence of withheld sound. To some
extent, then, language is as dependent upon the unspoken as the
spoken, and the rhythm of silence as well as of sound. In that
context, however, silence involves merely a pause of sound in
which sound is implied but withheld. Inner sound deals primarily
with that kind of relationship. Language is meaningful only because of the rhythm of the silence upon which it rides.

(11:33.) Its meaning comes from the pauses between the
sounds as much as it does from the sounds themselves. The flow
of breath is obviously important, regulating the rhythm and the
spacing of the words. The breath's integrity arises directly from the
proper give-and-take between cells, the functioning of the tissues;
and all that is the expression of molecular competence. That
competence is obviously responsible for language, but beyond
that it is intimately connected with the patterns of languages
themselves, the construction of syntax, and even with the figures
of speech used.

Again, you speak for yourselves; yet in doing so you speak a
language that is not yours alone, but the result of inner communications too swift for you to follow, involving corporal and
subjective realities alike. For this reason your languages have
meaning on several levels. The sounds you make have physical

effects on your own and other bodies. There is a sound value, then, as apart from a meaning value.

The words you speak to someone else are in certain terms broken down by the listener to basic components, and understood at different levels. There are psychological interpretations made, and molecular ones. The sounds and their pauses will express emotional states, and reactions to these will alter the body's condition to whatever degree.

The listener then breaks down the language. He builds up his own response. You have so connected words and images that language seems to consist of a sound that suggests an image. Yet some languages have had sounds for feelings and subjective states, and they had no subjects or predicates, nor even a sentence structure that you would recognize.

Your language must follow your perception, though the sound structure beneath need not. You say: "I am today, I was yesterday, and I will be tomorrow," yet some languages would find such utterances incomprehensible, and the words, "I am" would be used in all instances.

Take your break or end the session as you prefer.

("We'll take the break and see what happens.")

(11:55 P.M. At break Jane realized she felt tired, so she decided not to continue the session.)

SESSION 777, MAY 24, 1976
9:45 P.M. MONDAY

Now—good evening.

("Good evening, Seth.")

Dictation. Initially, however, before the birth of images and words—as you understand them (underlined)—the world existed in different terms from those you know. Images as you consider them had not taken the form that you recognize. It seems to you that visually, for example, the natural world must be put together or perceived in a certain fashion.

Whatever your language, you perceive trees, mountains, people, oceans. You never see a man merge with a tree, for example. This would be considered an hallucinatory image. Your visual data are learned and interpreted so that they appear as the only possible results of those data. Inner vision can confound you, because in your mind you often see images quite clearly that you would dismiss if your eyes were open. In the terms of which we are speaking, however, the young species utilized what I have called the "inner senses" to a far greater degree than you do. Visually, early man did not perceive the physical world in the way that seems natural to you.

You will have to give us time . . . *(Pause, one of many.)* When a man's consciousness, for example, blended with that of a tree, those data became "visual" for others to perceive. When a man's consciousness merged with an animal's, that blending became visual data also.

In a manner of speaking, the brain put visual information together so that the visual contents of the world were not as stationary as they are now. You have learned to be highly specific in your physical sight and interpretations. Your mental vision holds hints as to data that could be, but are not visually, physically perceived. You have trained yourselves to react to certain visual cues which trigger your mental interpretations, and to ignore other variations.

These latter can be described as too subtle. Yet actually they are no more subtle than those cues you acknowledge.

(Long pause at 10:05.) Data, you say, are stored in the chromosomes, strung together in a certain fashion. Now biologically that is direct cognition. The inner senses perceive directly in the same fashion. To you, language means words. Words are always symbols for emotions or feelings, intents or desires. Direct cognition did not need the symbols. The first language, the initial language, did not involve images or words, but dealt with a free flow of directly cognitive material.

A man, wondering what a tree was like, became one, and let his own consciousness flow into the tree. Man's consciousness mixed and merged with other kinds of consciousness with the great curiosity of love. A child did not simply look at an animal, but let its consciousness merge with the animal's, and so to some extent the animal looked out through the child's eyes.

(Long pause.) In ways most difficult to explain, man "absorbed" an animal's spirit before he killed it, so that the spirit of the animal merged with his own. In using the animal's flesh, then, the hunter believed that he was giving the animal a new focus of existence. He could draw on the animal's strength, and the animal could join in human consciousness. Nature and spirit therefore were one.

(A two-minute pause at 10:22. The last paragraph of material may give clues to human behavior today: Man kills animals—and eats them—for

reasons he's consciously forgotten. His killing today would be based on at least intuitive understanding . . . One wonders whether the same reasoning might apply when man kills man. . . .)

Your own kind of focus emerged from such a background, so that within yourselves you contain myriad consciousnesses of which you are unaware. Through your own particular focus, the consciousnesses of the natural world merged to form a synthesis in which, for example, symphonies can emerge. You act not only for yourselves, but also for other kinds of consciousness that you have purposefully forgotten. In following your own purposes, which are yours, you also serve the purposes of others you have forgotten.

In thinking your own private thoughts, you also add to a larger psychic and mental reality of which you are part. Your languages program your perceptions, and limit your communications in certain terms (underlined) as much as they facilitate it.

(Pause.) A musician writing a symphony, however, does not use all of the notes that are available to him. He chooses and discriminates. His discrimination is based upon his knowledge of the information available, however. In the same way, your languages are based upon an inner knowledge of larger available communications. The "secrets" of languages are not to be found, then, in the available sounds, accents, root words or syllables, but in the rhythms between the words; the pauses and hesitations; the flow with which the words are put together, and the unsaid inferences that connect verbal and visual data.

(Long pause at 10:37.) As a species "you" sought certain kinds of experience. Individually, and as tribes or nations, you follow certain "progressions"—and yet in so doing you act also on the part of the whole of nature. You take into your bodies in transmuted form the consciousnesses of all the things you consume.

(10:41.) Those consciousnesses then merge to perceive the world in a fashion you call your own. Through your eyes the beasts, vegetables, birds, and dust perceive the dawn and sunlight as you do—as you, and yet on the other hand your experience is your own.

(10:44.) To some extent it is true to say that languages emerged as you began to lose direct communication with your own experience, and with that of others. Language is therefore a substitute for direct communication. The symbols of the words stand for your own or someone else's experience, while protecting you or them from it at the same time.

Visual data as you perceive them amount to visual language; the images perceived are like visual words. An object is presented to your visual perception so that you can safely perceive it from the outside. Objects as you see them are also symbols.

Take your break.

(10:50. Jane had "strange feelings" connected with tonight's session. She felt somewhat disoriented, yet couldn't explain very well in just what way. She'd taken many long pauses in delivering the material—a few of which I've indicated—but hadn't been at all concerned about them while in trance. She said that at such times she was "waiting for the material to assemble and translate itself." Originally it wasn't verbal at all. Resume at 11:13.)

Now: Ruburt's sense of strangeness is indeed connected with this evening's material. He was, however briefly, involved in a process that enabled him to reach beneath verbal or imagery language.

In a manner of speaking he approached other thresholds of perception, and with my help translated those data into the material given. He felt as if he had been on a long journey—and he was, though it was not a conscious one in the terms you recognize. The training that connects your visual and verbal culture prevents full translation, but Ruburt was putting together, with my help, information not usually available. There are gaps in your awareness that are actually filled with data, and Ruburt was letting these pool up, so to speak. He will become more proficient, but for that reason I will now end the session.

He feels as if his consciousness were stretched out of shape in a certain way, as muscles might be if you used them in a new manner.

Let him rest. he has become aware of <u>distances</u> in his own consciousness, in a fashion difficult to describe. Neurologically he became familiar to some extent with the stuff beneath language, the inner rhythms unexpressed, and felt the odd connections that exist between words and your sense of time. This confused him, for this was material directly felt but verbally inexpressible. He will readjust "in no time."

End of session.

("Thank you, Seth."

(11:25 P.M. "I just feel funny," Jane said, "as if I've been where it was too smooth for my consciousness to get a grip on anything." It wasn't easy

for her to put her feelings into words. "Yet I feel as though I've been doing things there—perceiving in a different way while Seth was giving the session." She also felt that Seth had translated some of those now-forgotten experiences into the session's material.

(Jane's strange feelings were over by the time we went to bed. The next morning, though, she reported dream experiences that had been brilliantly clear at the time; in them she'd been "perceiving images or objects as language.")

Chapter 7
The Psyche,
Languages, and gods

SESSION 779, JUNE 14, 1976
9:17 P.M. MONDAY

(No dictation for Psyche *was given in the 778th session. Instead, Seth discussed the use of X rays in relation to health matters. We'd like to publish his information eventually.*

(As mentioned in other Seth books, Jane has her own physical hassles. During this spring she began to enjoy long periods of general relaxation and physical improvements, and no sessions were held last week as she "went along with" another series of such beneficial events.

(She also had a profound healing session last night while in bed—she "swooned" in a state of near-ecstasy, she said, for over two hours while she felt healing effects surge through her. I reminded her this morning to write an account of the experience, but the aftereffects, plus new healing sensations, were so strong that she couldn't concentrate enough to do the job; she wrote but a paragraph or two.

(In fact, Jane was fairly well "out of it" before tonight's session, but decided to give it a try.)

Good evening.

("Good evening, Seth.")

Dictation, while Ruburt continues his recovery. We will begin the next chapter, entitled: "The Psyche, Languages, and gods"—with a small "g."

Almost any question that you can ask about God, with a capital, can be legitimately asked of the psyche as well. It seems to you that you know yourself, but that you take the existence of your psyche on faith. At best, it often seems that you are all that you know of your psyche, and you will complain that you do not know yourself to begin with. When you say: "I want to find myself," you usually take it for granted that there is a completed, done, finished version of yourself that you have mislaid somewhere. When you think of finding God, you often think in the same terms.

Now you are "around yourself" all of the time. You are ever becoming yourself. In a manner of speaking you are "composed" of those patterns of yourself that are everywhere coming together. You cannot help but be yourself. Biologically, mentally, and spiritually you are marked as apart from all others, and no cloak of conventionality can ever hide that unutterable uniqueness. You cannot help but be yourself, then.

(Long pause at 9:27.) In a way, physically you are a molecular language that communicates to others, but a language with its own peculiarities, as if speaking an accepted tongue you spoke with a biological accent that carried its own flavor and meaning.

When you ask: "What is my psyche, or my soul, or who am I?" you are seeking of course for your own meaning as apart from what you already know about yourself. In that context, God is as known and as unknown as you are to yourself. Both God and the psyche are constantly expanding—unutterable, and always becoming.

You will question, most likely, "Becoming what?" for to you it usually seems that all motion tends toward a state of completion of one kind or another. You think, therefore, in terms of becoming perfect, or becoming free. The word "becoming" by itself seems to leave you up in the air, so to speak, suspended without definitions. If I say: "You are becoming what you already are," then my remark sounds meaningless, for if you already are, how can you become what is already accomplished? In larger terms, however, what you are is always vaster than your knowledge of yourself, for in physical life you cannot keep up with your own psychological and psychic activity.

Again, in a way your bodies speak a biological language, but in those terms you are bilingual, to say the least. You deal with certain kinds of organizations. They can be equated with biological verbs, adjectives, and nouns. These result in certain time sequences that can be compared to sentences, written and read from one side, say, to the other.

Pretend that your life's experience is a page of a book that you write, read, and experience from top to bottom, left to right, sentence by sentence, paragraph by paragraph. That is the you that you know—the world view that you understand. But other quite as legitimate you's may write, read and experience the same page backwards, or read each letter downward and back up again, as you would a column of figures. Or others might mix and match the letters in entirely different fashions altogether, forming entirely different sentences. Still another, vaster you might be aware of all the different methods of experiencing that particular page, which is your life as you understand it.

You think that your own consciousness is the only logical culmination of your body's reality. You read yourself in a certain accepted fashion. In the "entire book of life," however, just physically speaking, there are interrelationships on adjacent levels that you do not perceive, as other portions of your own biological consciousness or biological language relate to the entire living fabric of the world. In physical terms you are alive because of substructures—psychic, spiritual, and biological—of which you have hardly any comprehension at all.

These are implied, however, in the nature of your own consciousness, which could not exist otherwise as you know it. As language gains and attains its meaning not only by what is included in it, but also by what is excluded, so your consciousness attains its stability also by exclusions.

(9:55.) What you are is implied in the nature of what you are not. By the same token, you are what you are because of the existence of what you are not.

(Long pause.) You read yourselves from the top of the page to the bottom, or from what you think of as the beginning to the end. Your greater reality, however, is read in terms of intensities, so that the psyche puts you together in a different way. The psyche does not mark time. To it the intense experiences of your life exist simultaneously. In your terms they would be the psyche's present. The psyche deals with probable events, however, so some events— perhaps some that you dreamed of but did not materialize—are quite real to the psyche. They are far more real to it than most

innocuous but definite physical events, as for example yesterday morning's breakfast.

The inner events of the psyche compose the greater experience from which physical events arrive. They cast an aura that almost magically makes your life your own. Even if two people encountered precisely the same events in their lives at precisely the same time, their experiences of reality would still hardly be approximately connected.

Take your break.

(10:09 to 10:30.)

Again, you read your own identities in a particular, specialized fashion.

Within your biological experience, however, plant, mineral, animal, and human consciousness intersect. They encounter each other. In the language of the self that you speak, these encounters are like the implied pauses in your verbal language. These other kinds of consciousness then form inner rhythms upon which you superimpose your own.

These encounters of consciousness go on constantly. They form their own kind of adjacent identities. You would call them subspecies of consciousness, perhaps, but they are really identities that operate in a trans-species fashion.

If you "read yourselves" sideways in such a manner, you would discover portions of your own consciousness stretching out across the entire fabric of the earth as you understand it—becoming a part of the earth's material, even as those materials become part of the self that you recognize. Your consciousness would be far less hemmed in. Time would expand adjacently. You think of yourselves physically as "top dogs," however, separate from the other species and kinds of life, so that in effect you limit your own experience of your psyche.

If you thought or felt in such a fashion, then you would appreciate the fact that biologically your body is yours by virtue of the mineral, plant and animal life from which it gains its sustenance. You would not feel imprisoned as you often do within one corporal form, for you would understand that the body itself maintains its relative stability because of its constant give-and-take with the materials of the earth that are themselves possessed of consciousness.

You could to some extent feel your body coming together and dispersing constantly, and understand how you hover within it without fearing your own annihilation upon its dismantlement.

(Long pause at 10:47.) When you ask: "Who am I?" you are

trying to read yourself as if you were a simple sentence already written. Instead, you write yourself as you go along. The sentence that you recognize is only one of many probable variations. You and no other choose which experiences you want to actualize. You do this as spontaneously as you speak words. You take it for granted that a sentence begun will be finished. You are in the midst of speaking yourself. The speaking, which is your life, seems to happen by itself, since you are not aware of keeping yourself alive. Your heart beats whether or not you understand anatomy.

(Long pause at 10:55.) Give us a moment . . . You read yourself in too-narrow terms. Much of the pain connected with serious illness and death results because you have no faith in your own continuing reality. You fight pain because you have not learned to transcend it, or rather to use it. You do not trust the natural consciousness of the body, so that when its end nears—and such an end is inevitable—you do not trust the signals that the body gives, that are meant to free you.

Certain kinds of pain automatically eject consciousness from the body. Such pain cannot be verbalized, for it is a mixture of pain and pleasure, a tearing free, and it automatically brings about an almost exhilarating release of consciousness. Such pain is also very brief. Under your present system, however, drugs are usually administered, in which case pain is somewhat minimized, but prolonged—not triggering the natural release mechanisms.

If you read your selves adjacently, you would build up confidence in the body, and in those cooperative consciousnesses that form it. You would have an intimate awareness of the body's healing processes also. You would not fear death as annihilation, and would feel your own consciousness gently disentangle itself from those others that so graciously couched it.

Take a brief break and we shall continue.

(11:09. Seth called for a break here because the telephone started ringing; we'd forgotten to turn it off before the session. He returned at 11:23 with a page or two for Jane and me, and then ended the session at 11:45 P.M.)

SESSION 780, JUNE 22, 1976
9:19 P.M. TUESDAY

(As we sat for the session, Jane reminded me that she thought Seth would do an introduction tonight for her own book on Paul Cézanne. This feeling had first come to her earlier today.

("Wouldn't that be a riot?" she laughed. "But I've done introductions

for Seth's books, so why shouldn't he do one for mine?" And yes, the Cézanne material mentioned earlier—see Jane's introduction for Psyche—*had developed into a full-fledged book of its own.*

(A note of interest: The area immediately surrounding Elmira had some considerable flooding today, although the city itself wasn't affected to any great degree. In any case, Jane and I were safe and dry on our little hill this time—a far cry from our experiences in the great flood of 1972, as described in The Nature of Personal Reality. *After that event, we decided that a flood was one reality we could do without!)*

Good evening.

("Good evening, Seth.")

Dictation. *(Long pause.)* You are a part of the world, and yet you are yourself. This does not confuse you, and you follow your own sense of identity without difficulty, even though you are everywhere surrounded by other individuals.

Using this as an analogy, you are a part of your psyche or your soul, dwelling within it, easily following your own sense of identity even though that psyche also contains other identities beside the one that you think of as your own. You draw sustenance from the world, and grow through its medium. You contribute your abilities and experience, helping to form the world's civilization and culture. To some strong degree you bear the same kind of relationship to your own psyche.

Through ordinary methods of communication you are able to tell what is going on in other countries beside your own, even without traveling to them. News telecasts acquaint you with conditions around the world.

Now there are also inner "broadcasts" going on constantly—to which, however, you are not <u>consciously</u> attuned. These keep you in constant touch with the other portions of your own psyche. You are so a part of the world that your slightest action contributes to its reality. Your breath changes the atmosphere. Your encounters with others alter the fabrics of their lives, and the lives of those who come in contact with them.

It is easy for you to see how the cells of the body form it— that is, you understand at least the cooperative nature of the cell's activities. An alteration on the part of one cell immediately causes changes in the others, and brings about a difference in body behavior. It is somewhat more difficult for you to understand the ways in which your own actions and those of others combine to bring about world events. On the one hand, each of my readers is but one individual alive on the planet at any given "time." It may seem that the individual has little power. On the other hand, each individual alive is a necessary one. It is true to say that the world begins and ends with each person. That is, each of your actions is so important, contributing to the experience of others whom you do not know, that each individual is like a center about which the world revolves.

If you did not do what you did today, for example, the entire world would be in some way different.

Your acts ripple outward in ways that you do not understand, interacting with the experience of others, and hence forming world events. The most famous and the most anonymous person are connected through such a fabric, and an action seemingly small and innocuous can end up changing history as you understand it.

(9:41.) Children often feel that the world and time began with their birth. They take the world's past on faith. In very important terms this is quite a legitimate feeling, for no one else can experience the world from any other viewpoint except from his or her own, or affect it except through private action. *En masse,* that individual action obviously causes world events.

In metaphysical terms, you have your being in your psyche or soul in somewhat the same manner. Identities are obviously psychic environments, primarily, rather than physical ones. Physical objects cannot move through each other, as a table cannot move through a chair. Mental events behave differently. They can mix and merge, move through each other while still maintaining their own focus. They can interact on psychic levels in the way that events do on physical levels, but without physical restrictions. Though you are a portion of your psyche, then, your identity is still inviolate. It will not be submerged or annihilated in a greater self. It carries a stamp—a divine mark—of its own integrity. It follows its own focus, and knows itself as itself, even while its own existence as itself may be but a portion of another "identity."

Moreover, there is nothing to stop it from exploring this other greater identity, or moving into it, so to speak. When this happens both identities are changed. In greater terms, the psyche or soul nowhere exists as a finished product or entity. On the other hand it is always becoming, and that becoming happens on the part of each of its own portions.

Your very physical stance and existence are dependent

upon portions of your psyche's reality, or your soul's existence, of which you are normally unaware. Those portions are also dependent upon your existence, however.

(Long pause at 10:01.) You take your breathing, your moving, for granted, though they are unconsciously produced. In certain terms, however, "at one time" you had to learn how to do these things that you are not now consciously concerned with. At still other levels of reality, activities that you now consciously claim as your own have—in those same terms and from another viewpoint—become unconscious, providing a psychic history from which other identities emerge, as it seems that your own identities emerge from unconscious bodily activity.

Take your break.

(10:05. "It's hard material to get," Jane said, in spite of her delivery, which had moved right along. "It's one of those things where it's unraveling as you go along. Very difficult to verbalize. . . ." Resume in the same manner at 10:25.)

In certain very definite terms the existence of one person implies the existence of all others who have lived or will live. Your own existence is implied therefore in everyone else's and theirs is implied in yours.

I said that languages gain their meaning largely from the pauses and hesitations between sounds. They obviously gain their meaning also because of the sounds not used, so that any one language also implies the existence of all others. To that extent, all other languages reside silently within any given spoken language. The same applies to language written upon a page. The written characters make sense because of their arrangement, and precisely because they are chosen over other characters that do not appear.

In the same kind of manner, your focused existence is dependent upon all those other existences that are not you. You are a part of them. You ride upon their existences, though you are primarily you and no other.

The same applies, however, to every other person. Each of them becomes a primary focus or identity within which all others are implied. In ordinary terms, you do not "make yourselves." You are like a living language spoken by someone who did not originate it—the language was there for you to use. The language in this case is a molecular one that speaks your physical being. The components of that language or the earth elements that form the body were already created when you were born, as the alphabet of your particular language was waiting to be used.

Your very physical life, then, implies a "source," a life out of which the physical one emerges, dash—the implied, unspoken, unmaterialized, unsounded vitality that supplied the ingredients for the physical, bodily, molecular "alphabet." Your physical life therefore implies a nonphysical one. You take your particular "language" so for granted, and use it so effortlessly, that you give no thought at all to the fact that it implies other languages also, or that it gains its meaning because of inner assumptions that are never spoken, or by the use of pauses in which no sounds are made. You live your lives in the same fashion.

(10:49.) There are many languages, though most people speak one, or two, or three at most. Languages also have accents, each somewhat different while still maintaining the original integrity of any given language. To some extent you can learn to speak yourself with an accent, so to speak—say that I smiled—in which case, still being yourself, you allow yourself to take on some of the attributes of another "language."

You can read the world in a different way, while still maintaining your own identity, or you can move into a different country of yourself that speaks your native language but with a different slant. You do this to some extent or another whenever you tune in to broadcasts to which you usually pay no attention. The news is slightly foreign, while it is still interpreted through the language that you know. You are getting a translation of reality.

The psyche, always in a state of becoming, obviously has no precise boundaries. The existence of one, again, implies the existence of all, and so any one given psyche comes into prominence also because of the existence of the others upon which its reality rides. One television station exists in the same manner, for if one could not be tuned in to, theoretically speaking, none could.

These inner communications, then, reach outward in all directions. Each identity has eternal validity within the psyche's greater reality. At one level, then (underlined), any person contacting his or her own psyche can theoretically contact any other psyche. Life implies death, and death implies life—that is, in the terms of your world. In those terms life is a spoken element, while death is the unspoken but still-present element "beneath," upon which life rides. Both are equally present.

To obtain knowledge consciously other than that usually available, you pay attention to the pauses, to the implied elements in language, to any felt or sensed quality upon which the recognizable experiences of life reside. There are all kinds of information available to you, but it must still be perceived through your own focus or identity.

I have said that all events occur at once—a difficult statement to understand. All identities occur at once also. Each event
changes every other. Present ones alter past ones. Any one event
implies the existence of probable events which do not "emerge,"
which are not "spoken." Physical world events therefore rest upon
the existence of implied probable events. Different languages use
sounds in their own peculiar manners, with their own rhythms,
one emphasizing what another ignores. Other probabilities, therefore, emphasize events that are only implied (as pauses) in your
reality, so that your physical events become the implied probable
ones upon which other worlds reside.

Take your break.

(11:13 to 11:23.)

Now: Dictation—of a different kind—for Ruburt's book.
We will begin an Introduction.

(Now Seth moved from his own book to this new subject—Jane's The
World View of Paul Cézanne—*with ease and obvious zest. This was the
first time in our sessions that he's delivered material on two books in one
night. He didn't finish his work for* Cézanne *tonight, though.*

(The session ended at 11:41 P.M.)

SESSION 781, JUNE 28, 1976
9:15 P.M. MONDAY

*(Seth devoted the first part of the session to a continuation of his
introduction for Jane's "Cézanne" book—and he has yet to complete that
material. Then at 10:01:)*

Now—dictation for the book—my book.

In a manner of speaking, then, you use the language of the
atoms and molecules in your own private way. You mark the
universe. You impress it, or "stamp" it, or imprint it with your
own identity. Henceforth (in parenthesis: in those terms) it always
recognizes you as you and no other. You are then known.

In larger terms, while you speak your own language, the
universe also speaks "your" language as it constantly translates
itself into your private perception. Remember, I said that you
lived in your psyche somewhat in the same way that physically you
dwell in the world.

That world has many languages. Physically you are like one
country within your psyche, with a language of your own. People
are always searching for master languages, or for one in particular
out of which all others emerged. In a way, Latin is a master

language. In the same manner people search for gods, or a God, out of which all psyches emerged. Here you are searching for the implied source, the unspoken, invisible "pause," the inner organization that gives language or the self a vehicle of expression. Languages finally become archaic. Some words are entirely forgotten in one language, but spring up in altered form in another. All of the earth's languages, however, are united because of characteristic pauses and hesitations upon which the different sounds ride.

Even the alterations of obvious pauses between languages make sense only because of an implied, unstated inner rhythm. The historic gods become equally archaic. Their differences are often obvious. When you are learning a language, great mystery seems involved. When you are learning about the nature of the psyche, an even greater aura of the unknown exists. The unknown portions of the psyche and its greater horizons, therefore, have often been perceived as gods or as the greater psyches out of which the self emerged—as for example Latin is a source for the Romance languages.

(10:40.) Give us a moment . . . Using ordinary language, you speak with your fellows. You write histories and communications. Many books are meant to be read and never to be spoken aloud. Through written language, then, communication is vastly extended. In direct contact, however, you encounter not only the spoken language of another, but you are presented with the communicator's person as well. Spoken language is embellished with smiles, frowns, or other gestures, and these add to the meaning of the spoken word.

Often when you read a book you silently mouth the words, as if to reinforce their symbolic content with a more emotional immediacy. The language of the psyche, however, is far richer and more varied. Its "words" spring alive. Its "verbs" really move, and do not simply signify, or stand for, motion (emphatically).

Its "nouns" become what they signify. Its declensions are multidimensional. Its verbs and nouns can become interchangeable. In a way (underlined), the psyche is its own language. "At any given time," all of its tenses are present tense. In other words, it has multitudinous tenses, all in the present, or it has multitudinous present tenses. Within it no "word" dies or becomes archaic. This language is experience. Psychically, then, you can and you cannot say that there is a source. The very fact that you question: "Is there a God, or a Source?" shows that you misunderstand the issues.

In the same manner, when you ask: "Is there a master language?" it is apparent that you do not understand what language itself is. Otherwise you would know that language is dependent upon other implied ones; and that the two, or all of them, are themselves and yet inseparable, so closely connected that it is impossible to separate them even though your focus may be upon one language alone.

So the psyche and its source, or the individual and the God, are so inseparable and interconnected that an attempt to find one apart from the other automatically confuses the issue.

Take your break.

(11:01. Jane's delivery was quite intent. During break she picked up that the Cézanne material from Seth would be in two parts—one of these being on world views, the other more on Cézanne-and-world-views. "So what do I call the book?" she asked. 11:25.)

The physical world implies the existence of a god. God's existence also implies the existence of a physical world.

This statement implies the unstated, and the reverse also applies.

To deny the validity or importance of the individual is, therefore, also to deny the importance or validity of God, for the two exist one within the other, and you cannot separate them.

From one end of reality you shout:"Where is God?" and from the other end the answer comes: "I am Me." Capitalize "Me." From the other end of reality, God goes shouting: "Who am I?" and finds himself in you. You are therefore a part of the source, and so is everything else manifest. Because God is, you are. Because you are, God is.

On a conscious level certainly you are not all that God is, for that is the unstated, unmanifest portion of yourself. Your being rides upon that unstated reality, as a letter of the alphabet rides upon the inner organizations that are implied by its existence. In those terms your unstated portions "reach backwards to a Source called God," as various languages can be traced back to their source. Master languages can be compared to the historic gods. Each person alive is a part of the living God, supported in life by the magnificent power of nature, which is God translated into the elements of the earth and the universe.

End of dictation. Give us a moment. . . .

(11:40. Now Seth delivered some material for Jane, then closed out the session at 12:09 A.M.)

SESSION 782, JULY 5, 1976
9:56 P.M. MONDAY

Now: Dictation.

Your daily language deals with separations, divisions, and distinctions. To some extent your language organizes your feelings and emotions. The language of the psyche, however, has at its command many more symbols that can be combined in many more ways, say, than mere letters of an alphabet.

In daily language, objects have certain names. Obviously the names are not the objects, but symbols for them. Even these symbols, however, divide you as the perceiver from the rest of the world, which becomes objectified. You can yourself understand far more about the nature of the psyche, for example, than you think that you can. To do this, however, you must leave your daily language behind at least momentarily, and pay attention to your own feelings and imagination. Your language tells you that certain things are true, or facts, and that certain things are not. Many of your most vivid and moving feelings do not fit the facts of your language, so you disregard them.

These emotional experiences, however, often express the language of the psyche. It is not that an understanding of your psyche is beyond you: It is usually that you try to understand or experience it in one of the most difficult ways—through the use of daily language.

The imagination belongs to the language of the psyche. For this reason it often gives experiences that conflict with the basic assumptions upon which daily language is based. Therefore the imagination is often considered suspect.

You might stand alone in your doorway, or in a field—or even on a street, surrounded by many people in a large city—look upward, suddenly struck by the great sweeping clouds above, and feel yourself a part of them. You might momentarily experience a great yearning or feel your own emotions suddenly filled with that same moving majesty, so that for an instant you and the sky seem to be one.

(Pause at 10:12.) Mundane language tells you, as you think with its patterns, that your imagination is running away with you, for obviously you are one thing and the sky is another. You and sky do not equate—or *(amused)* as friend Spock would say: "It is not logical." The feeling swiftly fades after bemusing you briefly.

You might be spiritually refreshed, yet as a rule you would not consider the feeling to be a statement of any legitimate reality, or a representation of your psyche's existence.

The emotions and the imagination, however, give you your closest contact with other portions of your own reality. They also liberate your intellect so that its powers are not limited by concepts it has been taught are true. Instead, such concepts are relatively true—operationally true. For example, the physical laws that you are familiar with operate where you are. They are true, relatively speaking. In those terms you are one person physically objectified, staring upward in the scene just mentioned at an objectified sky. You weigh so many pounds, tilt your head at such-and-such an angle to peer upward at the skyscape, and physically speaking, you can be categorized.

In those same terms the clouds could be physically measured, and shown to be so far above you—composed of, say, winds of a certain velocity, ready to pour down a precise amount of rain or whatever. Physically speaking then, obviously, you are separate from the clouds, and so in those terms your momentary experience of uniting with them would seem to be a lie—at least not factual, or "the product of your imagination."

Instead, such an event is a direct expression of the psyche's knowledge. It senses its quite legitimate identification with nature, exercises its mobility, and feels its own emotional power leap. Your emotions in such a case would be momentarily magnified—raised, say, to a higher power. There are multitudinous such examples that could be given, as in each day your psyche presents evidence of its own greater being—evidence that you are taught to overlook, or to dismiss because it is not factual.

What is imaginary is not true: You are taught this as children. The imagination, however, brings you into connection with a different kind of truth, or a different framework in which experience can be legitimately perceived. The larger truths of the psyche exist in that dimension.

(10:32.) From it you choose physical facts. Thoughts are real. Only some thoughts turn into physical actions, of course. Despite distorted versions of that last statement, however, there is still obviously a distinct difference, say, between the thought of adultery and its physical expression.

You cannot treat thoughts and imagination in such a literal manner, nor in a large respect should you try to "guard your thoughts" as if they were herds of animals that you wanted to keep purely bred. Your thoughts <u>do</u> form your reality. If you do not fear them, however, they create their own balances. The psyche dwells in a reality so different from the world you usually recognize that <u>there</u> good and evil, <u>as you think of them</u>, are also seen to be as operationally or relatively true as the difference between the perceiver and the object perceived.

Take your break.

(10:42. "I didn't feel that I was necessarily with it tonight," Jane said, although her delivery had moved along well enough, and the material was good. Resume at 11:05.)

Dreams, you have been taught, are imaginary events.

In larger terms it is futile to question whether or not dreams are true, for they simply are. You <u>do</u> consider a dream true, however, if its events later occur in fact.

In the life of the psyche a dream is no more or less "true," whether or not it is duplicated in waking life. Dream events happen in a different context— one, you might say, of the imagination. Here you experience a valid reality that exists on its own, so to speak; one in which the psyche's own language is given greater freedom.

Some of you may try to remember your dreams, but none of you <u>have</u> to relate to dream reality as you must to physical life.

To some extent, however, you form physical events while you are dreaming. Then, freed from waking limitations, you process your experience, weigh it according to your own intents and purposes, correlate it with information so vast you could not be consciously aware of it. In most dreams you do not simply think of a situation. You imaginatively become part of it. It is real in every fashion except that of physical fact.

When you meet with any fact, you encounter the tail end of a certain kind of creativity. The psyche, however, is responsible for bringing facts into existence. In <u>that</u> reality a so-called fact is equally true or equally false. The dream that you remember is already a translation of a deeper experience.

It is cast for you so that it bridges the perception of the psyche and the perception of the dreaming self. Dreams serve as dramas, transferring experience from one level of the psyche to another. In certain portions of sleep, your experience reaches into areas of being so vast that the dream is used to translate it for you.

The power to dream springs from that source. Dreaming is

not a passive activity. It demands a peculiar and distinctive mixture of various kinds of consciousness, and the transformation of "nonphysical perception" into symbols and codes that will be sensually understood, though not directly experienced as in waking experience.

You take dreaming for granted, yet it is the result of a characteristic ability that is responsible for the very subjective feeling that you call conscious life. Without it your normal consciousness would not be possible.

A spoken language is, again, dependent upon all other languages that could possibly be spoken, and thus its sounds rise into prominence and order because of the silences and pauses between them; so your waking consciousness is dependent upon what you think of as sleeping or dreaming consciousness. It rises into prominence in somewhat the same fashion, riding upon other possible versions of itself; alert only because—in your terms—of hidden pauses within its alertness.

(11:33.) The ability to dream presupposes the existence of experience that is not defined as physical fact. It presupposes a far greater freedom in which perception is not dependent upon space or time, a reality in which objects appear or are dismissed with equal ease, a subjective framework in which the individual freely expresses what he or she will in the most direct of fashions, yet without physical contact in usual terms.

That reality represents your origin, and is the natural environment in which the psyche resides. Your beliefs, cultural background, and to some extent your languages, set up barriers so that this dream dimension seems unreal to you. Even when you catch yourselves in the most vivid of dream adventures, or find yourselves traveling outside of your bodies while dreaming, you still do not give such experiences equal validity with waking ones.

Take your break.

(11:42 to 11:55.)

Subjectively speaking, you are everywhere surrounded by your own greater reality, but you do not look in the right places. You have been taught not to trust your feelings, your dreams, or your imagination precisely because these do not often fit the accepted reality of facts.

They are the creators of facts, however. In no way do I mean to demean the intellect. It is here, however, that the tyranny of the fact world holds greatest sway. The intellect has been denied its wings. Its field of activity has been limited because you have given it only facts to go on.

Biologically, you are quite capable of dealing with dreaming and waking reality both, and of forming a far more effective synthesis in that regard. All of your creative impulses arise from that hidden dimension—the very impulses that formed your greatest cities, your technology, and the physical cement that binds your culturally organized world.

The creative impulses are behind your languages, yet often you use the languages to silence rather than free inner communication. There have always been rhythms in consciousness that are not historically obvious. At certain times some behavior has been primarily expressed in the waking state, and sometimes in the dream state. The emphasis is never static, but ever-changing. In some periods, then, the normal behavior was "more dreamlike," while more specific developments occurred in the dream state, which was then the more clear or specified of the two. Men went to sleep to do their work, in other words, and the realm of dreams was considered more real than waking reality. Now the opposite is true.

End of session. My heartiest regards. I wish you exciting experiences in the dreams you will have tonight, now that I'm telling you all about how to do it *(amused)*.

("Okay. Thank you, Seth. Good night." 12:09 A.M.)

Chapter 8
Dreams, Creativity, Languages, and "Cordellas"

SESSION 783, JULY 12, 1976
9:25 P.M. MONDAY

Now: Dictation.

("Okay.")

Next chapter, which I believe is eight: "Dreams, Creativity, Languages, and 'Cordellas.' " You may put Cordellas in quotes.

Though you may not realize it, you really manage your subjective lives in a rather circular fashion. Pretend that the present moment is like a wheel, with your concentration at the hub. To maintain what you think of as time momentum, the hub is connected by spokes to the exterior circular framework. Otherwise the hub alone would get you nowhere, and your "moment" would not even give you a bumpy ride.

Your journey through time, however, seems to go smoothly, colon: The wheel rolls ever forward. It *can* roll backward as well, but in your intentness you have a forward direction in mind, and to go backward would seem to divert you from your purpose.

The forward motion brings you into the future, out of the past from which it seems you are emerging. So you plot a straight course, it seems, through time, never realizing in our analogy that the wheel's circular motion allows you to transverse this ongoing road. The hub of the present, therefore, is held together by "spokes." These have nothing to do with your ideas of cause and effect at all. Instead they refer to the circular motion of your own psyche as it seems to progress in time. Each present moment of your experience is dependent upon the future as well as the past, your death as well as your birth. Your birth and your death are built in, so to speak, together, one implied in the other.

You could not die unless you were the kind of creature who was born, nor could you have a present moment as you consider it. Your body is aware of the fact of its death at birth, and of its birth at its death, for all of its possibilities for action take place in the area between. Death is therefore as creative as birth, and as necessary for action and consciousness, in your terms.

(*Pause at 9:40.*) It is not quite that simple, however, for you live in the midst of multitudinous small deaths and births all of the time, that are registered by the body and the psyche. Consciously you are usually unaware of them. Logical thought, using usual definitions, deals with cause and effect, and depends upon a straight sequence of time for its framework. It builds step upon step. It is woven into your language. According to logical thought and language you may say: "I am going to a party today because I was invited last week, and said I would attend." That makes sense. You cannot say: "I am going to a party today because I am going to meet an individual there who will be very important to my life five years from now." That does not make sense in terms of logical thought or language, for in the last example cause and effect would exist simultaneously—or worse, the effect would exist before the cause.

On all other-than-normally conscious levels, however, you deal very effectively with probabilities. The cells maintain their integrity by choosing one probability above the others. The present hub of the wheel, therefore, is but one prominent present, operationally valid. Cause and effect as you think of them appear only because of the motion, the relative motion, of the wheel in our analogy.

When your eyes are on the road of time, therefore, you forget the circular motion of your being. When you dream or sleep, however, the world of cause and effect either vanishes or appears confused and chaotic. Normal daytime images are mixed and matched, so that combinations are formed quite different from those seen in the daylight. The known rules that govern the behavior of creatures and objects in dreams seem no longer to apply. Past, present, and future merge in a seemingly bizarre alliance in which, were you waking, you would lose all mental footing. The circular nature of the psyche to some extent makes itself known. When you think of dreams you usually consider those aspects of it only, commenting perhaps upon the strange activities, the odd juxtapositions and the strange character of dream life itself. Few are struck by the fact of their dreams' own order, or impressed by the ultimate restraint that allows such sometimes-spectacular events to occur in such a relatively restricted physical framework.

For example, in a dream of 20 minutes, events that would ordinarily take years can be experienced. The body ages its 20 minutes of time, and that is all. In dreams, experience is peripheral, in that it dips into your time and touches it, leaving ripples; but the dream events themselves exist largely out of time. Dream experience is ordered in a circular fashion. Sometimes it never touches the hub of your present moment at all, as you think of it, as far as your memory is concerned; yet the dream is, and it is registered at all other levels of your existence, including the cellular.

(Long pause.) You always translate experience into terms you can understand. Of course the translation is real. The dream as you recall it is already a translation, then, but an experienced one. As a language that you know is, again, dependent upon other languages, and implied pauses and silences, so the dream that you experience and recall is also one statement of the psyche, coming into prominence; but it is also dependent upon other events that you do not recall, and that your consciousness, as it now operates, must automatically translate into its own terms.

Take your break.

(10:15 to 10:33.)

Now: On a physical level your body reacts to information about the environment with which you are not consciously concerned. That same information is highly important to the body's integrity, however, and therefore to your own mental stance.

On cellular levels the body has a picture not only of its own present condition, but of all those aspects of the physical environment that affect its own condition. In its own codified fashion it is not only aware of local weather conditions, for example, but of all those world patterns of weather upon which the local area is dependent. It then prepares itself ahead of time to meet whatever challenges of adjustment will be necessary. It weighs probabilities; it reacts to pressures of various kinds.

You are aware of pressure through touch, for instance, but in another version of that sense entirely, the cells react to air pressure. The body knows to the most precise degree the measurements involving radiation of all kinds. At one level, then, the body itself has a picture of reality of its own, upon which your conscious reality must be based—and yet the body's terms of recognition or knowledge exist in terms so alien to your conscious ones as to be incomprehensible. Your conscious order, therefore, rides upon this greater circular kind of knowledge.

Generally speaking, the psyche has the same kind of instant overall comprehension of psychological events and environments as your body has of physical ones. It is then aware of your overall psychological climate locally, as it involves you personally, and in world terms.

Your actions take place with such seeming smoothness that you do not realize the order involved. A volcanic eruption in one corner of the world will ultimately affect the entire earth in varying degrees. An emotional eruption will do the same thing on another level, altering the local area primarily but also sending out its ripples into the mass psychological environment. The psyche's picture of reality, then, would be equally incomprehensible to the conscious mind because of the intense focus upon singularity that your usual consciousness requires.

Your dreams often give you glimpses, however, of the psyche's picture of reality in that regard.

(Long pause at 10:51.) You become aware of probabilities, as actions sometimes that seem to have no connection with your own, but which are still related to them in that greater scheme of interaction that ordinarily you do not comprehend.

New paragraph. When you grow from a baby to an adult you do not just grow tall: You grow all about yourself, adding weight and thickness as well. To some extent events "grow" in the same fashion, and from the inside out, as you do. In a dream you are closer to those stages in which events are born. In your terms they emerge from the future and form the past, and are given vitality because of creative tension that exists between what you think of as your birth and your death.

Take your break.

(10:57 to 11:12.)

You make sentences out of the alphabet of your language. You speak these or write them, and use them to communicate. Events can be considered in the same fashion, as psychological sentences put together from the alphabet of the senses—experienced sentences that are lived instead of written, formed into perceived history instead of just being penned, for example, into a book about history.

I said that your language to some extent programs your experience. There is a language of the senses, however, that gives you biological perception, experience, and communication. It forms the nature of the events that you can perceive. It puts experience together so that it is physically felt. All of your written or verbal languages have to be based upon this biological "alphabet." There is far greater leeway here than there is in any of your spoken or written languages.

I use the word "cordella" to express the source out of which such languages spring. There are many correlations of course between your language and your body. Your spoken language is dependent upon your breath, and even written language is dependent upon the rapidity with which messages can leap the nerve endings. Biological cordellas then must be the source for physical languages, but the cordellas themselves arise from the psyche's greater knowledge as it forms the physical mechanism to begin with.

Dreams are a language of the psyche, in which man's nature merges in time and out of it. He has sense experiences. He runs, though he lies in bed. He shouts, though no word is spoken. He still has the language of the flesh, and yet that language is only opaquely connected with the body's mechanisms. He deals with events, yet they do not happen in his bedroom, or <u>necessarily</u> in any place that he can find upon awakening.

(Louder:) That is the end of dictation—end of session, and a hearty good evening to you both.

("Thank you very much, Seth."

(11:26 P.M. Jane said that it was as though Seth had just so much material planned for this evening's session, and when he'd covered everything he called it a night.)

SESSION 784, JULY 19, 1976
9:23 P.M. MONDAY

Once again Seth devoted the first delivery of the session to his introduction for Jane's "Cézanne" book. She's been busy typing that manuscript in its final form. As for me, I'm still "grappling" with my notes for "Unknown" Reality.

(We took a break from 10:15 to 10:30. Then:)

<u>Our</u> book.

Information flows through the universe at such a rate and in such quantities that you could not possibly process any but a small portion of it.

Your physical senses, again, act almost like a biological alphabet, allowing you to organize and perceive certain kinds of information from which you form the events of your world and the contours of your reality.

Your conscious knowledge rests upon an invisible, unspoken, psychological <u>and</u> physical language that provides the inner support for the communications and recognized happenings of conscious life. These inner languages are built up as cordellas, and cordellas are psychic organizational units from which, then, all alphabets are born. Alphabets imply cordellas, but cannot contain them, any more than English can <u>contain</u> Russian, French, Chinese, or any combination. If you try to speak English you cannot speak Chinese at the same time. One precludes the other, even while one implies the existence of the other, for to that degree all languages have some common roots.

In a way events are like the spoken components of language, yet voiced in a living form—and not for example only sounded. These are based upon the sensual alphabet, which itself emerges from nonsensual cordellas. A sentence is built up as words, parts of speech, verbs, and adjectives, subjects and predicates, vowels and syllables, and underneath there is the entire structure that allows you to speak or read to begin with. To some extent, events are built up in the same fashion. <u>You</u> form and organize sentences, yet you speak on faith, without actually knowing the methods involved in your speaking. So you only recognize the surface of that activity.

In the same way you form events, often without being aware that you do so. It seems that events happen as it seems words are spoken. You were taught how to construct sentences in school, and you learned how to speak from your elders. You were involved with event-making before the time of your birth, however. The psyche forms events in the same way that the ocean forms waves— except that the ocean's waves are confined to its surface or to its basin, while the psyche's events are instantly translated, and splash out into mass psychological reality. In waking life you meet the completed event, so to speak. You encounter events in the arena of waking consciousness. In the dream state, and at other levels of consciousness, you deal more directly with the formation of events. You are usually as unaware of this process as you are in normal practice of the ways in which you form your sentences, which seem to flow from you so automatically.

(10:56.) The psyche, as it is turned toward physical reality, is a creator of events, and through them it experiences its own reality as through your own speech you hear your voice.

In dreams, then, you are involved in the inner process by which physical events are formed. You deal with the psychological components of actions which you will, awake, form into the consecutive corporal "language" that results in the action of your days.

The events that you recognize as official have a unitary nature in time that precludes those probable versions of them, from which they arose—versions that appeared to one extent or another in the dream state. Again, if you speak the English sentence "I am here," you cannot speak the Chinese version at the same time. In that regard, in your framework of action you choose to "speak" one event rather than another. Your formation of events, however, does not simply reside in your unique psychological properties, of course, but is possible because of the corporal alphabet of the flesh.

(Long pause.) Now as it is possible for any one human being to speak more than one language, it is also possible for you to put physical data together in other ways than those usually used. The body is capable then of putting together different languages of reality. In usual terms, for example, your body can only be in one place at one time, and your experience of events is determined in large measure by your body's position. Yet there are biological mechanisms that allow you to send versions or patterns of your body outside of its prime position, and to perceive from those locations. In sleep and dream states you do this often, correlating the newly perceived data with usual sense information, and organizing it all without a qualm. For that matter, the preciseness of your ordinary sense perception rests firmly upon this greater inner flexibility, which gives you a broad base from which to form your secure focus

(Long pause.) Events emerge like spoken words, then, into your awareness. You speak, yet who speaks, and in your briefest phrase, what happens? The atoms and molecules within your vocal cords, and lungs and lips, do not understand one word of the language they allow you to speak so liquidly. Without their cooperation and awareness, however, not a word would be spoken.

(11:15.) Yet each of those nameless atoms and molecules cooperates in a vast venture, incomprehensible to you, that makes your speech possible, and your reality of events is built up from a cordella of activity in which each spoken word has a history that stretches further back into the annals of time than the most ancient of fossils could remember. I am speaking in your terms of experience, for in each word spoken in your present, you evoke that past time, or you stimulate it into existence so that its reality and yours are coexistent.

In dreams even the past is in present tense. Events are everywhere forming. You make and remake the past as well as the future. You choose from those experiences certain ones as events in normal waking reality.

Are your hands tired?

("No.")

(11:22.) While you can only speak one sentence at a time, and in but one language, and while that sentence must be sounded one vowel or syllable at a time, still it is the result of a kind of circular knowledge or experience in which the sentence's beginning and end is known simultaneously. If the end of it were not known, the beginning could not be started so expertly.

In the same way the experienced event occurring in time is dependent upon a circular happening, in which beginning and end are entwined, not one occurring before the other, but coexistent.

End of dictation—some personal remarks. Take a brief break first if you prefer.

("Okay.")

(11:28. Seth returned at 11:35, and delivered material for Jane until ending the session at 12:13 A.M.)

SESSION 785, AUGUST 2, 1976
9:32 P.M. MONDAY

(The weather has been excellent lately. We've been holding the sessions with the front and back doors opened so that the cool winds from the hills blow through the house. So far, no one has interrupted us at such times, though more and more visitors are finding their ways to our door. While we enjoy meeting

people, we're getting somewhat concerned because such encounters do cut into our worktime.

(With some amusement: Even if Jane is bothered by the summer heat on a particular night, Seth is never affected. In trance Jane is as "cool as a cucumber"—until break, that is, when she has to contend with the temperature like the rest of us.)

Now: Good evening—

("Good evening, Seth.")

—dictation, our book.

On a conscious level, again, you could not possibly handle all of the information that is available to you on other levels— information upon which your very physical survival depends. To some extent then language operates as a screening device, enabling you to communicate certain data while effectively blocking out other kinds.

When you speak a sentence you do not stop to consider all of the rules of grammar. You do not mentally diagram the sentence ahead of time. You simply speak more or less automatically. This involves the utmost precision, both mentally and physically. When you experience an event, you do not usually stop either to examine the rules of perception or to wonder what these are. You simply experience or perceive.

Those experienced events, however, are also the result of a screening process. They attain their focus, brilliance, and physical validity because they rise into prominence on the backs of other seemingly unperceived events. In the dream state you work inti- mately with the "inner grammar" of events. In dreams you find the unspoken sentence and the physically unexperienced act. The skeletons of the inner workings of events are there more obvious. Actions are not yet fully fleshed out. The mechanics of your waking psychological behavior are brilliantly delineated. That state can be explored and utilized far more fully than it is, and should be. Yet there will always be a veil between the waking and sleeping consciousness, for while you are physical, the waking mind can only deal with so much information. It would simply forget what it cannot hold.

Your dreams affect your cellular reality, even as that reality is also largely responsible for the fact that you dream, in your terms, at all. Dreams are a natural "product" of cellularly tuned con- sciousness. As fire gives off light, cellularly tuned consciousness gives off dreams.

Such a consciousness is at a state of being in which its reality generates more energy and power than it can physically express in its brilliant intersection with physical reality. The "sparks" generated by each instant of its existence cause additional experiences, perceptions, that will not fit in the <u>known</u> moment of the present— for by then in your terms that present has already vanished into the past.

(9:53.) These events and responses continue to operate, however, particularly in the dream state where they do not intersect directly with full physical experience, as waking events do. All of these parallel or alternate experiences are then used to construct the physical events that you recognize. Again, you speak a sentence truly so that the end of it comes smoothly, though when you begin it you may not have known consciously what you were going to say. Some part of you knew the sentence's beginning and end at once, however.

In dreams you know the beginning and end of events in the same fashion. Any one action in your life is taken in context with all of the other events from your birth to your death. Now it seems to you that because you speak one sentence at any given time, rather than ten other possible versions of it, the sentence as spoken is the "correct" one. Its probable variations in grammar or tense or inflection escape you entirely. Yet unconsciously you may have tried out and discarded all of those, even though you have no memory of such experiences. So even in forming sentences you deal with probabilities, and to some extent or another your body mimics, say, the various muscular responses that might be involved with each unspoken sentence.

Even as you speak your sentence with such fine conscious nonchalance, inner choices are still being made, as you unconsciously check your communications against events occurring outside you as you speak.

So, while each action of your life is taken in context with all other actions of your life until your death, this does not mean that your death is predestined to occur at any given time. As you might change your sentence in the middle from one version to another without even being consciously aware of it, so as you live your life you also work with probabilities. You are the self who speaks the sentence, and you are the self who lives the life. You are larger than the sentence that you speak, and larger than the life you live.

You cannot remember all of the sentences you spoke today.

You may have a general idea of what you said. It certainly seems to you that you said one thing at any given time rather than something else. It also seems that witnesses would back you up. It certainly seems that waking events are more steady and dependable than dream events.

Take your break.

(10:12 to 10:32.)

Waking events happen and vanish quickly. They are experienced directly with the senses fully participating, but for the instant involvement you give up larger dimensions of the same actions that exist, but beneath the senses' active participation.

In dreams the preparations for experienced events take place, not only in the most minute details but in the larger context of the world scene. Events fit together, forming a cohesive whole that gives you a global scale of activities. The "future" history of the world, for example, is worked out now, as in the dream state each individual works with the probable events of private life. That private life exists, however, in a context—social, political, and economic—which is unconsciously apprehended. When a person constructs various probable realities in the dream state, he or she does so also in this larger context, in which the probable status of the world is known.

Here, events are connected one to the other in a psychic webwork that is far more effective than your physical technological system of communication. Here, reality codes are utilized. Knowledge is received and transmitted in electromagnetic patterns so that one pattern can carry far more units of information than anything you have, technologically speaking. Each cell in the body does its part in picking up such signals and transmitting them. Some decoding also takes place at that level, so that pertinent information is sent where it belongs, physically speaking.

Much information does not even reach the brain (the mind is aware of such data, however). In man, the psychic-physical structure has at every moment a complete up-to-date picture of pertinent information about all events that will in any way affect the organism. All actions are taken with this information available. In the dream state such data become transformed, again, into pseudophysical pictures—reflections of events that might occur, previews of probable sequences. These are flashed before a consciousness that momentarily focuses upon the inner rather than the outer arena of reality.

Now these previews are played out not only for the mind but for the body as well. In sleep, again, each cell calculates the effect of various probable events upon its own reality. Computations are made so that the body's entire response can be ascertained ahead of time, and the advantages and disadvantages weighed. The body participates in dreaming at the most minute levels.

The atoms and molecules themselves possess kinds of consciousness impossible for you to analyze, because the scales of your activities are so different. They are information-gathering processes, however, containing codified electromagnetic properties that slip between all of your devices. The atoms and molecules and all of the seemingly smaller "particles" within them are, again, information-carrying processes, and upon them depends your entire interpretation of the nature of events.

Again, cellularly-attuned consciousness generates dreams. Consciousness, riding on a molecular back, generates a physical reality and events suited to it.

Take your break.

(11:00 to 11:20.)

Thinking also rests firmly in the reality of cellularly attuned consciousness.

Thought takes time, and exists by virtue of cellular composition. Consciousness not focused in cellular construction involves itself with a kind of direct cognition, involving comprehensions that come in a more circular fashion.

The creative act is your closest experience to direct cognition. While your consciousness thinks of itself in physical terms, whether you are living or dead, then you will still largely utilize thinking patterns with which you are familiar. Your consciousness is cellularly attuned in life, in that it perceives its own reality through cellular function that forms the bodily apparatus. The psyche is larger than that physically attuned consciousness, however. It is the larger context in which you exist. It is intertwined with your own reality as you think of it. On those occasions when you are able to alter your focus momentarily, then the psyche's greater experiences come into play. You are able to at least sense your existence apart from its cellular orientation. The experience, however, is circular, and therefore very difficult to verbalize or to organize into your normal patterns of information.

(11:32. This was the end of book dictation. Seth came through with a page for Jane and me, and ended the session at 11:45 P.M.)

SESSION 786, AUGUST 16, 1976
9:19 P.M. MONDAY

*(It was a beautiful evening. Most enjoyable. Jane and I were both
somewhat tired, though; indeed, we held no sessions last week. Over the
summer we'd scheduled meetings with professionals in various fields who are
interested in our work, and these had taken time and concentration. We're
curious about all of those other disciplines in the arts, sciences, and human-
ities, of course, so we always look forward to such visitors—though sometimes
any new relationship "takes," and sometimes it doesn't.*

*(In any case, we felt a bit weary this evening, and decided that for a
while at least we'd had our fill of personal encounters. Yet, paradoxically, Seth
seemed to be as energetic as ever:)*

Good evening—book dictation.

("Good evening, Seth.")

You recognize that earth has an atmosphere. In your limited
space travel you take for granted the fact that different conditions
will be met from those encountered upon your planet.

There are alterations taken into your calculations, so astro-
nauts know ahead of time that they can expect to encounter
weightlessness, for example. Your ideas and experiences with space
and matter, however, are determined by your own sense apparatus.
What is matter to you might be "empty space" for beings equipped
in an entirely different fashion. Your conscious mind as you
understand it is the "psychological structure" that deals with
conditions on a physical basis. Sense data are served up, so to
speak, more or less already packaged. The greater inner reality of
the psyche, however, is as extensive as outer space seems to be.

When information "falls" into your conscious mind from
those vaster areas, then it also is changed as it travels through
various levels of psychological atmosphere, until it finally lands or
explodes in a series of images or thoughts. Period.

You are bombarded with such "alien intrusions" constantly.
The focus of your consciousness blots these out while you are in the
normal waking state. There are falling stars everywhere tumbling
through the heavens, for example, though you only see some of
these in the night sky. It is important during the day that a
screening process be used, so that the precision of your actions can
be maintained. Again, however, that fine precision rests upon an
endless amount of information that impinges onto other levels of
your psychological reality. Those data then become the raw material, so to speak, from which your physical events are formed.

In the dream state, with your body more or less safe and at rest, and without the necessity for precise action, these psychological intrusions become more apparent. Many of your dreams are like the tail end of a comet: Their real life is over, and you see the flash of their disappearance as they strike your own mental atmosphere and explode in a spark of dream images. They are transformed, therefore, as they travel through your own psychological atmosphere. You could not perceive them in your own state—nor can they maintain their native state as they plunge through the far reaches of the psyche. They fall in patterns, forming themselves naturally into the dream contents that fit the contours of your own mind. The resulting structure of the dream suits your reality and no other: As this intrusive matter falls, plummets, or shifts through the levels of your own psychological atmosphere, it is transformed by the conditions it meets.

Raindrop patterns in a puddle follow certain laws having to do with the contours of the land, the weather, the nature of the rain, of the clouds, the height from which the raindrops fall, and the conditions operating in the nearby and far portions of the world. If you could properly understand all of that, then by looking into a single puddle you could tell the past and present weather conditions for the entire planet, and follow the probabilities in terms of storms, or volcanic eruptions. You cannot do this, of course, yet it is possible.

(9:44.) Dreams patter down into psychological puddles. They follow the contours of your psychological reality. They make ever-moving psychic patterns in your mind, rippling outward. The rain that hits your backyard as warm drops, soft and clear, may be hail in areas far above your rooftop, but it changes its form as it falls—again, according to the conditions that it encounters. So these "alien intrusions" do the same, and the dreams are like the raindrops, for at other "higher" levels they may have quite a different form indeed.

There are gullies, hills, mountains, valleys, large continents, small islands upon the earth, and the falling rain fits itself to those contours. Your own thoughts, dreams, intents, emotions, beliefs— these are the natural features of your mind, so that information, impinging upon your mental world, also follows those contours.

If there is a gully in your backyard, it will always collect the rain that falls. Your beliefs are like receptive areas—open basins— that you use to collect information. Intrusive data will often fall into such basins, taking on their contours, of course. Beliefs are ways of structuring reality. If you overstructure reality, however, then you will end up with a formal mental garden—whose precise display may be so rigidly structured that the natural aspect of the plants and the flowers is completely obscured. Even your dream information, then, will flow into structured patterns.

(Long pause.) You know that the natural world changes its form constantly. Objects, however, follow certain laws of a physical nature as you experience them, just as violets on the ground do not suddenly change into rocks.

These conditions, however, only exist at the conscious level of your perception. The larger psyche deals with the greater dimension of events, and the dream state itself is like a laboratory in which your waking reality is constructed. The physical earth is bombarded by cosmic rays, and by other phenomena that you do not perceive, yet they are highly important to your survival. The psyche is bombarded in the same way by phenomena important to your survival. In the laboratory of dreams this information is processed, collected, and finally formed into the dreams that you may or may not remember; dreams that are already translations of other events, shaped into forms that you recognize.

Each dream you remember is quite legitimate in the form in which you recall it, for the information has broken down, so to speak, fitting the contours of your own intents and purposes. But such a dream is also a symbol for another unrecalled event, a consciously unrecorded "falling star," and a clue as to how any environment is formed.

Take your break.

(10:10 to 10:25.)

In a manner of speaking, dream reality is closer to the true nature of events than your experience with physical events leads you to suppose.

Dreams often seem chaotic because your point of reference is too small to contain the added dimensions of actuality. Again, in a manner of speaking, events are far more circular in nature. In dreams you can experience the past or future. Physical events are actually formed now, in your terms, because of the interactions between past and future, which are not separate in actuality, but only in your perception.

A dream is like the snap of a rubber band, but it is not the rubber band. You read newspapers and keep in constant physical communication with others of your kind. The news affects "future" events. Individuals and governments take such communications into consideration when they make their decisions. The newspapers are not the events they discuss, though they are their own kind of events. The written news story is actually composed of a group of symbols. Through reading you learn how to interpret these. If you watch news on television you have a larger view of a given news event. When you are viewing a war in a newscast, however, you are still not watching people die. You are watching symbols translated into images that are then visually perceived. The images stand for the people, but they are not the people. The symbols carry the message, but they are not the event they depict.

Some of your dreams are like newspaper stories, informing you of events that have happened in other portions of the psyche. Others are like the televised news picture, carrying perhaps more information about the event but still not containing it.

Psychologically and physically, however, you send out dream bulletins all the while in a constant inner communication. On this level individual dreams help form mass reality, yet also to some extent arise from it in the same way that local weather conditions contribute to world weather conditions, while they are formed by them at the same time.

(Long pause at 10:44.) Your earth exists in the context of the physical universe. You exist in the context of your psyche. The events that you recognize as real are dependent upon all of the other events occurring within your psyche, even as the existence of the earth is dependent upon the other aspects of the physical universe.

Events as you understand them are only intrusions of multidimensional activities into space and time. Events are reflections of your dreams even as your dreams reflect the events you know; those you experienced, and those you anticipate in one way or another. In a manner of speaking, then, and without denying the great validity of your experience, events as you know them are but fragments of other happenings in which you are also intimately involved. The inner multidimensional shape of events occurs in a framework that you cannot structure, however, because as a rule you are not focused in that direction. You prefer to deal with activities that can be physically manipulated.

The physical manipulation of events is indeed a psychological knack of considerable merit, in which consciousness and attention are exuberantly and wholeheartedly focused, bringing vitality and meaning to one relatively small range of activity.

Again, I do not mean to deny the validity of that experience, but to point out its specialized nature. By its nature, however, that precise specialization and tuning of consciousness in to space and time largely precludes other less-specialized encounters with realities. Dreams often present you with what seems to be an ambiguity, an opaqueness, since they lack the immediate impact of psychological activity with space and time. From your viewpoint it seems often that dreams are not events, or that they happen but do not happen. The lack of normal time and space intersections means that you cannot share your dreams with others in the way that you can share waking events. Nor can you remember dream events—or so it seems—as you do your normal conscious experience. In actual fact you remember consciously only certain highlighted events of your lives, and ordinary details of your days vanish as dreams seem to.

You have a dream memory, of course, though you are not aware of it as a rule. There is a craft involved in the formation of events. You perform this craft well when dreaming. Event-making begins before your birth, and the dreams of unborn children and their mothers often merge. The dreams of those about to die often involve dream structures that already prepare them for future existence. In fact, towards death a great dream acceleration is involved as new probabilities are considered—a dream acceleration that provides psychic impetus for new birth.

Take your break.

(11:07 to 11:34.)

Some of this is most difficult to explain, yet it is true to say that no event has a beginning or ending.

This is true of a life. It is true of a dream. The information is not practical in your terms, because it denies your direct experience. Upon request, however, and with some practice, you can suggest in the middle of a dream that it expand to its larger proportions. You would then experience one dream wrapped in another, or several occurring at one time—all involving aspects of a particular theme or probability, with each connected to the others, although to you the connections might not be apparent.

Each event of your life is contained within each other event. In the same way, each lifetime is contained in each other lifetime. The feeling of reality is "truer" then in the dream state. You can become consciously aware of your dreams to some extent—that is, consciously aware of your own dreaming. You can also allow your "dream self" greater expression in the waking state. This can be done through techniques that are largely connected with creativity.

Creativity connects waking and dreaming reality, and is in itself a threshhold in which the waking and dreaming selves merge to form constructs that belong equally to each reality. You cannot begin to understand how you form the physical events of your lives unless you understand the connections between creativity, dreams, play, and those events that form your waking hours. In one respect dreams are a kind of structured unconscious play. Your mind dreams in joyful pleasure at using itself, freed from the concerns of practical living. Dreams are the mind's free play. The spontaneous activity, however, is at the same time training in the art of forming practical events.

Probabilities can be juggled, tried out without physical consequences. The mind follows its natural bents. It has far more energy than you allow it to use, and it releases this in great "fantasies"—fantasies from which you will choose facts that you will experience. At the same time dreaming is an art of the highest nature, in which all are proficient. There are structured dreams as there are structured games in waking life. There are mass dreams "attended by many." There are themes, both mass and private, that serve as a basis or framework. Yet overall, the mind's spontaneous activity continues because it enjoys its own activities.

End of dictation. Give us a moment. . . .

(11:55. As Seth, Jane delivered a few paragraphs of material for herself now, and the session ended at 12:08 A.M.)

Chapter 9

Characteristics of Pure Energy, the Energetic Psyche, and the Birth of Events

SESSION 787, AUGUST 23, 1976
9:40 P.M. MONDAY

Good evening—dictation.

("Good evening, Seth.")

Our book. New chapter. Heading: "Characteristics of Pure Energy, the Energetic Psyche, and the Birth of Events."

When people profess an interest in the nature of dreams, they usually have certain set questions in mind, such as: "How real are dream events?" "What do dreams mean?" "How do they affect daily life?" Each person is aware of the astonishingly intimate nature of dreams. Despite this, certain symbols seem to be fairly universal in your experience.

Such issues, however, while obviously of concern, do not touch upon the greater events behind dream activity, or begin to touch upon the mysterious psychological actions that are behind the perception of any event. Dreams are primarily events, of course. Their importance to you lies precisely in the similarities and differences that characterize them in contrast to waking events.

Behind all of these issues are far deeper considerations. The nature of creativity itself is involved, and the characteristics of energy, without which no action is possible.

Basically, the psyche is a manifestation of pure energy in a particular form. It is very difficult to consider its experience outside of the framework familiar to you. You demand a certain preciseness of definition and terminology. That vocabulary automatically structures the information, of course. The psyche is a conglomeration of energy gestalts. To understand that, you must realize that pure energy has such transforming pattern-forming propensities that it always appears as its manifestations. It becomes its "camouflages."

It may form particles, but it would be itself whether or not particles existed. In the most basic of terms, almost incomprehensible in your vocabulary, energy is not divided. There can be no portions or parts of it, because it is not an entity like a pie, to be cut or divided. For purposes of discussion, however, we must say that in your terms each smallest portion—each smallest unit of pure energy—contains within it the propelling force toward the formation of all possible variations of itself.

The smallest unit of pure energy, therefore, weighing nothing in your terms, containing within itself no mass, would hold within its own nature the propensity for the creation of matter in all of its forms, the impetus to create all possible universes. In those terms, energy cannot be considered without bringing to the forefront questions concerning the nature of God or All That Is, for the terms are synonymous.

(10:02.) I can say precisely that pure energy is everywhere within itself conscious, but the very words themselves somewhat distort my meaning, for I am speaking of a consciousness most difficult to describe.

Pure energy, or any "portion" of it, contains within itself the creative propensity toward individuation, so that within any given portion all individually conscious life is implied, created, sustained. Pure energy cannot be destroyed, and is "at every point" simultaneously being created. Your physical universe and laws give you little evidence of this kind of activity, for at that level the evidence shows you the appearance of time or decay. Your own psychological activity is the closest evidence you have, though you do not use it as such. Pure energy has no beginning or end. The psyche, your psyche, is being freshly created "at every point" of its existence. For that matter, despite all appearances, the physical universe was not born through some explosion of energy which is being dispersed, but is everywhere being created at all of its points "at each moment."

The psyche's basic experience, then, deals with a kind of activity that you cannot directly perceive, yet that existence is responsible for the events that you do perceive, and therefore acts as the medium in which your dreaming and waking events occur.

In that respect you cannot rip apart your events to find the reality behind them, for that reality is not so much a glue that holds events together, but is invisibly entwined within your own psychological being. There are obvious differences between what you think of as waking and dream events. You differentiate definitely between the two, making great efforts to see that they are neatly divided. In your world, conventional and practical sanity and physical manipulation are dependent upon your ability to discriminate, accepting as real only those events with which others more or less agree.

These so-called real events, however, have changed radically through the ages. "Once" the gods walked the earth, and waged battles in the skies and seas. People who believed such things were considered sane—and <u>were</u> sane, for the accepted framework of events was far different from your own. In historic terms the changing nature of accepted events provides far more than, say, a history of civilization, but mirrors the ever-creative nature of the psyche.

(Pause at 10:23.) All of the elements of physical experience at any given time are present in the dream state. Practically speaking, however, the species accepts certain portions of dream reality as its so-called real events at any particular time, and about those specialized events it forms its "current" civilizations. Historically speaking, early men dreamed of airplanes and rocket ships. For that matter, their natural television operated better in some ways than your technological version, for their mental images allowed them to perceive events in neighboring areas or in other portions of the world. They could not simply press a button to bring this about, however. The psychic and biological mechanisms were there, permitting the species to know, particularly in time of stress or danger, what normally unperceived events might threaten survival. But in the dream state, then as now, all such issues were contemporary, acting as models from which the species then chose the practical events that formed its physical experience.

To that extent a study of the dream state gives you some important insights as to the nature of the psyche. In certain terms you are "prepackaged." You always recognize one package of psychological reality as "you.' In basic terms you are always arriving by a kind of instantaneous mail into that package, however. You are unknowingly immersed in and a part of pure energy, being newly created in each moment, so that the energy of your atoms and molecules and of your physical universal system is being replenished at every conceivable moment.

Your psyche is being drawn back into itself, into All That Is, and "out of itself" into your individuation, in psychological pulses of activity that have a correlation with the behavior of electrons in your world. In the dream or sleep state, when you do not meet as directly with physical activity, there is the opportunity to learn more about the psyche by a study of dreams—those events that are so like and so dissimilar to your waking experience.

Take your break.

(10:44 to 11:10.)

Now: All of the probable events of your life exist at once, at certain levels that are connected to the dream state. Since your activities physically must be fitted into a space-time framework, only a minimum of those probable events will physically occur.

Those that do are chosen with great discrimination, dreams serving as one of the methods by which you ascertain the desirability of any given probable act. There is basically no difference at these other levels of existence between waking and dream events. Creatively, then, you organize your experience in such a fashion, with the conscious mind as you think of it also carrying its own responsibility. Those events that you do not accept as physical ones, however, also exist and join their own organizations. They do not simply fall away from your experience, but serve as focus points for events that do not concern you directly, while indirectly they form a definite psychological background. To a certain extent they become the invisible medium of experience from which your own specialized activities emerge, so that their nature is implied in your own life—and so that your life is implied in those other frameworks.

To that extent the dream also serves as a drama of interweaving probabilities, a springboard from which events emerge in all directions. Each aspect of a dream, while having personal meaning, is also your version of a symbol that stands for a corresponding kind of event, but in a different level of reality entirely.

(Long pause.) If you numbered each aspect of a dream, then each number would represent itself in a different numerical system entirely. The surface numbers, or the familiar ones, would still

serve to explain the dream in the context of your own world. As you live in an obvious physical universe, sharing in its reality, so each of you exists in a far vaster psychological or psychic universe—surrounded by, supported by, and part of psychic or psychological entities *(long pause)* infinite in their variety. Your smallest action affects their reality, as theirs does yours. To some extent in the dream state you can perceive such entities more clearly, as at night the stars become more apparent, physically speaking. Psychological realities cannot be compared in terms of size, or bigger or smaller, for the validity and brilliance of each existence carries a personalized intensity so unique that it overshadows any such considerations.

(11:35.) The life of a star, the life of a flower, are entirely different in your terms of duration, size, and characteristics; yet each exists in a validity of experience that ultimately makes such comparisons meaningless. In the same way, it does not help to compare your own consciousness to one of starlike psychological or psychic properties. The psychological mobility of consciousness, however, allows for an inner kind of communication impossible to verbalize, an interlocking spiritual and biological language by which experience is directly transmuted. Many of your dreams therefore are translations of events occurring in other levels of the greater psyche.

There, events are not dependent upon time. You, on the other hand, must work with the time version of events. Dreams provide an elegant framework that allows you to break down timeless events, placing them properly in the context of your own world. This proper placement is quite dependent upon an inner knowledge of probable future events, and your present time would be an impossible achievement were it not for this unconscious knowledge of the "future."

The dreams are often a synthesis of past, present, and future, where one main event is used as a focus point around which "present" events will be collected.

Take your break.

(11:47. The next two pages of the session were given over to material for Jane. The session ended then at 12:21 A.M.)

SESSION 788, SEPTEMBER 6, 1976
9:27 P.M. MONDAY

(Jane has just finished the final typing of her own The World View of Paul Cézanne, *and now I'm ready to type the finished version of Volume 1 of*

Seth's "Unknown" Reality. As I explain in the Introductory Notes for his book, we decided to publish Seth's very long manuscript for "Unknown" in two volumes. This means that our readers can have access to somewhat less than half of that material while I prepare the much longer Volume 2 for later publication. Quite to my surprise, since typing isn't one of her favorite activities, Jane announced that she's going to help me type the final copy for Volume 1 — so each of us spent most of the day at our respective machines.

(At the same time, Seth marched right along on this book, Psyche. Jane jokingly commented that she wished Seth could type too.)

Good evening.

("Good evening, Seth.")

Dictation: Basically, events have nothing to do with what you think of as cause and effect. This is perhaps apparent to some degree when you study dream events, for there the kind of continuity you are used to, connecting events, largely vanishes.

Instead events are built up, so to speak, from significances. But let us forget that term for a moment and considcr association, with which you are already familiar, since your stream of consciousness operates in that fashion. By its very nature each consciousness is a particular, peculiar, and unique focus of awareness which will experience any possible realities through its own characteristics.

It also "stamps" or "impresses" the universe with its own imprint. No portion of the universe is inactive or passive, regardless of its seeming organization or its seeming lack of organization. Each consciousness, then, impresses the universe in its own fashion. Its very existence sets up a kind of significance, in whose light the rest of the universe will be interpreted. The universe knows itself through such significances. Each consciousness is endowed with creativity of a multidimensional nature, so that it will seek to create as many possible realities for itself as it can, using its own significance as a focus to draw into its experience whatever events are possible for it from the universe itself. It will then attract events from the universe, even as its own existence imprints the universe as an event with the indelible stamp of its own nature.

Put more simply from another viewpoint, each of you as you know yourselves has certain abilities and characteristics of your own. You experience reality through the cast of those abilities and characteristics, but you also stamp the universe with that particular imprint of individuality that is your own, and you attract those events that are suited to your nature and no other.

Significances fall or happen in certain patterns, and when

these become very obvious they appear as cause and effect. They are simply heavy-handed significances. Your associative processes and habits are perhaps the closest examples that can give clues of how significances operate. Even then, however, associations deal with the passage of time, and basically significances do not. You might think of your aunt Sarah, for example, and in a few moments the associative process might bring you images of periods in the past when you visited your aunt, of her friends and neighbors, the articles in her house, and episodes connected with your relationship.

(9:49.) At the same time Aunt Sarah, unbeknown to you, might pick up a blue vase, one that you had just seen in your mind as belonging on a shelf in her living room. Touching the vase, your aunt Sarah might think of the person who gave it to her, now on the other side of the continent. That person, perhaps thinking of buying a present for someone, might settle upon a vase in a flash of inspiration, or suddenly begin humming a song with the name "Sarah" in the title, or possibly even think of your aunt. If on the other hand any opposing associations existed anywhere along the line, the "chain" of association could be broken. The last lady might consider a vase, for example, but reject the idea. Because of the time element, it seems to you that the first episode caused the others, and that your first association concerning your aunt brought about the "following" events.

The inner significances, however, the associations, existed all at once, to be tuned in to at any point of time. They had their reality basically apart from time, even though they appeared within it.

Actually the three sets of events could easily occur to the three people at once, and if no normal communication happened no one would be the wiser. The inner tapestry of events deals with just this kind of association. Emotional intensities and significances compose the nature of events. In dreams you work with the kind of intensities involved, exploring multitudinous significances. These are like charged emotional patterns, formed of your own highly personal emotions and intents.

Using such significances as yardsticks, you accept or reject probable events. You imprint the universe with your own significance, and using that as a focus you draw from it, or attract, those events that fit your unique purposes and needs. In doing so, to some extent you multiply the creative possibilities of the universe, forming from it a personal reality that would otherwise be absent, in those terms; and in so doing you also add in an immeasurable fashion to the reality of all other consciousness by increasing the bank of reality from which all consciousness draws.

Take your break.

(10:10 to 10:23.)

Now: There is no such thing, basically, as random motion. There is no such thing as chaos. The universe, by whatever name and in whatever manifestation, attains its reality through ordered sequences of significances.

These are kept separate in various systems of actuality, while still combining in an overall fashion. You understand the cause-and-effect kind of order, but this is built upon the noncausal aspect of significances. In a way the dreams that you recall are like numbered paintings, tailored to fit your own intents and purposes, fitting the contours of your mind so perfectly that you forget the larger experiences from which they were drawn.

Physically and psychically the dream itself is the result of the most precise kind of calculation and activity, in which complicated dramas and interactions occur, often highly charged and intense, and yet cut off from the body's full participation. These significances, then, involve from your end certain biological cues that regulate the intersection of psychological events with physical activity in time and space. Only when all conditions match your own highly specific requirements are the necessary cues activated to give you physical experience. To that extent in dreams you are "on hold," involved with a range of action too wide to fit the contours of practical earth experience.

These significances set up their own codes, then, so that physical events must be coded in a certain fashion, and dreams in another. There is, then, what can be called a predream state, or a state of experience from which the dream will be formed. Such experience will carry a different kind of code, further divorcing it from that acceptable intersection with bodily activity, space, and time.

Your physical events happen to you as you. In dreams you may experience an event seemingly as someone else, or you may find yourself in the past or future instead of the present. In waking life you have the family that you recognize, or group of friends, or profession, or what have you. In dreams you may find yourself married to someone else, or living an entirely different kind of life. In a way dreams are like variations of the theme of your life, though in reality your life is the theme you have chosen from those possible versions.

To some extent, however, dream events are like physical

ones a good deal of the time. Your dream perceptions seem physical—you walk, run, eat, and perform other physical functions. There are actually many other conditions of existence, but for now we will speak of a predream state, which is actually composed of several conditions of actuality. Here the physical aspects of events largely vanish, comparatively speaking, the farther away you go from the dream state into inner reality. It would seem to you that experience becomes broader but less specific, but such is not the case. Experience does become broader, but it changes in quality so that, for example, one moment in your terms of such experience would provide the working material for five years of dreams.

This is simply an analogy because you are steeped in that other reality constantly; but its illuminations and nature are transmitted to the self that you know through the formation of dreams, and in your terms, "it takes time to dream." This larger experience, from which your dreams are finally formed, involves you in a kind of journey. Period. Using another analogy, it is as if you joyfully leave the normal paraphernalia of usual life behind, and ride aboard your own greater psyche into vaster seas of experience.

(10:55.) You leave behind the physical nature of events and go into those areas in which events are formed. In ways most difficult to describe, you encounter the universe in a more direct fashion, using inner senses that are far more ranging. Using your own indestructible validity as "bait," you go forth to draw from the universe the raw material of experience. You are yourself, yet at that level you are also a part of that universe from which that self springs, and its power and vitality are your own, to be uniquely focused. In your terms, you literally look backward and forward in time at your individual self and your civilization, seeing where they merge, and feeling the infinite connections, so that each event you choose as your own will also be chosen as a world event— participated in to whatever extent by others, and adding to the available experience of the species from which others can also draw.

A direct cognition is involved in which each consciousness knows what each other one is doing, its "position," and the implications of its experience. The entire fabric and framework of time and reality at each point is ascertained, and the probabilities probed and understood.

Now: All of this sounds very complicated. Yet in a different way the same processes occur at other levels, as in its way cellular consciousness perceives all of the probabilities concerned with physical survival in its most far-reaching complications. At this moment the cells within your body know the life conditions of any place on the planet, and compute these, ascertaining the ways in which they require action on the body's part. Your cells are aware of the motion of the planets and of all circumstances regarding the body's equilibrium, stability, and survival. The body is then formed constantly as the result of these computations.

In larger terms, in the predream states you are aware of all of the activities of your own greater psyche as it participates in—and contributes to—the infinite existence of psychic consciousness as you understand it, and becomes aware of the psychological realities that form the framework of its own stability.

Take a break or end the session as you prefer. I did not go to the dentist.

("We'll take the break."

(11:12. Seth made his humorous remark because I'd had a tooth out last Friday. I still wasn't up to par. Resume at 11:30.)

Now: Events do not become physical, then, unless certain requirements are met, and certain codes activated.

Experiences at predream levels occur at their own intensities. The knowledge is translated into information that is broken down in the dream state into more specific data, highly symbolized, suiting individual requirements and "run through the body" in a kind of ghostly trial fashion.

It is then further processed into individual significances, drives, or intents, which convert it into the required codes that will then determine the nature of actualized waking events. Data must be of particular kinds of intensity before they register as physical matter, or are experienced as physical events. Part of this processing occurs in the dream state, and creativity plays a large part in the preliminary process.

End of session, and a good start for the next one. My heartiest best wishes, and a fond good evening.

("Thank you very much, Seth. Good night."

(11:36 P.M. Jane said that Seth's material was going to lead into the formation of EE units—electromagnetic energy units—and their collective role in the creation of physical matter.)

SESSION 789, SEPTEMBER 27, 1976
9:30 P.M. MONDAY

(Jane received her first press copy of Psychic Politics *in the mail two days ago. She was delighted, and so was I.*

(Because we have been so busy, I haven't written any elaborate notes

for Psyche, *as I did for the other Seth books. As he promised he'd do early in this work, Seth himself does "set the scene" now and then by mentioning our activities, but obviously—and rightly—he's more interested in delivering his material. Nor has Jane had that much time to provide notes of her own.*

(We feel that the importance of Seth's work far surpasses our own comments, of course, yet I do like to remind the reader now and then of Seth-Jane's spontaneous delivery of these sessions.

(No matter what we may have been doing earlier that day, when the session begins—there's Seth. He may be joking or serious, dictating a chapter or making remarks about our lives or the world in general. Whatever, he's always ready to share his perceptions and knowledge with us, as far as he can translate them into words so that we can understand them. When Jane speaks for him her eyes are always much darker and seemingly larger, with a compelling luminous quality that's both mysterious and evocative. Seth's voice, coming through her in his own unique accent, can be as gentle as a whisper or as ear-splitting as he desires when he wants to make a point. When she comes out of trance Jane can remember what he's said, or have no recollection at all of his material.

(Tonight, Seth launched right into dictation for Psyche:*)*

Now: Good evening—

("Good evening, Seth.")

—dictation. What I have called the predream state here is actually one in which you are always immersed whether you are waking or sleeping, or whether in your terms you are alive or dead. It involves conditions in which direct knowing primarily operates.

It is your <u>natural</u> state of being. In its larger aspects, then, nature involves states that include both life and death in far more expansive frameworks of reference.

Give us a moment . . . This is characterized perhaps most of all by more perceptive psychological organizations. In the predream state you participate in such organizations, although you bring back home to your physical self—in the form of dreams—only data that can be recognized and used in physical terms. It is highly important to remember that your experience and knowledge grow at those other levels of actuality. Even during your physical lifetime your experience is not confined to conventional physical events alone. Those usual events arise from the creative impetus that occurs at these other levels.

Please understand: I am not saying here that you have no conscious control over events, for they <u>are</u> formed by you in accordance with your feelings, beliefs, purposes, and intents.

The inner material that "makes events real" comes from

these other sources, however. Most of you are not aware of this basic, mysterious nature of events, because it does not occur to you to study the inner fabric. The past and future of any given event provides a kind of thickness, a kind of depth-in-time. The probabilities of an event escape you in practical terms.

In the predream state you directly encounter a reality in which those probabilities exist all at once to your perception. In a dazzling display you are aware of such events from infinite perspectives. Consciously you could not grasp such information, much less act upon it, nor could you maintain your particular, unique, psychological stance. You still take advantage of that level of being, however, using that immeasurable data as a basis to form the reality that you know.

To some extent your dreaming state is a connective between the kind of life you recognize and this far vaster dimension that is its source. Dreaming involves a far greater input of information than is realized, then—that is, you take in far more data when you are dreaming than when you are awake, although the data are of a different kind. You form your dreams in part from that information. The dreams themselves are further processed so that they become a fabric for recognizable waking events.

(9:48.) Dream dramas are highly complicated, artistic productions. On the one hand they represent other events of the predream state, events beyond your comprehension in their "natural condition." Such events are not lost, however, but translated into dreams as your own consciousness returns closer to its "home base." Each aspect of a dream stands in coded form as a symbol for greater, undecipherable events.

The symbols are so precisely and accurately produced that they simultaneously serve as aspects relating to your intimate daily life as well. Since everyday events are formed in part as a result of such dream information, then each event of your physical life is also a symbol for another otherwise undecipherable event that occurs in those levels of the psyche in which your own being is immersed.

This in no way denies the validity of events as you think of them, for all of your physical activity immediately alters all other relationships at all levels of being. Most of you are familiar with inspiration in one form or another. People who are not writers or artists, or poets or musicians, often suddenly find themselves almost transformed for a brief period of time—suddenly struck by a poem or a song or a snatch of music, or by a sketch—that seems to come from nowhere, that seems to emerge outside of the context of usual thought patterns, and that brings with it an understanding, a joy, a compassion, or an artistic bent that seemingly did not exist a moment earlier. Where did the song or poem or music come from? Such individuals feel that they suddenly "know" in a direct manner. They experience knowledge that comes from within rather than information that comes from without.

Now the dream comes in the same fashion. You do not have to wonder about how to form a dream before you go to bed at night. You do not have to know any of the mechanisms involved, so dreaming often seems to "just happen" in the same way that an inspiration seems to just come.

Books have been written about the nature of dreams. There are classic accounts of precognitive dreams, or prophetic dreams involving saints and honored personages in the Bible. Yet each dream alters the physical world to some extent. A creative idea might lead to a book—certainly a physical-enough production. Dreams involve you with the most intimate mechanics by which physical events are formed. There are hormonal and chemical changes occurring in the body—often at minute but important levels—in direct response to dream experience. Your dreams then are tied into your biological makeup. There are also coded biological connections within dream images themselves that relate to cellular activity—not generally, but specifically.

Each dream object is chosen with the highest discrimination so that it serves as a symbol at many levels, and also sends pertinent messages to the individual cells and organs of your body as well.

Take your break.

(10:15 to 10:38.)

Dictation. I want to discuss the connections between creativity, dreams, and the actual formation of physical events. At the same time I understand your need for some kind of precise terminology, even while I know that in certain terms the more "precise" I become for your benefit, the more we may miss of greater issues that escape such boundaries. I also want to avoid many preconceptions that are connected with certain words.

Nevertheless, in dreams you are intimately connected with the processes by which physical events are formed. Events, again, gain their characteristics from those significances that you place upon the universe as your own being impresses it with your beliefs, desires, and individual nature.

As a continent does not exist alone, but also in relationship to other physical formations, so in your terms you form events so that they fit into a mass framework. You form your own reality. You do not form it isolated and alone, however. You are aware of other events, and take them into consideration, for example, regardless of appearances. You cannot force another person to experience an event he or she rejects. Nor can anyone act in like manner against you. So-called good or bad events each faithfully follow the inner mechanics.

In order to become physical, probable events must meet certain conditions, as it were. They must fall into the proper time and space slots. There must be a psychological fit also, certain intensities reached in terms of desire, belief, or intent. By intensity I do not necessarily mean effort, vehement desire, or determined conscious intent. I mean instead the collection of certain intangible qualities, precisely focused toward physical activity.

Physical events imply the collection of basically nonphysical forces into an organization that exists initially outside of the time-space context. This is a psychological organization, consisting of a selection of chosen probable events. These wait in the wings, so to speak, for physical actualization. The final trigger for that actualization may come from the waking or dream states, but it will represent the final factor needed—the quickening of inspiration, desire, or purpose—that will suddenly activate the initial psychological organization as a physical occurrence.

(Pause at 10:56.) The EE units which I have mentioned in other material are important because they exist in an electromagnetic sphere of activity, and they trigger certain responses in the brain and nervous system. Events themselves involve a steady condition of highly related fields of activity, however, that exist between the EE units, so to speak.

These fields involve psychological reactions, not physically perceivable, and yet as explosive in their way as a nuclear detonation. That is, these psychological activities "explode" into physical events by virtue of a transformation and a charge that allows purely mental acts to "break the time-space barrier" and emerge as realities in a physical world. In a way, the EE units occur on the furthest reaches of this activity. If an event were a physical craft such as a spaceship, the EE units would allow it to land in your world, but would not be the original propellants. Those propellants are psychic fields of interrelationship.

Let us use an analogy. Pretend that you are a planet, as indeed in certain terms you are. You exist in a highly complicated and sophisticated universe. You know that space is filled with all kinds of inhabitants, and we will compare these space inhabitants to probable events. As a planet you have certain characteristics. Some space inhabitants would not be able to land under those conditions at all. The conditions represent your own psychological individuality. You send out messages to the stars because you are lonely, and events or visitors are one of your main methods of gaining experience and knowledge. To land their own rocket ships, space travelers must enter your atmosphere and use its conditions while maintaining their own integrity. They must also have their own reasons for such a visit.

Now any physical event is something like the impact of a rocket ship entering your world from "somewhere else." Thoughts often seem to swim in and out of your system of consciousness, and you barely notice. Events often appear and disappear in the same manner, yet they have impressed your reality. You have attracted them to one extent or another, and they have been attracted to you. Momentarily a field of relatedness is set up that is highly charged, one that provides an inner path by which probable events can flow into your area of recognized events.

This path exists on psychological levels, and triggers your perceptive mechanisms, which then of course react and dutifully perceive. Your intent or purpose or belief is one of the main attractions. These serve as beams searching the universe, but the conditions of manifestation also exist. There must be a proper fit.

Take your break.

(11:21 to 11:40.)

Now: Dictation. First of all, your own universe is not isolated, either. It is simply the one that you perceive.

There are in a basic sense other universes within the one that you recognize, and constantly happening in those universes are other events of which you are unaware. The universes exist one within the other, so to speak, and their events also one within the other, so that while any given event seems itself only in the terms that you recognize, it is a part of endless others that exist one within the other, and it is impossible at certain levels to separate the "portions."

Your daily life seems to give you little evidence of this. Your dreams, however, often contain this kind of interrelatedness. Because you perceive events in the way that you do, of course, you see the familiar physical universe. Dream events, not as precise in space and time, often serve as a framework through which some evidence of other universes can be glimpsed. No system is closed, so there are interactions, so to speak, between all universes. No psychological system is closed either, even while it retains an inviolate nature that is indestructible.

Dreams, then, operate as vast mass communicative networks, far more effective at certain levels of the psyche than, for example, television is at a physical level.

The dream state can be used then as a psychological or psychic platform to view other realities, and to glimpse the inner mechanics by which nonphysical events become actualized in your world.

End of dictation. End of session unless you have questions.

(11:50. Seth came through with a paragraph of information for Jane in response to my question about her writing, then ended the session at 11:54 P.M.)

SESSION 790, JANUARY 3, 1977
9:20 P.M. MONDAY

(Tonight we started the sessions up again after a three-month layoff. During that time I typed the final manuscript for Volume 1 of Seth's "Unknown" Reality, with Jane's help, and we've just mailed it to her publisher, Prentice-Hall, Inc. I can now begin finishing Volume 2.

(It's been a very busy period for us otherwise, too. Among many events, we saw the last several professional people whose visits we'd scheduled late last summer. Few weeks went by without unexpected guests as well.

(With all of our outgoing activities, though, the month of November was also a sad—and educational—one for us. Our 16-year-old cat, Willy, had first shown signs of illness last summer. The veterinarian told us that the cat's heart was failing. As Jane worked on "Unknown" Reality, Willy often lay on her lap, and we felt his approaching death with heavy hearts of our own.

(He died on November 5, 1976, while at home with us. The courageous acquiescence of his death made us feel humble and ignorant—and in awe of nature's mysteries—because certainly Willy died with a kind of absolute trust that people find most difficult to achieve. I buried him in the backyard. Now seldom do we go in or out of the driveway without glancing at the group of rocks I placed upon his grave.

(The weekend following Willy's death, though, Jane insisted that we get a "new" kitten at once. She was afraid that if we didn't, she, at least,

would never have another pet—so we found "Willy Two" at an area humane society. He's so small, he still almost fits in just one of my hands. During this evening's session, he slept curled up on the couch beside me.

(Seth opened the session by finishing his Introduction to Jane's The World View of Paul Cézanne, *which Prentice-Hall will publish later this year. In that piece Seth has come through with an excellent capsule explanation of his theory of "world views." He sees Jane's book as a prime example of what can be done in that area.*

(Then, back to Psyche *at 9:33:)*

Dictation: There are vast distances of a psychological and psychic nature separating my reality from your own. To some degree Ruburt's mind is the connective between us. As I speak in sessions, therefore, I am not entirely myself.

I am what I am, interpreted through your reality. I have personality characteristics by which those who have come to sessions can identify me. I have a peculiarity of <u>voice</u> and <u>accent</u> that is, if I may say so myself, unique and individualistic. Yet I come to your reality by a strange route—one that does not involve roads or highways but psychological dramas that wind backward like paths into the "psychological history" of your species. To some extent, I am <u>like</u> a particularly vivid, persistent, recurring dream image, visiting the mass psyche, only with a reality that is not confined to dreams—a dream image that attains a psychological fullness that <u>can</u> seem to make ordinary consciousness a weak apparition by contrast, psychologically speaking.

We have been speaking of dream events and waking reality, the nature of creativity and the formation of events. We have also touched upon psychological entities of vast proportions, in your terms, that form psychological structures from which your own reality emerges. In that connection, the nature of my reality becomes pertinent.

I am not speaking here of gods, but of psychological structures different from the ones you know. They cannot directly perceive or experience your reality in their "present" form of organization. In a manner of speaking they are in the background, from which the foreground of your experience emerges. They appear in your dreams in various ways. They are like the cloth from which you are cut. They are forces which have no need of names except for your convenience.

(9:50.) Those psychological structures are also great energy activators, and as such are important initiators of events. They are

seldom if ever physically materialized. Yet they are very responsive to the psychic needs of the people, and so they "appear" at various times in history with certain messages, in the same way that certain dreams might reoccur in a private mind.

In the most cosmic and most minute ways, physical experience springs from inner reality. Events are initiated from within and then appear without. In your terms I have no physical existence. These books, however, initiate quite physical events as readers learn to take better control of their lives, expand their consciousnesses, and become aware of their own greater abilities.

You may say if you wish that I am a dream image lacking even an image—but if so, then each individual whose life is changed by my words must question: "What is a dream?" In the same way that my personality exists without physical manifestation, so does your own. Your dreaming and waking experience has a direct effect upon the entire universe. The difference is that you are not consciously aware of what you are doing, but I am. I change a world to some extent, though in your terms I will not actually sit in a chair or walk the streets, or shake your hand, or see the twilight come, or the sunrise.

To me your world is a dream universe which I visit by invitation, a probable reality that I find unique and very dear—but one in which I can no longer have direct experience. Because I am not as immersed in it as you, I can tell you much about it, since your precise orientation necessitates a more narrow, concentrated view.

Now in your dreams you often visit other such realities, but you have not learned to organize your perception, or direct it. If entities like myself form the background of your own existence, so do entities like yourselves act as the background psychological structures in which other such organizations exist. There is always a give-and-take in all such relationships.

Your kind of psychological reality is therefore implied in my own, and mine in yours, even as your kind of reality is implied in that of Willy Two (our kitten)—and his in yours.

Take your break.

(10:07 to 10:20.)

It is not easy to explain the workings of the inner psyche, or the activity behind dreams, for such experience exists beyond the framework of verbalization or images, and deals basically with the nature and behavior of psychological and psychic energy.

I am a personified energy source—but so are you. I have had many lives, in your terms, yet in other terms I have not lived physically, but rather lent or loaned my energy to lives that rose from my reality but were not me. In the same way you give birth to dream images of your own—hardly aware that you have done so, unconscious of the fact that you have provided impetus for a kind of psychological reality that quite escapes your notice. The dream stories you begin continue on their own. No dream is stillborn. Each chapter of this book is written in such a way that the ideas presented will activate your own intuitions, and open pathways between your dreaming and waking states.

Your own greater reality hovers about you in each instant. If you knew in precise terminology how you grew physically from a fetus to an adult, if you could consciously follow that process, you would not necessarily be better off, but possibly hindered in your growth; for you would begin to question: "Am I doing this right?" The perfection of the process would make you ill at ease.

In the same way, a step-by-step illustration of the nature of the dream state might well make you too self-conscious. *(Humorously:)* You would begin to question: "Am I dreaming right?"

(10:32.) Many people are in awe of their dreams. They are afraid of anything they do not consciously control. Yet if you think of your dreams as extensions of your own experience in another context, then you can indeed learn to gain ease with them. You will recall them more easily, and as you do you will be able to maintain a sense of continuity between the waking and dream states.

As this happens the contours of your own psyche will appear more clearly. Those contours will not show themselves in terms of definite mathematical-like propositions, however, but will emerge through the techniques, symbols, feelings, and desires usually attributed to creativity.

The characteristics of creativity appear most clearly in children. Creativity implies abandon within a framework that is accepted for itself, and itself only.

If in your waking hours you playfully make up a <u>dream</u> for yourself, and then playfully interpret it without worrying about implications, but for itself only, you will unwittingly touch upon the nature of your own nightly dreaming. Your regular dreams and your "manufactured" ones will have much in common, and the process of manufacturing dreams will acquaint you with the alterations of consciousness that to a greater degree happen nightly. This is an excellent exercise. It is particularly beneficial for those who have a too-rigid mental framework.

The playfulness and creativity of dreams are vastly underrated in most dream studies. Children often frighten themselves on purpose through games, knowing the game's framework all the time. The bogeyman in the garden vanishes at the sound of the supper bell. The child returns to the safe universe of tea and biscuits. Dreams often serve the same purpose. Fears are encountered, but the dawn breaks. The dreamer awakes for breakfast. The fears, after all, are seen as groundless. This is not an explanation for all unpleasant dreams by any means, yet it is a reminder that not all such events are neurotic or indicative of future physical problems.

Ruburt and Joseph have a kitten. In its great exuberant physical energy it chases its own tail, scales the furniture, tires itself out—and man's mind exuberantly plays with itself in somewhat the same fashion. In dreams it uses all those splendid energetic abilities freely, without the necessity for physical feedback, caution, or questioning. It seeks realities, giving birth to psychological patterns. It uses itself fully in mental activity in the same way that the kitten does in physical play.

When you try to explore the psyche in deadly seriousness, it will always escape you. Your dreams can be interpreted as dramas, perhaps, but never as diagrams.

Do not try to bring "dream interpretation"—and kindly, now—down to your level, but instead try to playfully enter that reality imaginatively, and allow your own waking consciousness to rise into a freer kind of interpretation of events, in which energy is not bounded by space, time, or limitations.

End of dictation. Give us a moment. . . .

(10:57. Seth gave a page of material for Jane and me, then ended the session at 11:12 P.M.)

SESSION 791, JANUARY 17, 1977
9:42 P.M. MONDAY

(Although we hated to do it, Jane and I have finally arranged to have an unlisted telephone number. Up to twenty calls a day have been coming in—and sometimes many more, day and night. It can be quickly calculated that such a rate adds up to 600 or so messages a month. Jane was the one

who took most of the calls, for she was usually the one people wanted to talk to. She enjoyed the personal interactions most of the time, and often spent a half hour or so trying to help someone in that way. But finally she reached the point where there just wasn't enough time for her to answer the telephone that often and get her own work done too.)

Now: Dictation. *(Long pause.)* Pretend that you are a fine actor, playing in a multidimensional theater, so that each role you take attains a vitality far surpassing the creative powers of any ordinary play.

Each of you is embarked upon such an endeavor. You lose yourselves in your parts. You are also involved in a kind of creative dilemma, since in a manner of speaking you confuse yourself as the actor with the character you play so convincingly that you are fooled.

You say: "I must maintain my individuality after death," as if after the play the actor playing Hamlet stayed in that role, refused to study other parts or go on in his career, and said: "I am Hamlet, forever bound to follow the dilemmas and the challenges of my way. I insist upon maintaining my individuality."

In the dream state the actors become aware to some extent of the parts they play, and sense the true personal identity that is behind the artist's craft. I have spoken of this before, but it is important to remember that you impose a certain kind of "artificial" sense of exaggerated continuity even to the self you know. Your experience changes constantly, and so does the intimate context of your life—but you concentrate upon points of order, <u>in your terms</u>, that actually serve to scale down the context of your experience to make it more comprehensible. There are no such limits naturally set about your consciousness.

You have a mass psychological environment that forms your worldly culture, and corresponds to a worldly stage set in which experience then occurs. Certain psychological conventions act as props. There are, then, more or less formal psychological arrangements that are used as reference points, or settings. You group your experience within those arrangements. They serve to shape mental events as you physically perceive them.

The last sentence is important, for in your lifetimes your experience must be physically felt and interpreted. Despite this, however, events spring from a nonphysical source. As mentioned earlier, your recalled dreams are already interpretations of other nonphysical events.

Putting this as simply as possible, your actual experience is far too vast for you to physically follow. Your particular kind of consciousness is the result of specialized focus within a particular area. You imagine it to be "absolute," in that it seems to involve an all-exclusive state that includes your identity as you think of it—only you give it boundaries like a kingdom. It is, instead, a certain kind of organization that is indeed inviolate even while it is itself a portion of other kinds of consciousnesses, with their own points of focus. Your body itself is composed of self-aware organizations of consciousness that escape your notice and deal with perceptual material utterly alien to your own ways.

(10:10.) There are affiliations of a most "sophisticated" fashion that leap even the boundaries of the species. You look upon your cultural world with its art and manufacture, its cities, technology, and the cultivated use of the intellectual mind. You count your religions, sciences, archeologies, and triumphs over the environment, and it seems to you that no other consciousness has wrought what man's has produced. Those "products" of your consciousness are indeed unique, creative, and form a characteristic mosaic that has its own beauty and elegance.

There are organizations of consciousness, however, that leapfrog the species, that produce no arts or sciences per se—yet these together form the living body of the earth and the physical creatures thereon. Their products are the seas upon which you sail your ships, the skies through which your airplanes fly, the land upon which your cities sprawl, and the very reality that makes your culture, or any culture, possible.

Man is a part of that trans-species consciousness also, as are the plants and animals. Also, part of man's reality contributes to that trans-species organization, but he has not chosen to focus his practical daily consciousness in that direction, or to identify his individuality with it. As a result he does not understand the greater natural mobility he himself possesses, nor can he practically perceive the natural psychological gestalts of which he is a part, that form all of your natural—meaning physical—world.

In dreams this relationship often is revealed. The truth behind such relationships is inherent in all God-Man, God-Woman, Animal-Man, or Animal-Woman legends and mythology. There are connections, then, between man and the animals and the so-called gods (in small letters), that hint at psychological and natural realities.

Any section of the land has an identity, so to speak, and I am not talking symbolically. Such identities represent the combined organizations of consciousness of land, man, and animal, within any given realm. Simply enough put, there are as many kinds of consciousnesses as there are particles, and these are combined in infinite fashions. *(Long pause.)* In the dream state some of that experience, otherwise closed to you, forms the background of the dream drama. *(A one-minute pause.)* Your consciousness is not one thing like a flashlight, that you possess. It is instead a literally endless conglomeration of points of consciousness, swarming together to form your validity—stamped, as it were, with your identity.

(Intently:) Whether dispersed, concentrated in a tight grouping, appearing "alone" or flying through other larger swarms, that particular organization represents your identity.

Using an analogy, its "particles" could be dispersed throughout the universe, with galaxies between, yet the identity would be retained. So unknowingly, now, portions of your consciousness mix and merge with those of other species without jarring your own sense of individuality one whit—yet forming other psychological realities upon which you do not concentrate.

In the dream state, animals, men, and plants merge their realities to some extent so that information belonging to one species is transferred to others in an inner communication and perception otherwise unknown in your world.

Take your break.

(10:45 to 11:05.)

The natural structures of the earth are formed as the result of the biological cooperation of all species, and consciousness itself is independent of any of the forms that it may at one time or another assume.

Therefore, at levels that would appear chaotic to you, there is a great mixing and merging of consciousness, a continual exchange of information, so to speak; an open-ended exploration of possibilities, from which in your terms events privately and *en masse* emerge.

I am simply explaining the characteristics, aptitudes, abilities, and tendencies of Nature, with a capital N. There are so many different levels in what you call the dream state that they are impossible to list, except in stereotyped ways. This is particularly because some dream sequences involve biological comprehensions that are not literally translatable.

It has been truthfully said that the "unconscious" is intimately aware of the most minute details of your health, state of mind, and relationships. "It" is also aware of the state of the earth's health—even of the environmental conditions on the other side of the planet. It is familiar with the cultural climate also. Your recognized consciousness operates as it does because of immense information-gathering procedures—procedures that unite all species. Biologically such information is coded, but that physical information, such as in the genes and chromosomes, can be altered through experience and mental activity in other species as well as your own.

(11:23.) On the one hand, dreaming on the part of animals—and men in particular—involves not only information processing, but information gathering. Dreaming prevents life from becoming closed-ended by opening sources of information not practically available in the waking state, and by providing feedback from other than the conventional world. Data gained through waking learning endeavor and experience are checked in dreaming, not only against physical experience, but are also processed according to those "biological" and "spiritual" data, colon: Again, that information is acquired as the sleeping consciousness disperses itself, in a manner of speaking, and merges with other consciousnesses of its own and other species while still retaining its overall identity. These [other consciousnesses] are dispersed in like manner.

In such ways each individual maintains a picture of the ever-changing physical and psychological mass environment. Physical events as you understand them could not exist otherwise. *(Long pause)* Basically, information is experience. In dreams you attain the necessary information to form your lives. That state of sleep, therefore, is not simply the other side of your consciousness, but makes your waking life and culture possible.

Death operates in the same fashion. The animals in particular realize this because they organize time differently from you. Dreaming provides all the conditions of life and death, therefore—a fact that often frightens the waking self. But here is a creative mixture: the perceptive organizations from which prosaically tuned conscious life emerges. Here are the raw materials for all the daily events you recognize privately and on a world scale.

In nature nothing is wasted, so the luxurious growth of man's dream landscapes are also utilized. Whether or not these are physically actualized, they have their own reality. Your own personalities are to some extent the result of your waking experience. But they are also formed equally by your dreaming experience, by the learning and knowledge and encounters that occur when many would tell you that you are beyond legitimate perception. Dreams, then, are deeply involved with the learning processes. Dreams of walking and running occur in infants long before they crawl, and serve as impetuses.

In rudimentary form children's dreams also involve mathematical concepts, so that formal mathematical training falls on already fertile ground. The arts, sciences, agriculture—all of these reflect natural contours and tendencies inherent in man's mind, as general rather than specific attributes emerging first in the dream state, and then sparking specialized intellectual tendencies in the waking state.

Cities, therefore, existed in dreams before the time of tribes. The dream state provides the impetus for growth, and opens up to the earth-tuned consciousness avenues of information for its physical survival.

(11:59.) Because that state is also connected with waking life, you also take into it many of the elements of your daily existence, so that your recalled dreams are often cast in fairly conventionalized terms. As a rule you remember the dream's outer veneer, or what it turns into as you approach your usual level of consciousness. In a dream you are basically aware of so many facets of an event that many of them must necessarily escape your waking memory. Yet any real education must take into consideration the learning processes within dreams, and no one can hope to glimpse the nature of the psyche without encouraging dream experience, recall, and the creative use of dream education in waking life.

(Louder:) Do you have any questions?

("No. . . . ")

Then I will return you to your pussycat—who is doing exactly what you want him to do—both of you.

("Okay.")

He is reminding you of life's natural spontaneous creativity—the source of your own creativity, purposes, and intents. So that life can intrude upon your art *(with amusement).*

My heartiest regards and a fond good evening.

("Thank you very much, Seth. Good night.")

(12:18 A.M. We laughed. Seth's remarks about Willy Two, or Billy, as we sometimes call him now, were obviously made in response to the funny annoyance we'd felt before the session, when the kitten had been in great form;

jumping all over the furniture, pawing at the curtains—as well as Jane and me—getting in our papers, and so forth.)

SESSION 792, JANUARY 24, 1977
9:22 P.M. MONDAY

Now: Dictation.

In waking reality you obviously share a mass world experience as well as a physical world environment.

Again, the events that you perceive come packaged in time sequences, so that you are used to a certain kind of before-and-after order. When you build physical structures you pile brick upon brick. It may seem that psychological events have the same kind of structure, since after all you <u>do</u> perceive them in time.

When you ask: "How are events formed?" you more or less expect an answer couched in those terms. The answer is not that simple. The origin of events lies in that creative, subjective realm of being with which you are usually least concerned. This state of dreaming provides an inner network of communication, that in its way far surpasses your technological communications. The inner network deals with another kind of perceptual organization entirely. A rose is a rose is a rose. In the dream state, however, a rose can be an orange, a song, a grave, or a child as well, and be each equally.

In dreams you deal with symbols, of course. Yet symbols are simply examples of other kinds of quite "objective" events. They are events that are what they seem to be, and they are equally events that do not "immediately" show themselves. One so-called event, therefore, may be a container of many others, while you only perceive its exterior face—and you call that face a symbol.

The other events within the symbol are as legitimate as the one event you perceive.

Basically, events are not built one <u>upon</u> the other. They grow <u>out of</u> each other in a kind of spontaneous expansion, a profusion of creativity, while the conscious mind chooses which aspects to experience—and those aspects then become what you call an objective event.

(9:40.) Events obviously are not formed by your species alone, so that, as I mentioned in our last session, there is a level of the dream state in which all earth-tuned consciousnesses of all species and degrees come together. From your standpoint this

represents a deep state of unconscious creativity—at the cellular levels particularly—by which all cellular life communicates and forms a vital biological network that provides the very basis for any "higher" experience at all.

What you call dreaming is obviously dependent upon this cellular communication, which distributes the life force throughout the planet. The formation of any psychological event therefore depends upon this interspecies relationship.

The psychological symbols with which you are familiar in natural terms rise up like smoke, inherent in cellular structure itself. In deepest terms animals and plants also possess symbols and react to them.

Symbols can be called psychic codes that are interpreted in infinite fashion according to the circumstances in which consciousness finds itself. Dream events "come together" in the same way that the universe does. Events, therefore, cannot be precisely defined. You can explore your own experience of an event, and that exploration itself alters the nature of the seemingly separate event that you began to investigate. You share, then, a mass dream experience as you share a mass waking world. Your daily experience is private and uniquely yours, yet it happens within the context of a shared environment. The same applies to the dream state.

Your dreams are also uniquely yours, yet they happen within a shared context, an environment in which the dreams of the world occur. In that context your own existence is "forever" assured. You are the physical event of yourself put into a given space and time, and because of the conditions of that framework, within it you automatically exclude other experience of your own selfhood. The greater event of yourself exists in a context that is beyond your usual perception of events. That greater portion of yourself, however, forms the self that you know.

In the dream state you step into a larger context to some extent. For that reason you also lose the special kind of precise orientation with which you are familiar. Yet you begin to sense, sometimes, the larger shape of events and the timeless nature of your own existence.

Individually and *en masse,* in the dream state you change the orientation of your consciousness, and deal with the birth of events which are only later time-structured or physically experienced.

Take your break.

(10:07 to 10:29.)

First of all, physical events are the end products of non-physical properties.

The formation of events is initially an emotional, psychic, or psychological function. Events are physical interpretations, conventionalized versions of inner perceptive experiences that are then "coalesced" in space and time. Events are organized according to laws that involve love, belief, intent, and the intensities with which these are entertained.

Events are attracted or repelled by you according to your loves, beliefs, intents, and purposes. Your world provides a theater in which certain events can or cannot occur. Wars, violence, disasters—these are obviously shared by many, and are a part of your shared psychological and physical environment.

Some people encounter war directly, however, in terms of hand-to-hand combat, or bombing. Others are only inconvenienced by it. Here the mass shared environment is encountered as physical reality according to individual belief, love, and intent. In the deepest meaning there is no such thing as a victim, either of war, poverty, or disease. This does not mean that those negative qualities should not be combated, for in the terms of conventional understanding it certainly appears that men and women are victims in many such cases.Therefore they behave like victims, and their beliefs reinforce such experience.

Certainly for more than the hundredth time I say: "Your beliefs form your reality," and this means that your beliefs structure the events you know.

Such experience then convinces you more thoroughly of the reality you perceive until a vicious circle is formed, in which all events mirror beliefs so perfectly that no leeway seems to appear between the two.

If this were really the case, however, mankind's history would never change in any true regard. Alternate paths of experience—new possibilities and intuitive solutions—constantly appear in the dream state, so that man's learning is not simply dependent upon a feedback system that does not allow for the insertion of creative material. Dreaming then provides the species with learning experience not otherwise available, in which behavior and events can be judged against more developed and higher understanding than that present in conventional daily reality at any level.

There may be, for example, complications arising from a person's intents, loves, and desires that cause the individual to seek certain events that his or her very beliefs make impossible. Current experience will provide a dilemma in which a desired goal seems impossible.

In such instances a dream, or a series of them, will often then alter the person's beliefs in a way that could not otherwise occur, by providing new information. The same data might come in a state of inspiration, but they would in any case be the result of an acquisition of knowledge otherwise inaccessible. Love, purpose, belief, and intent—these shape your physical body and work upon it and with it even as at other levels cellular consciousness forms it.

(10:59.) Love is a biological as well as a spiritual characteristic. Basically, love and creativity are synonymous. Love exists without an object. It is the impetus by which all being becomes manifest. Desire, love, intent, belief and purpose—these form the experience of your body and all the events it perceives. You cannot change one belief but it alters your body experience. The great give-and-take between biological and psychological integrity occurs constantly. Your thoughts are as active as your cells, and as important in maintaining your physical being.

Your thoughts are also as <u>natural</u> as your cells. Your thoughts propel you toward survival and growth also, and in the same way that your cells do. If you find yourself in physical difficulties healthwise, you cannot say: "Why doesn't my body stop me and assert its own wisdom?" because in the truest sense there <u>is no division</u> between your thoughts and your body. You are given the ability to think, as you are given the ability to move. Your thoughts multiply even as your cells do. Your thinking <u>is</u> meant to ensure your survival in those terms, as much as your body mechanism.

The give-and-take between the two occurs largely in the dream state, where constant translations of data occur. Your thoughts and your body cells are reflected one in the other.

I am going to suggest a series of exercises. They should be regarded as creative exuberant games. They will acquaint you with your psyche, or your own greater experience of yourself, by helping you shift your attention to aspects of your own experience that usually escape your notice.

The exercises will not work, however, in the way they are meant to if they are embarked upon with too serious an air or intent. They should be considered as creative play, though of a mental nature, and they actually consist of mental endeavors tried quite spontaneously by children. So they are not to be regarded as esoteric accomplishments. They represent the intent to discover once again the true transparent delight that you once felt in the manipulation of your own consciousness, as you looped and unlooped it like a child's jumping rope.

Take your break.

(11:15 to 11:30.)

The dream state is the source of all physical events, in that it provides the great creative framework from which you choose your daily actuality.

Children quickly learn from their parents that experience must be structured in a certain conventional pattern. In their own periods of imaginative play, however, children utilize dream events, or events perceived in dreams, while clearly realizing that these are not considered actual in the "real" world.

Physical play is pleasant, and accompanied by high imaginative activity. Muscles and mind are both exercised. The same kind of activity occurs in the child's dream state as it learns to handle events before they are physically encountered. Intense dream activity is involved. Some dream events are more real to the child than some waking events are—not because the child does not understand the nature of experience, but because he or she is still so close to the emotional basis behind events. Some of the exercises I will suggest will put you in touch with the way events are formed.

Children's play, creativity, and dreams all involve you with the birth of events in the most direct of fashions. The games that you play or habitually observe will, of course, tell you much about the kind of organization that occurs in your own experience. Overall, you organize events around certain emotions. These can be combative, in which there will always be good teams and bad teams, salvation or destruction, winning or losing.

The events of your life will follow a similar structure. Before conditioning, children's play follows the love of performance, of body or imagination, for performance's sake only; the expansion of mental or physical abilities. The most satisfying of events involve those characteristics. The exercises I will suggest have to do with games "that anybody can play," then —with the natural joyful manipulation of the imagination that children employ.

End of dictation. The next chapter will be called: "Games That Anybody Can Play. Dreams and the Formation of Events."

(11:47. After giving a page or so of information for Jane and me, as usual, Seth ended the session at 11:55 P.M.

(The next morning, Jane awakened with the title of a book in mind:

The Afterdeath Journal of an American Philosopher. *She knew that it referred to William James—the American psychologist and philosopher who'd lived from 1842 to 1910—and that a dream had been involved, though she'd forgotten it. The title was all that remained.*

(As mentioned earlier in this manuscript, Jane had received several pages of "James material" which she'd included in Psychic Politics, *and Seth had given a session last year explaining her "subjective connections" with James. He hadn't mentioned anything about a future James book, though.*

(Nevertheless, during the morning Jane suddenly felt that "something was ready." She put fresh paper in her typewriter and at once began what may very well be a new book. I watched, bemused and certainly delighted, as she got to work. Again, like the Cézanne manuscript, this morning's material "came" so quickly that she had to type as quickly as she could to keep up with its flow.

(It will be most interesting to see what develops.)

Chapter 10

Games That Anybody Can Play. Dreams and the Formation of Events

SESSION 793, FEBRUARY 14, 1977
9:28 P.M. MONDAY

Good evening.

("Good evening, Seth.")

Dictation. The brain is primarily an event-forming psycho-mechanism through which consciousness operates. Its propensity for event-forming is obvious even in young children. By obvious, I mean active, when fantasies occur involving activities far beyond the physical abilities as they are thus far developed.

Children's dreams are more intense than those of adults because the brain is practicing its event-forming activities. These must be developed before certain physical faculties can be activated. Infants play in their dreams, performing physical actions beyond their present physical capacities. While external stimuli are highly important, the inner stimuli of dream play are even more so.

Children practice using all of their senses in play-dreams, which then stimulate the senses themselves, and actually help ensure their coordination. In your terms, events are still plastic to young children, in that they have not as yet learned to apply your stringent structure. There is an interesting point connected with the necessity to coordinate the workings of the senses, in that before this process occurs there is no rigid placement of events. That placement is acquired. The uncoordinated child's senses, for example, may actually hear words that will be spoken tomorrow, while seeing the person who will speak them today.

Focusing the senses in time and space is to some extent an acquired art, then—one that is of course necessary for precise physical manipulation. But before that focusing occurs, children, particularly in the dream state, enjoy an overall version of events that gradually becomes sharper and narrower in scope.

A certain amount of leeway in space and time lingers, for even biologically the child is innately equipped with a "forevision" that allows it some "unconscious" view of immediate future events that forewarn it, say, of danger. From this more plastic, looser experience, the child in dreams begins to choose more specific elements, and in so doing trains the senses themselves toward a more narrow sensitivity.

In periods of play the child actually often continues some games initiated quite naturally in the dream state. These include role-playing, and also games that quite simply involve physical muscular activity. All of this teaches a specification. In dreams the mind is free to play with events, and with their formation. The actualization of those events, however, requires certain practical circumstances. In play the children try out events initiated in the dream state, and "judge" these against the practical conditions. In such a way the child juggles probabilities, and also brings his physical structure precisely into line with a given niche of probability. Basically (underlined twice) in dreaming the brain is not limited to physically encountered experience.

(9:58.) Mentally it can form an infinite number of events, and consciousness can take an infinite number of roles. The child may easily dream of being its own mother or father, sister or brother, the family dog, a fly, a soldier. In waking play the child will then try out those roles, and quickly see that they do not fit physical conditions.

Before a child has seen mountains it can dream of them. A knowledge of the planet's environment is an unconscious portion of your heritage. You possess an unconscious environment, a given psychological world attuned to the physical one, and your learning takes place in it subjectively even as objectively you learn exterior manipulation.

The imagination is highly involved with event-forming. Children's imaginations prevent them from being too limited by their parents' world. Waking or dreaming, children "pretend." In their pretending they exercise their consciousness in a particularly advantageous way. While accepting a given reality for themselves, they nevertheless reserve the right, so to speak, to experiment with other "secondary" states of being. To some extent they become what they are pretending to be, and in so doing they also increase their own knowledge and experience. Left alone, children would learn how to cope with animals by pretending to be animals, for example. Through experiencing the animals' reactions, they would understand how to react themselves.

In play, particularly, children try on any conceivable situation for size. In the dream state adults and children alike do the same thing, and many dreams are indeed a kind of play. The brain itself is never satisfied with one version of an event, but will always use the imagination to form other versions in an activity quite as spontaneous as play. It also practices forming events as the muscles practice motion.

The brain seeks the richest form of an event. I am speaking specifically of the brain, as separated from the mind, to emphasize the point that these abilities are of creaturehood. The brain's genius comes from the mind, which can be called the brain's biophysical counterpart.

Take your break.

(10:15 to 10:31.)

You have inner senses that roughly correlate with your physical ones. These, however, do not have to be trained to a particular space-time orientation.

When children dream, they utilize these inner senses as adults do, and then through dreaming they learn to translate such material into the precise framework of the exterior senses. Children's games are always "in the present"—that is, they are immediately experienced, though the play events may involve the future or the past. The phrase "once upon a time" is strongly evocative and moving, even to adults, because children play with time in a way that adults have forgotten. If you want to sense the motion of your psyche, it is perhaps easiest to imagine a situation either in the past or the future, for this automatically moves your mental sense-perceptions in a new way.

Children try to imagine what the world was like before they entered it. Do the same thing. The way you follow these directions can be illuminating, for the areas of activity you choose will tell you something about the unique qualities of your own consciousness. Adult games deal largely with manipulations in space, while children's play, again, often involves variations in time. Look at a natural object, say a tree; if it is spring now, then imagine that you see it in the fall.

Alter your time orientation in other such exercises. This will automatically allow you to break away from too narrow a focus. It will to some extent break apart the rigid interlocking of your perception into reality as you have learned how to perceive it. Children can play so vividly that they might, for example, imagine themselves parched under a desert sun, though they are in the middle of the coolest air-conditioned living room. They are on the one hand completely involved in their activity, yet on the other hand they are quite aware of their "normal" environment. Yet the adult often fears that any such playful unofficial alteration of consciousness is dangerous, and becomes worried that the imagined situation will supersede the real one.

(10:49.) Through training, many adults have been taught that the imagination itself is suspicious. Such attitudes not only drastically impede any artistic creativity, but the imaginative creativity necessary to deal with the nature of physical events themselves.

Man's creative alertness, his precise sensual focus in space and time, and his ability to react quickly to events, are of course all highly important characteristics. His imagination allowed him to develop the use of tools, and gave birth to his inventiveness. That imagination allows him to plan in the present for what might occur in the future.

This means that to some extent the imagination must operate outside of the senses' precise orientation. For that reason, it is most freely used in the dream state. Basically speaking, imagination cannot be tied to practicalities, for when it is man has only physical feedback. If that were all, then there would be no inventions. There is always additional information available other than that in the physical environment.

These additional data come as a result of the brain's high

play as it experiments with the formation of events, using the inner senses that are not structured in time or space.

Put another time on. Just before you sleep, see yourself as you are, but living in a past or future century—or simply pretend that you were born 10 or 20 years earlier or later. Done playfully, such exercises will allow you a good subjective feel for your own inner existence as it is apart from the time context.

(11:04. Now Seth digressed from book dictation to discuss some questions we had about our rather voluminous—and still growing—correspondence. Then we took a break from 11:20 to 11:30.)

Dictation: To encourage creativity, exert your imagination through breaking up your usual space-time focus. As you fall to sleep, imagine that you are in the same place, exactly in the same spot, but at some point in the <u>distant</u> past or future. What do you see, or hear? What is there?

For another exercise, imagine that you are in another part of the world entirely, but in present time, and ask yourself the same questions. For variety, in your mind's eye follow your own activities of the previous day. Place yourself a week ahead in time. Conduct your own variations of these exercises. What they will teach you cannot be explained, for they will provide a dimension of experience, a feeling about yourself that may make sense only to you.

They will teach you to find your own sensations of yourself, as divorced from the official context of reality, in which you usually perceive your being. Additionally, you will be better able to deal with current events, for your exercised imagination will bring information to you that will be increasingly valuable.

Do not begin by using your imagination only to solve current problems, for again, you will tie your creativity to them, and hamper it because of your beliefs about what is practical.

Playfully done, these exercises will set into action other creative events. These will involve the utilization of some of the inner senses, for which you have no objective sense-correlations. You will understand situations better in daily life, because you will have activated inner abilities that allow you to subjectively perceive the reality of other people in a way that children do.

There is an inner knack, allowing for greater sensitivity to the feelings of others than you presently acknowledge. That knack will be activated. Again, the powers of the brain come from the mind, so while you learn to center your consciousness in your body—and necessarily so—nevertheless your inner perceptions roam a far greater range. Before sleep, then, imagine your consciousness traveling down a road, or across the world—whatever you want. Forget your body. Do not try to leave it for this exercise. Tell yourself that you are imaginatively traveling.

If you have chosen a familiar destination, then imagine the houses you might pass. It is sometimes easier to choose an unfamiliar location, however, for then you are not tempted to test yourself as you go along by wondering whether or not the imagined scenes conform to your memory.

To one extent or another your consciousness will indeed be traveling. Again, a playful attitude is best. If you retain it and remember children's games, then the affair will be entirely enjoyable; and even if you experience events that seem frightening, you will recognize them as belonging to the same category as the frightening events of a child's game.

Children often scare themselves. A variety of reasons exist for such behavior. People often choose to watch horror films for the same reason. Usually the body and mind are bored, and actually seek out dramatic stress. Under usual conditions the body is restored—flushed out, so to speak—through the release of hormones that have been withheld, often through repressive habits.

The body will seek its release, and so will the mind. Dreams, or even daydreams of a frightening nature, can fulfill that purpose. The mind's creative play often serves up symbolic events that result in therapeutic physical reactions, and also function as post-dream suggestions that offer hints as to remedial action.

I mention this here simply to point out the similarity between some dreams and some children's games, and to show that all dreams and all games are intimately involved with the creation and experience of events.

And *(loudly)* the event of this session is finished. Do you have questions?

(12:01. I did have a couple on another matter. After giving half a page or so of material on them, Seth said good night at 12:12 A.M.)

SESSION 794, FEBRUARY 21, 1977
9:31 P.M. MONDAY

(Early last week a friend sent me a copy of a "double dream"

*experienced by his lady. Then as Jane and I were discussing the episode last
Friday night, I found myself saying that one explanation for double dreams—
that is, the awareness of experiencing two dreams at once, or a dream within
a dream—could be that each half of the brain has its own separate dream; the
two dreams then try to emerge together into ordinary consciousness.*

*(Each dream would be characteristic of the functions of the hemisphere
of the brain that experienced it, I added, as we think of those functions in the
light of current knowledge. The left hemisphere, being more analytical and
intellectual, would have dreams embodying those qualities; the more creative
right hemisphere would have dreams involving symbols, the arts, and the
emotions.*

*(As I talked so easily about this, without any conscious foreknowledge
or preparation, I realized I'd been mulling over our friend's letter, and that
this was the way my ideas spontaneously came out. I further said that
although the two hemispheres of the brain were separate, they were united at
the brain stem and by the corpus callosum, and so there were all kinds of
interchanges between them. In the same way, in the double dream there
would be relationships between the two dreams.*

*(Later, Jane suggested that I ask Seth to comment upon the ideas in a
session. There would also be a number of other reasons for double dreams, of
course. I briefly wrote about them in Volume 1 of "Unknown" Reality; see
the notes for Session 692.)*

Good evening.

("Good evening, Seth.")

Now: Leading up to your questions. First of all, your
memories, feelings, and emotions, while connected to the body
and while leaving traces, are separate.

It is as if the experiences of your life were captured on a film.
In this case the film would be the body tissue, the brain's tissue.
The experiences themselves, however, would exist independently
of the film, which in any case could not capture their entirety.

In a manner of speaking the activity of your brain adjusts
the speed with which you, as a physical creature, perceive life's
events. Theoretically, those events could be slowed down or run at
a quicker pace. Again in a manner of speaking, the sound, vision,
dimensional solidity and so forth are "dubbed in." The picture
runs at the same speed, more or less. The physical senses chime in
together to give you a dramatic sensual chorus, each "voice"
keeping perfect time with all the other sensual patterns so that as a
rule there is harmony and a sense of continuity, with no embar-
rassing lapses.

The same applies to your thoughts, which if you bother to

listen seem to come smoothly one after another, more or less
following the sequence of exterior activity. The brain like the
movie screen gives you a physical picture, in living stereo *(humorously)*, of inner activities that nowhere themselves physically
appear.

(*9:44.*) Your brain gives you a handy and quite necessary
reference system with which to conduct corporal life. It puts
together for you in their "proper" sequences events that could be
experienced in many other ways, using other kinds of organization. The brain, of course, and other portions of the body, tune
into your planet and connect you with numberless time sequences—molecular, cellular, and so forth—so that they are synchronized with the world's events.

The brain organizes activity and translates events, but it
does not initiate them. Events have an electromagnetic reality that
is then projected onto the brain for physical activation. Your
instruments only pick up certain levels of the brain's activity. They
do not perceive the mind's activity at all, except as it is imprinted
onto the brain.

Even dreams are so imprinted. When one portion or one
half of the brain is activated, for example, the corresponding
portion of the other half is also activated, but at levels scientists do
not perceive. It is ridiculous to call one side or the other of the
brain dominant, for the full richness of the entire earth experience
requires utilization of both halves, as does dreaming.

In dreaming, however, the full sense-picture usually projected by the brain, and reinforced by bodily action, is not necessary. Those dream experiences often seem out of joint or out of
focus in morning's hindsight, or in retrospect, simply because they
occur with a complexity that the brain could not handle in
ordinary waking terms.

The body obviously must react in your official present;
hence the brain neatly keeps its physical time sequences with
spaced neural responses. The entire package of physical reality is
dependent upon the senses' data being timed—synchronized—
giving the body an opportunity for precise action. In dreams the
senses are not so restrained. Events from past, present, and future
can be safely experienced, as can events that would be termed
probable from your usual viewpoint, since the body, again, is not
required to act upon them.

Because of the brain's necessary specifications, large portions of your own greater reality cannot appear through its auspices.

The brain might consider such extracurricular activity as background noise or clutter that it could not decipher. It is the mind, then, as the brain's nonphysical counterpart, that decides what data will activate the brain in that regard. The so-called ancient portions of the brain *(among them the brainstem—limbic system)* contain "the mind's memories." Generally speaking, this means important data to which, however, no conscious attention need be given.

None could be given, because the information deals with time scales that the more "sophisticated" portions of the brain can no longer handle.

(10:10.) The knowledge of the body's own biological probabilities takes place at those ancient levels, and at those levels there is activity that results in a cellular communication between all species. The brain has built-in powers of adaptation to an amazing degree, so that innately one portion can take over for any other portion, and perform its activities as well as its own. Beliefs in what is possible and not possible often dull that facility, however. While the neural connections are specific, and while learned biological behavior dominates basically, the portions of the brain are innately interchangeable, for they are directed by the mind's action.

This is most difficult to explain, but the capacity for full conscious life is inherent in each portion of the body itself. Otherwise, in fact, its smooth synchronicity would be impossible. The brain has abilities you do not use consciously because your beliefs prevent you from initiating the proper neural habits. Certain portions of the brain seem dominant only because of those neural habits that are adopted in any given civilization or time. But other cultures in your past have experienced reality quite differently as a result of encouraging different neural patterns, and putting experience together through other focuses.

Dreaming, for example, can be "brought into focus" in a far sharper fashion, so that at least some of those experiences can be consciously utilized. When this happens, you are consciously taking advantage of experience that is physically and logically extracurricular.

You are bringing into your consciousness traces of events that have not been registered in the same way that waking events are *(emphatically)* by the brain. The dream events are partially brain-recorded, but the brain separates such experience from waking events. Dreams can provide you with experience that in a manner of speaking, at least, is not encountered in time. The dream itself is recorded by the brain's time sequences, but in the dream itself there is a duration of time "that is timeless."

Theoretically, certain dreams can give you a lifetime's experience to draw upon, though the dream itself can take less than an hour in your time. In a way, dreams are the invisible thickness of your normal consciousness. They involve both portions of the brain. Many dreams do activate the brain in a ghostly fashion, sparking responses that are not practically pertinent in ordinary terms. That is, they do not require direct action but serve as anticipators of action, reminders to the brain to initiate certain actions in its future.

(10:33.) Dreams are so many-leveled that a full discussion requires an almost impossible verbal expertise. For while dreams do not necessitate action on the part of the whole body, and while the brain does not register the entire dream, the dream does serve to activate biological action—by releasing hormones, for example.

There are also what I will call body dreams. No consciousness, to whatever degree, is fully manifested in matter. There is always constant communication between all portions of the body, but when the conscious mind is diverted that activity often increases. Cellular consciousness at its own level then forms a body dream. These do not involve pictures or words, but are rather like the formations of electromagnetic intent, anticipating action to be taken, and these may then serve as initiators of therapeutic dreams, in which "higher" levels of consciousness are psychologically made aware of certain conditions.

Many problems, however, are anticipated through body dreams, and conditions cleared at that level alone.

Take your break.

(10:42 to 11:10.)

Now: While consciousness enjoys its physical orientation, it is also too creative to confine its activities in one direction. Dreams provide consciousness with its own creative play, therefore, when it need not be so practical or so "mundane," allowing it to use its innate characteristics more freely.

Many people are aware of double or triple dreams, when they seem to have two or three simultaneous dreams. Usually upon the point of awakening, such dreams suddenly telescope into one that is predominant, with the others taking subordinate positions, though the dreamer is certain that in the moment before the dreams were equal in intensity. Such dreams are representative of the great creativity of consciousness, and hint of its ability to carry on more than one line of experience at one time without losing track of itself.

In physical waking life, you must do one thing or another, generally speaking. Obviously I am simplifying, since you can eat an orange, watch television, scratch your foot, and yell at the dog—all more or less at the same time. You cannot, however, be in Boston and San Francisco at the same time, or be 21 years of age and 11 at the same time.

In double dreams and triple dreams consciousness shows its transparent, simultaneous nature. Several lines of dream experience can be encountered at the same time, each complete in itself, but when the dreamer wakes to the fact, the experience cannot be neurologically translated; so one dream usually predominates, with the others more like ghost images.

There are too many varieties of such dreams to discuss here, but they all involve consciousness dispersing, yet retaining its identity, consciousness making loops with itself. Such dreams involve other sequences than the ones with which you are familiar. They hint at the true dimensions of consciousness that are usually unavailable to you, for you actually form your own historical world in the same manner, in that above all other experiences that one world is predominant, and played on the screen of your brain.

Take a very simple event like the eating of an orange. Playfully imagine how that event is interpreted by the cells of your body. How is the orange perceived? It might be directly felt by the tip of your finger, but are the cells in your feet aware of it? Do the cells in your knee know you are eating an orange?

Take all the time you want to with this. Then explore your own conscious sense perceptions of the orange. Dwell on its taste, texture, odor, shape. Again, do this playfully, and take your time. Then let your own associations flow in your mind. What does the orange remind you of? When did you first see or taste one? Have you ever seen oranges grow, or orange blossoms? What does the color remind you of?

Then pretend you are having a dream that begins with the image of an orange. Follow the dream in your mind. Next, pretend that you are waking from the dream to realize that another dream was simultaneously occurring, and ask yourself quickly what that dream was. Followed in the same sequence given, the exercise will allow you to make loops with your own consciousness, so to speak, to catch it "coming and going." And the last question—what else were you dreaming of?—should bring an entirely new sequence of images and thoughts into your mind that were indeed happening at the same time as your daydream about the orange.

The feel and practice of these exercises are their important points—the manipulation of a creative consciousness. You exist outside of your present context, but such statements are meaningless, practically speaking, unless you give yourself some freedom to experience events outside of that rigid framework. These exercises alter your usual organizations, and hence allow you to encounter experience in a fresher fashion.

A double dream is like the double life lived by some people who have two families—one in each town—and who seemingly manipulate separate series of events that other people would find most confusing. If the body can only follow certain sequences, still consciousness has inner depths of action that do not show on the surface line of experience. Double dreams are clues to such activity.

While each person generally follows a given strand of consciousness, and identifies with it as "myself," there are other alternate lines beneath the surface. They are also quite as legitimately the same identity, but they are not focused upon because the body must have one clear, direct mode of action.

(11:41.) These strands are like double dreams that continue. They also serve as a framework to the recognized self. In periods of stress or challenge the recognized self may sense these other strains of consciousness, and realize that a fuller experience is possible, a greater psychological thickness. On some occasions in the dream state the recognized self may then enlarge its perception enough to take advantage of these other portions of its own identity. Double or triple dreams may represent such encounters at times. Consciousness always seeks the richest, most creative form, while ever maintaining its own integrity. The imagination, playing, the arts and dreaming, allow it to enrich its activities by providing feedback other than that received in the physical environment itself.

This session is dictation for the book—and in answer to your question at the same time. And *(humorously)* this is an example of a double session. Now if you have no questions—

("No . . .")

—I bid you a doubly fond good evening, and I hope you have some excellent double dreams.

("So do I, Seth. Thank you, and good night.")

(11:49 P.M. By now it should be obvious that this session is an excellent example of the way Seth often winds our questions and concerns into book dictation, couching his answers so that they also fit the larger framework he has in mind. But even if our private lives do sometimes influence the way Seth delivers his material, we've discovered that he still pretty much covers the subject matter he wants to.)

SESSION 795, FEBRUARY 28, 1977
9:33 P.M. MONDAY

(Jane and I have been reviewing the original manuscript for Volume 1 of "Unknown" Reality, which was returned to us for this purpose by Prentice-Hall after the editor and copyeditor had gone over it. Few realize the many stages involved in the production of a book, after the text itself has been written. Later, for example, the page proofs—those set in the actual type—for "Unknown" Reality will also be sent to us for minute checking.

(And someday, this session—indeed, Psyche itself, of course—will go through the same process.)

Now: Good evening.

("Good evening, Seth.")

Dictation: In their play children often imaginatively interchange their sexes. The young selfhood is freer in its identification, and as yet has not been taught to identify its own personality with its sex exclusively.

In the dreams of children this same activity continues, so that the boy may have many dream experiences as a girl, and the girl as a boy. More than this, however, in children's dreams as in their play activity, age variances are also frequent. The young child dreaming of its own future counterpart, for example, attains a kind of psychological projection into the future of its world. Adults censor many of their own dreams so that the frequent changes in sexual orientation are not remembered.

Play then at another game, and pretend that you are of the opposite sex. Do this after an encounter in which the conventions of sex have played a part. Ask yourself how many of your current beliefs would be different if your sex was. If you are a parent, imagine that you are your mate, and in that role imaginatively consider your children.

Your beliefs about dreams color your memory and interpretation of them, so that at the point of waking, with magnificent psychological duplicity, you often make last-minute adjustments that bring your dreams more in line with your conscious expectations. The sexual symbols usually attached to dream images are highly simplistic, for example. They program you to interpret your dreams in a given manner.

(9:45.) Give us a moment . . . You do have a "dream memory" as a species, with certain natural symbols. These are individually experienced, with great variations. The studies done on men and women dreamers are already prejudiced, however, both by the investigators and by the dreamers themselves. Men remember "manly" dreams—generally speaking, now—while women in the same manner remember dreams that they believe suit their sex according to their beliefs.

People often program their waking memory in quite the same fashion. The psyche, again, not only has no one sexual identification, but it is the larger psychic and psychological bank of potentials from which all gradations of sexuality emerge. It is not asexual, and yet it is the combination of those richest ingredients considered to be male and female.

The human personality is therefore endowed sexually and psychologically with a freedom from strict sexual orientation. This has contributed to the the survival of the species by not separating any of its mental or psychological abilities into two opposite camps. Except for the physical processes of reproduction, the species is free to arrange its psychological characteristics in whatever fashions it chooses. There is no inner programming that says otherwise.

In dreams this psychological complexity is more apparent. Because of programming, many people refrain from natural reactions of a most harmless nature, and these are often given expression in the dream state. Those dreams, however, are precisely the ones least remembered—the censoring is so habitual. The male's aggressive tendencies, often taken as basic characteristics of the species itself, are a case in point. This is an exaggerated, learned aggressive response, not natural in those terms in your species, or as interpreted in any other species.

This artificial aggressiveness has nothing to do either, basically, with the struggle for survival. It is the direct result of the fact that the male has been taught to deny the existence within himself of certain basic emotions. This means that he denies a certain portion of his own humanity, and then is forced to overreact in expressing those emotions left open to him. The reasons for such a lopsided focus have been discussed at various times in my works.

The male, however, chose to take upon himself a kind of specialization of consciousness that, carried too far, leads to a hard overobjectivity. Only in dreams in your time, in your society, is the male free to cry unabashedly, to admit any kind of dependency, and only at certain occasions and usually in relative privacy is he allowed to express feelings of love.

His rage turns outward as aggression. It is the highest idiocy, however, to project that artificial aggression outward upon the animal kingdom in general. Such beliefs invisibly affect all of your studies—and worse, they help you misread the activity in nature itself.

Those who imagine they look upon nature with the most objective of eyes are those whose subjective beliefs blind them most of all, for they cannot see through their own misinterpretations. It has been said that statistics can be made to say two things at once, both contradictory; so the facts of nature can be read in completely different fashions as they are put together with the organizational abilities of the mind operating through the brain's beliefs. The exterior core of dreams is also blemished to that degree, but the inner core of dreams provides a constant new influx of material, feedback, and insight from the psyche, so that the personality is not at the mercy of its exterior experience only—not confined to environmental feedback only, but ever provided with fresh intuitive data and direction.

Even if such dreams are not recalled, they circulate through the psychological system, so to speak. They are responsible for the inventiveness and creativity of the species, even bringing new comprehensions that can be used to bear upon the life of the physical world.

Take your break.

(10:17 to 10:39.)

Dictation: Now: Again, as in your terms the species has a physical past, so it has a psychological past. No experiences are ever lost. The most private event is still written in the mass psyche of the species.

I am explaining this for now in terms of past, present, and future. You can only understand some concepts when they are given in that fashion. Taking that for granted, then, you are each born with the conscious knowledge of what has come before. Your brain is far from an empty slate, waiting for the first imprint of experience; it is already equipped with complete "equations," telling you who you are and where you have come from. Nor do you wipe that slate clean, symbolically speaking, before you write your life upon it. Instead, you draw upon what has gone before: the experiences of your ancestors, back—in your terms now—through time immemorial.

The individual is born equipped with his humanness, with certain propensities and leanings toward development. He knows what human voices sound like even before his ear physically hears those sounds. He is born wanting to form civilizations as, for example, beavers want to form dams.

Children's dreams activate inner psychological mechanisms, and at a time when their age makes extensive physical knowledge of their world impossible. In dreams they are given information regarding that environment.

Physical feedback is of course necessary for development, and a child deprived of it will not fully mature. Yet the development of dreams follows inner patterns that activate the child's growth, and stimulate its development. There are even key dreams in infancy that serve to trigger necessary hormonal functioning. The child crawls and walks in dreams before those acts are physically executed—the dreams serving as impetus for muscular coordination and development.

Language is practiced by infants in the dream state, and it is indeed that mental practice that results in children speaking sentences far more quickly than otherwise would seem possible. The dream world, then, develops faster than physical experience. For some time the child is more secure there. Without dreaming there would be no learning, nor would there be memory.

Events are processed in dreams, put in the necessary perspective, sorted and arranged. This is done when the conscious mind is separated from direct involvement with physical events. Dreams serve to dull the impact of the day's events just past, while the meaning of those activities sifts through the various levels of the personality, settling into compartments of intent and belief. Often the true impact of an event does not occur until it has been interpreted or reexperienced through a dream.

Because dreams follow paths of association, they break through time barriers, allowing the individual to mix, match, and compare events from different periods of his life. All of this is done somewhat in the way that a child plays, through the formation of creative dream dramas in which the individual is free to play a million different roles and to examine the nature of probable events from the standpoint of "a game."

(11:05.) In play, children adopt certain rules and conditions "for a time." The child can stop at any time. Innumerable play events can occur with varying intensity, yet generally speaking the results cease when the game is over. The child plays at being an adult, and is a child again when his parents call, so the effects of the game are not long-lasting. Still, they are an important part of a child's daily life, and they affect the way he or she relates to others. So in dreams, the events have effects only while dreaming. They do not <u>practically</u> intrude into waking hours—the attacking bear vanishes when you open your eyes; it does not physically chase you around the bedroom.

The great versatility of the species in its reaction to events is highly dependent upon this kind of dreaming capacity. The species tries out its probable reactions to probable events in the dream state, and hence is better prepared for action "in the future."

To some extent dreams are participated in by cellular consciousness also, for the cells have an equal interest in the individual's psychic and body events. In a way dreams are of course composite behavior—mental and psychic games that suit the purposes of mind and body alike. Feedback from the physical environment may trigger an alarming dream that causes the individual to awaken.

Certain chemicals may affect dreaming by altering the cells' reality. Many sleeping pills are detrimental, in that they inhibit the body's natural response to its environment while an individual is sleeping, and deaden the intimate relationship between the dreaming mind and the sleeping body.

Because you have very limited ideas of what logic is, it seems to you that the dreaming self is not critical, or "logical"; yet it works with amazing discrimination, sifting data, sending some to certain portions of the body, and structuring memory. Sleeping pills also impede the critical functions of dreams that are so often overlooked. The facts are that dreams involve high acts of creativity. These are not only intuitively based, but formed with a logic far surpassing your ideas of that quality. These creative acts are then fitted together through associative processes that come together most precisely to form the dream events.

Take your break.

(11:25 to 11:33.)

It should certainly be obvious that dreams are not passive events. Some rival physical events in intensity and even effect.

They involve quite active coordination on the part of mind and body, and they bring to the individual experience otherwise unattainable.

Small amounts of ordinary stimulators, such as coffee or tea, taken before bed when you are already sleepy, have a beneficial effect in stimulating dream activity and aiding dream recall. Too large a serving, of course, could simply waken you, but small amounts taken if you are already drowsy allow you to take your conscious mind into the dream state more readily, where it can act as an observer.

A very small amount of alcohol can also serve. Anything that suppresses activity will also suppress your dreams. As is known, anyone deprived of sufficient dreaming will most likely begin to hallucinate while in the waking state, for too much experience has built up that needs processing. There are many secondary hormonal activities that take place in the dream state and at no other time. Even cellular growth and revitalization are accelerated while the body sleeps.

End of dictation. Give me a moment. . . .

(11:44. After giving a page of material for Jane and me, Seth ended the session at 11:56 P.M.)

Chapter 11

The Universe and the Psyche

SESSION 796, MARCH 7, 1977
9:52 P.M. MONDAY

(The first half of this session came through because of a dream Jane had last night, and interpreted on her own today. Although they aren't book dictation, we're presenting here some of Seth's own comments about the dream, since they have a general interest and also fit in with his earlier dream material.

(The balance of the session is in response to a discussion of evolution that Jane and I had before the session. This came about because of a note I'm writing for Volume 2 of "Unknown" Reality, and I may quote part of Seth's material on the subject in that note.

(We hadn't expected that he'd deal with either topic in tonight's session, since we hadn't asked that he consider them. Seth's presentations clearly illuminate the subject matter of both Jane's dream and our questions about evolution. First he went into Jane's dream per se, then continued as follows:)

It is often not enough—in fact, seldom enough—that deep

emotional fears simply be realized once or twice. They must be encountered more or less directly. Otherwise the old habits allow such fears to be buried again.

So Ruburt's dream made possible a conscious emotional realization of fear—but more, it provided for that fear's release, or gave the solution to a deep emotional equation. In this case it was the realization emotionally that life is not given by the parent, but through the parent—by LIFE (in capitals) itself, or All That Is, and "with no strings attached."

The second part of the dream, the solution, had not come consciously and emotionally to Ruburt before. Intellectually he had that solution, but it did not become part of the emotional equation until the dream put the two together. You cannot logically, mathematically explain such emotional reality.

On some occasions long-term illnesses, for instance, are resolved suddenly through a dream. However, in most cases dreams prevent such chronic illnesses, providing through small therapeutics a constant series of minor but important personal revelations.

That is, dreams are the best preventative medicine. Some psychological difficulties need clear conscious light and understanding. Others, however, operate even without conscious participation, and those are often solved, or remedied, at the same level without interfering with the conscious mind. As the body handles many physical manipulations without your own conscious knowledge of what is being done, or how, so the workings of your own psychological systems often automatically solve "their own problems" through dreams of which you are not aware.

You could not physically handle anything like complete dream recall. *(With a small laugh:)* You are not consciously capable of dealing with the psychological depths and riches that activity reveals. For one thing, your concepts of time, realistically or practically speaking, as utilized, would become more difficult to maintain in normal life. This does not mean that far greater dream recall than you have is not to your advantage, because it certainly is. I merely want to explain why so many dreams are not recalled.

While the large proportion remain relatively hidden, however, the average person often meets with dream fragments just below the normal threshold of consciousness—not recognizing them as what they are—experiencing instead the impulse to do this or that on a given day; to eat this or that, or to refrain from something else. An easy enough example is the case where an

individual with no memory [of such a dream] decides to cancel a
plane trip on a given day, and later discovers that the plane
crashed. The impulse to cancel may or may not seem to have an
acceptable, rational explanation; that is, for no seeming reason,
the individual may simply, impulsively, feel a premonition. On
the other hand the impulse might appear as a normal, logical
change of plan.

(10:17.) We are taking it for granted that a forgotten dream
stated the probable catastrophe. This information was unconsciously processed, the probability considered and rejected: Psychologically or physically, the person was not ready to die. Others
with the same knowledge found that death was the accepted
probability. This does not mean that any of those people could
bear consciously knowing their own decisions—or could board
that plane with the conscious consequences in mind.

Nor is such an inner decision forced upon the conscious
personality, for in all such instances, the conscious personality has
at various times come close to accepting the idea of death at the
particular time in life.

This does not mean that those people are committing
suicide in the same way that a person does who takes his life—but
that in a unique psychological manipulation they no longer hold
the same claim to life as they had before. They "throw their lives to
the Fates," so to speak, saying not as they did before: "I will live,"
but: "I will live or die as the Fates decide."

They may use other terms than Fate, of course, but the vital,
personal, direct, affirmative intent to live is not there. They are
headed for another reality, and ready for it.

The conscious mind, however, can only hold so much. Life
as you know it could not exist if everything was conscious in those
terms. The sweet parcel of physical existence, I have told you,
exists as much by merit of what it does not include as it does by
merit of your experience. In important ways your dreams make
your life possible by ordering your psychological life automatically, as your physical body is ordered automatically for you. You
can make great strides by understanding and recalling dreams,
and by consciously participating in them to a far greater degree.
But you cannot become completely aware of your dreams in their
entirety, and maintain your normal physical stance.

As a civilization you fail to reap dreams' greater benefit, and
the conscious mind is able to handle much more dream recall
than you allow. Such training would add immeasurably to the

dimensions of your life. Dreams educate you even in spatial relationships, and are far more related to the organism's stance in the
environment than is realized. The child learns spatial relationships in dreams.

Now give us a moment ... *(With much humor:)* The question
on dreams was a good one, and you see I had a good answer.

("Yes. ...")

Ruburt had to know what he was afraid of, and his dream
interpretation gave him that knowledge so that he could deal with
it. It was the fear of death—not chosen, of course—the fear that if
he did not deliver, work hard, and pay his mother back for a life
magically given, grudgingly given, then in a magical equation she,
the mother, could take it back. But the mother did not give the life.
The life came from All That Is, from the spirit of life itself, and was
freely given—to be taken away by no one, or threatened by no one
or no force, until that life fulfills its own purposes and decides to
travel on.

(As Seth, Jane delivered all of the above most forcefully.)

Ruburt did feel that it was not safe to let go, lest relaxation
mean death. Life is expression. It comes to be out of the force of
itself, and no force stands against it or threatens it. Death in your
terms certainly seems an end, but it is instead a translation of life
into another form.

This leads me rather naturally to my next topic *(which
concerns our questions about evolution).*

First of all, there are verbal difficulties having to do with the
definition of life. It appears that there is living matter and nonliving matter, leading to such questions as: "How does nonliving
matter become living?"

(With a laugh:) Take your break. That is the hanger-on.

(10:42 to 10:53.)

There is no such thing, in your terms, as nonliving matter.
There is simply a point that you recognize as having the characteristics that you have ascribed to life, or living conditions—a
point that meets the requirements that you have arbitrarily set.

This makes it highly difficult in a discussion, however, for
there is no particular point at which life was inserted into nonliving matter. There is no point at which consciousness emerged.
Consciousness is within the tiniest particle, whatever its life conditions seem to be, or however it might seem to lack those conditions you call living.

Give us a moment . . . If we must speak in terms of continuity, which I regret, then in those terms you could say that life in the physical universe, on your planet, "began" spontaneously in a given number of species at the same time. I am going slowly in order to get the material as clear as possible.

(11:01. Jane's delivery was very slow with this material. She took many pauses, some of them long. Her eyes remained closed for the most part. What Seth had to say about the spontaneous beginnings of life, in our terms, surprised me. . . .)

There were fully developed men—that is, of full intellect, emotion, and will—living at the same time, in your terms, as those creatures supposed to be man's evolutionary ancestors. Species have come and gone of which you have no knowledge. There are parallel developments. That is, there were "apes" who attained their own "civilizations," for example. They used tools. They were not men-to-be, nor did they evolve into men.

It is erroneous to say that they did not develop, or that their progress was stunted, for it was not. Their reality explored the ramifications of animalhood in a completely different fashion. Their development paralleled man's in many respects, in that they lived simultaneously upon the earth, and shared the environment.

I have referred to them at various times as animal medicine men, for man did learn from them. The impact of many of my statements of the past goes unrecognized, or perhaps the words sound pat, but there are other conditions of life that you do not perceive, sometimes because your time sequences are too different. Before the smallest cell appeared, in your terms, there was the consciousness that formed the cell.

(Long pause.) Words do nearly forsake me, the semantic differences are so vast. If I say to you: "Life came from a dream," such a statement sounds meaningless. Yet as your physical reality personally is largely dependent upon your dreaming state, and impossible without it, so in the same way the first cell was physically materialized and actual only because of its own inner reality of consciousness.

In those terms there was a point where consciousness impressed itself into matter through intent, or formed itself into matter. That "breakthrough" cannot be logically explained, but only compared to, say, an illumination—that is, a light everywhere occurring at once, that became a medium for life in your terms. It had nothing to do with the propensity of certain kinds of cells to reproduce, but with an overall illumination that set the conditions in which life as you think of it was possible—and at that imaginary hypothetical point, all species became latent.

There was no point at which consciousness was introduced, because consciousness was the illumination from which the first cells emerged. That illumination was everywhere then at every point aware of itself, and of the conditions formed by its presence. In your terms each species is aware of the conditions of each other species, and of the entire environment. In those terms the environment forms the species and the species forms the environment.

As hinted, there have been all kinds of species of animal-man, and man-animal, of which your sciences are not aware, and bones found thought to form, say, a man and an animal that were from the same creature. Afgastan—

("Afghanistan?" I asked, as Jane, in trance, had trouble with the word.)

Indeed: Afghanistan comes to mind here, as a particularly lucrative environment.

Your own kind of conscious mind is splendid and unique. It causes you, however, to interpret all other kinds of life according to your own specifications and experience. The complex nature of other animal consciousness escapes you completely. And when you compare your technologies, learning, logical thought, cultures and arts with what you understand of animal experience, there seems no doubt that you are superior and "the Flower of Evolution"—that all other kinds of life are topped by your existence.

You are closed to the intricate, voluptuous, sensuous, social experience of the animals, or even of the plants—not being able to perceive that different kind of biological emotion and belonging, that rich, sensual identification with earth, and cut off from a biologically oriented culture that is everywhere part and parcel of both plant and animal life.

You are a part of that also, but the conscious mind, with its own specifications, cannot manipulate with that kind of knowledge. *(Pause at 11:29.)* There have also been men—in your terms—more developed than you—in your terms—for your ideas of development are highly erroneous. But they topped you in technology, if that is your criterion.

I hesitate in many instances to say what I might, because it is so easy to misinterpret meanings; but when you ask what is the purpose of consciousness you take it for granted there must be one purpose—where the greater truth and creativity must be that consciousness itself cannot be aware of all of its own purposes, but ever discovers its own nature through its own manifestations.

To those who want easy answers, this is no answer, I admit. There is, I know, in heroic terms a love, a knowledge, a compassion, a creativity that can be assigned to All That Is, which is within each creature. I know that each smallest "particle" of consciousness can never be broken down, and that each contains an infinite capacity for creativity and development—and that each is innately blessed.

There is a design and a designer, but they are so combined, the one within and the one without, that it is impossible to separate them. The Creator is also within its creations, and the creations themselves are gifted with creativity.

If you have more questions on this subject, give them to me at our next session. *(Loudly:)* End of session.

("Thank you, Seth. It's very good.")

(With amusement:) Naturally.

Now: A tiny note to you. You did very well this past winter, avoiding the malaise that sometimes affects you in January and February. My congratulations.

("Thank you.")

(11:40 P.M. I was surprised at Seth's remark, since it seems to me that my energy has been "good" for as long as I can remember. And it developed that I did quote portions of Seth's material on evolution and time in Volume 2 of "Unknown" Reality. See Appendix 12.)

SESSION 797,   MARCH 14, 1977
9:32 P.M. MONDAY

(The page proofs for Jane's The World View of Paul Cézanne *arrived in the mail from her publisher this morning, and she's been busy correcting them most of the day since—checking the type for errors in spelling, punctuation, omission, and so forth.)*

Good evening.

("Good evening, Seth.")

Now, in continuation: When you ask about the beginning of a universe, you are speaking of a visible universe.

There is consciousness within each conceivable hypothetical point within the universe. There is therefore "an invisible universe" out of which the visible or objective universe springs.

I do not mean to overemphasize the point that this particular material is most difficult to explain, yet I can hardly stress the issue too strongly.

Give us a moment . . . Your universe did not emerge at any one point, therefore, or with any one initial cell—but everywhere it began to exist at once, as the inner pulsations of the invisible universe reached certain intensities that "impregnated" the entire physical system simultaneously.

In this case, first of all light appeared. At the same time EE *(electromagnetic energy)* units became manifest, impinging from the invisible universe into definition. Again, because of the psychological strength of preconceived notions, I have to work my way around many of your concepts. Yet in much of my material I have definitely implied what I am saying now, but the implications must have passed you by.

(Not at all, at least from Jane's and my viewpoints. . . .)

I have said, for example, that the universe expands as an idea does, and so the visible universe sprang into being in the same manner. The whole affair is quite complicated since—again as I have intimated—the world freshly springs into new creativity at each moment. No matter <u>what</u> your version of creativity, or the creation of the world, you are stuck with questions of where such energy came from, for it seems that unimaginable energy was released more or less at one time, and that this energy must then run out.

The <u>same</u> energy, however, still gives birth anew to the universe. In those terms, it is still being created. The EE units, impressing a probable physical field, contain within them the latent knowledge of all of the various species that can emerge under those conditions. The groupings "begin" in the invisible universe. You can say that it took untold centuries for the EE units "initially" to combine, form classifications of matter and various species; or you can say that this process happened at once. It is according to your relative position, but the physical universe was everywhere seeded, impregnated, simultaneously. On the other hand, this still happens, and there is no real "coming-in" point.

(9:53.) Give us a moment . . . You distinguish between consciousness and your own version, which you consider consciousness of self. When I speak of atoms and molecules having consciousness, I mean that they possess a consciousness of themselves as identities. I do not mean that they love or hate, in your terms, but that they are aware of their own separateness, and aware

of the ways in which that separateness cooperates to form other organizations.

They are innately aware, in fact, of all such probable cooperative ventures, and imbued with the "drive" for value fulfillment. Every known species was inherently "present" with the overall impregnation of the visible universe, then.

If the universe were a painting, for example, the painter would not have first painted darkness, then an explosion, then a cell, then the joining together of groups of cells into a simple organism, then that organism's multiplication into others like it, or traced a pattern from an amoeba or a paramecium on upward—but he or she would have instead begun with a panel of light, an underpainting, in which all of the world's organisms were included, though not in detail. Then in a creativity that came from the painting itself the colors would grow rich, the species attain their delineations, the winds blow and the seas move with the tides.

The motion and energy of the universe still come from within. I certainly realize that this is hardly a scientific statement—yet the moment that All That Is conceived of a physical universe it was invisibly created, endowed with creativity, and bound to emerge.

Because each hypothetical, conceivable portion of the universe is conscious, the Planner is within the plan itself in the greatest of terms—perhaps basically inconceivable to you. There is of course no "outside" into which the invisible universe materialized, since all does indeed exist in a mental, psychic, or spiritual realm quite impossible to describe. To you your universe seems, now, objective and real, and it seems to you that at one time at least this was not the case, so you ask about its creation and the evolution of the species. My answer has been couched in the terms in which the question is generally asked.

While you believe in and experience the passage of time, then such questions will naturally occur to you, and in that fashion. Within that framework they make sense. When you begin to question the nature of time itself, then the "when" of the universe is beside the point.

Almost anyone will agree, I should hope, that the universe is a most splendid example of creativity. Few would agree, however, that you can learn more about the nature of the universe by examining your own creativity than you can by examining the world through instruments—and here is exquisite irony, for you create the instruments of creativity, even while at the same time you often spout theories that deny to man all but the most mechanical of reactions.

In other terms, the world comes to know itself, to discover itself, for the Planner left room for divine surprise, and the plan was nowhere foreordained; nor is there anywhere within it anything that corresponds to your survival-of-the-fittest theories.

These are creative distortions on your part, directly related to specializations of consciousness that cut you off from the greater concourse existing at other levels between the species and the land. Again, consciousness everywhere pervades the universe, and is aware of all conditions. The balance of nature upon your planet is no chance occurrence, but the result of constant, instant computations on the part of each most minute consciousness, whether it forms part of a rock, a person, an animal, a plant. Each invisibly "holds space together," whatever its station. This is a cooperative venture. Your own consciousness has its particular unique qualities, in that like other comparatively long-lived species, you associate your identity with your form far more rigidly. Other kinds of consciousness "leap in and out of forms" with greatest leeway. There is a biological understanding that exists, for example, when one animal kills another one for food. The consciousness of the prey leaves its body under the impetus of a kind of stimulus unknown to you.

I want to be very careful here, for I am speaking of natural interplay among the animals. This is not anywhere meant to justify the cruel slaughtering of animals by man under many circumstances.

Take your break.

(10:35. Seth's next material came through because of some angry comments I made during break. Because of news reports and my own negative thinking today, I was filled with rage, actually, about what appeared to be the generally chaotic state of the world of man. Before the session we'd read a couple of book reviews that also helped set me off now. One piece had been written by a brain "researcher" who, we thought, exhibited remarkably little understanding of the human condition. Almost in spite of myself, I thought it quite humorous that the reviewer himself had written books on the brain—that had in their turns been attacked by other reviewers.

(I'm sure that Jane tires of hearing me periodically rehash views that the species has engaged in at least three major wars in a little more than half a century, plus a number of "smaller" ones. Furthermore, I added, since in our "practical" world we generally renounce all belief in anything like reincarnation, or what I consider to be a true religious stance, we place all of life

within each individual living "now." To send our young to the battlefield under those circumstances, then, to deprive individuals of the one life—the one priceless, irreplaceable attribute—seems the worst crime imaginable, I told Jane. I said more in a similar vein, while all the time a basic part of me knew that I was oversimplifying the human condition by far.

(Resume at 10:58.)

An impartial, guarded reply to your discussion.

The historical and cultural world as you know it appears to be the only one objective world, of course, with its history already written, its present, and hopefully its probable future.

It seems also that the future must be built upon that one known species or world past. Often it may simply sound like a figure of speech when I talk about probabilities. In many ways it may indeed appear to be almost outrageous to consider the possibility that "there is more than one earth," or that there are many earths, each similar enough to be recognizable, yet each different in the most vital respects.

This particular house exists. Yet you may open the door on any given day to a probable world from your immediate standpoint, and never know the difference. This happens all the time, and I mean <u>all the time</u>.

You move through probabilities without knowing it. The transitions are literally invisible to you, though they may appear as trace elements in your dreams. As a diamond has many facets, so does your reality in that regard.

(To me:) Since your birth a probability has occurred that you could have followed, in which your wars did not happen. There is another probability in which the Second World War ended in nuclear destruction, and you did not enter that one either. You chose "this" probable reality in order to ask certain questions about the nature of man—seeing him where he wavered equally between creativity and destruction, knowledge and ignorance; but a point that contained potentials for the most auspicious kinds of development, in your eyes. The same applies to Ruburt.

In a way, man is <u>trans-species</u> at this point in probability. It is a time and a probability in which every bit of help is needed, and your talents, abilities, and <u>prejudices</u> made you both uniquely fitted for such a drama. At the same time, do not dwell <u>too much</u> upon that world situation, for a concentration upon your own nature and upon the physical nature of your world—the seasons, and so forth—allows you to refresh your own energy, and frees you to take advantage of that clear vision that is <u>so</u> necessary.

(A point I mentioned at break—the difficulty of seeing clearly just what man is up to as a species.)

You each also became involved in this probability precisely to use it as a creative stimulus that would make you seek for a certain kind of understanding. There is always a creative give-and-take between the individual and his world. To some extent or another each of those involved in this probability chose it for their own reasons. Saying this, however, I also say that many leave this probability for another when they have learned and contributed.

For now I bid you a fond good evening, unless you have questions. I have a remark. *(To me:)* You are personally inhibiting your dream recall because you do not want to take the time to remember and interpret the dreams. Knowing this, you may want to change your ways.

(Now Seth came through with some other material for Jane and me, and finally ended the session at 11:22 P.M.)

SESSION 798, MARCH 21, 1977
9:54 P.M. MONDAY

Good evening.

("Good evening, Seth.")

Now: The last two sessions, more or less on evolution, can be included in this book, and serve as the opening sessions of a new chapter, entitled: "The Universe and the Psyche."

Dictation: Your next question is easy to anticipate, of course, for you will want to know the origin of that "interior" universe from which I have said the exterior one ever emerges—and here we must part company with treasured objectivity, and enter instead a mental domain, in which it is seen that contradictions are not errors; an inner domain large enough to contain contradictions at one level, for at another level they are seen to be no contradictions at all.

In science as it stands, it is necessary that self-contradictions do not arise. If a hypothesis is "proven true," then it cannot be proven false—or, of course, it was never true to begin with.

In those terms, therefore, the universe either had "a Creator," or it had none; or it came into being as stated in the Big Bang theory, and is either constantly expanding or it is not. Evolution exists or it does not. As a rule such theories are proven "true" by the simple process of excluding anything else that seems contradictory, and so generally your scientific theories carry the weight of strong validity within their own frameworks.

In those frameworks you have made certain classifications that now appear quite obvious. Common sense upholds them, and it seems impossible to consider reality otherwise. Yet by their nature such categories structure your experience of reality itself to such an extent that any alternate ways of perceiving life seem not only untrustworthy, but completely impossible.

Thusly, your classifications of various species appear to you as the only logical kinds of divisions that could be made among living things. Quite the contrary is the case, however. That particular overall method of separation leads to such questions as: "Which species came first, and which came later, and how did the various species emerge—one from the other?" Those questions are further brought about by your time classifications, without which they would be meaningless.

Your classifications in such respects set up exterior divisions. Now these serve as quite handy reference points, but basically speaking they in no way affect the natural experience of those various living creatures that you refer to as "other species."

Your specializations work as long as you stay within the framework, though then you must wrestle with the questions that such divisions automatically entail. It is perhaps difficult for you to realize that these are written and verbalized categories that in no real manner tell you anything about the actual experience of other creatures—but only note habits, tendencies, and separations of the most exterior nature.

If your purpose is to comprehend what other living creatures perceive, then the methods you are using are at the best short-sighted, and at the worst they completely defeat your purpose. For example: No matter what information or data you receive as the result of animal experimentation or dissection for scientific purposes, and no matter how valuable the results appear to be, the consequences of such methods are so distorted that you comprehend less of life than you did before.

(10:17.) The answers to the origins of the universe and of the species lie, I'm afraid, in realms that you have largely ignored—precisely in those domains that you have considered least scientific, and in those that it appeared would yield the least practical results.

Your present methods will simply bring you pat, manufactured results and answers. They will satisfy neither the intellect nor the soul. Since your universe springs from an inner one, and since that inner one pervades each nook and cranny of your own existence, you must look where you have not before—into the reality of your own minds and emotions. You must look to the natural universe that you know. You must look with your intuitions and creative instincts at the creatures about you, seeing them not as other species with certain habits, not as inferior properties of the earth, to be dissected, but as living examples of the nature of the universe, in constant being and transformation.

You must study the quality of life, dare to follow the patterns of your own thoughts and emotions, and to ride that mobility, for in that mobility there are hints of the origin of the universe and of the psyche. The poet's view of the universe and of nature is more scientific, then, than the scientists', for more of nature is comprehended.

The child, laughing with joy and awe at the sight of the first violet, understands far more in the deepest terms than a botanist who has long since forgotten the experience of perceiving one violet, though he has at his mental fingertips the names and classifications of all the world's flowers. Information is not necessarily knowledge or comprehension.

Thoughts spring into your mind as the objective universe swims into reality—that is, in the same fashion. Diagramming sentences tells you little about the spoken language, and nothing about those miraculous physical and mental performances that allow you to speak—and so diagramming the species of the world is, in the same way, quite divorced from any true understanding.

The subjective feeling of your being, your intimate experience from moment to moment—these possess the same mysterious quality that it seems to you the universe possesses. You are mortal, and everywhere encounter evidence of that mortality, and yet within its framework your feelings and thoughts have a reality to you personally that transcends all such classifications. You know that physically you will die, yet each person at one time or another is secretly sure that he or she will not meet such a fate, and that life is somehow eternal.

Through such feelings the psyche breaks through all misconceptions, hinting at the nature of the self and of the universe at once.

In a larger level of actuality, then, there is no beginning or end to the universe, and at that level there are no contradictions. There is no beginning or end to the psyche, either. You may say: "Granted," yet persist, saying: "In our terms, however, when did the world begin, and in what manner?" Yet the very attempt to place such an origin in time makes almost any answer distorted.

The truth is that the answers lie in your own experience. They are implied in your own spontaneous behavior—that is, in the wondrous activity of your bodies and minds.

Take your break.

(10:41 to 10:58.)

You walk quite well without having at your fingertips any conscious knowledge of the inner mechanism's activity. You may have been told, or you may have read about the body's anatomy, and the interaction of its parts. Yet whether or not you have such information, you walk quite as well. Such data therefore do not help your walking performance any.

For that matter, an athlete may have a great zest for motion and an impatience with reading, caring not what within the body makes it move as long as its performance is superb—while an invalid with great book knowledge about all of the body's parts is quite unable to physically perform in a normal manner.

Your body knows how to walk. The knowledge is built-in and acted upon. The body knows how to heal itself, how to use its nourishment, how to replace its tissues, yet in your terms the <u>body itself has no access</u> to the kind of information the mind possesses. Being so ignorant, how does it perform so well?

If it were scientifically inclined, the body would know that such spontaneous performance was impossible, for science cannot explain the reality of life itself in its present form, much less its origins.

Consciousness within the body knows that its existence is within the body's context, and <u>apart</u> from it at the same time. In ordinary life during the day consciousness often takes a recess, so to speak—it daydreams, or otherwise experiences itself as somewhat apart from the body's reality. At night, in sleep, the self's consciousness takes longer, freer recesses from physical reality, and does this as spontaneously as the body itself walks. These experiences are not hypothetical. They happen to each person. On such occasions, each person is to some extent aware of a kind of comprehension that is not dependent upon the accumulation of data, but of a deeper kind of experience and direct encounter with the reality from which the world emerges.

This is the kind of <u>wordless</u> knowledge the body possesses, that brings forth your physical motion and results in the spectacular preciseness of bodily response. It is, then, highly practical. In your terms, the same force that formed the world forms your subjective reality now, and is a source of the natural universe.

Exploring those realities lovingly will bring you into direct contact with inner dimensions of your being, providing intuitive understandings that are of greatest import.

The motion of the universe appears in the motion of your own intimate experience, and in that <u>seemingly</u> most nebulous area the answers will be found.

End of dictation. Give us a moment. . . .

(11:19. After delivering a couple of pages on other matters, Seth closed out the session at 11:40 P.M..

(Once again Seth surprised us by indicating that the previous two sessions should be considered a part of Psyche—and once again we saw that he'd let our questions lead him precisely where he intended to go in any case! We've also discovered over the years that more often than not our questions reflect those of many readers at any given point.)

SESSION 799, MARCH 28, 1977
9:42 P.M. MONDAY

(A few days ago Jane received in the mail a combination date book and calendar—quite an elaborate job, in color. The sponsor had sent her one for 1976, also, in which a passage from Seth was given. Below each date is a page of ruled lines for notes and appointments, then opposite each date is a page of news items and quotations of various kinds. Leafing through it yesterday to see if Jane was mentioned—she wasn't—I began reading some of the short items. I thought the book's editor had changed his slant in the new work, for now I came across many more pieces about foolish governmental spending, corruption, and so forth. I read some of them aloud to Jane. They seemed both ridiculous and tragic.

(They also fit in beautifully with my own recent feelings and questions about the behavior of our species, and Seth's answering material. In fact, Seth had much more to present on the subject this evening, so even though he didn't say so Jane and I take it for granted that this session belongs in Psyche.)

Now: Good evening.

("Good evening, Seth.")

(With elaborate humor:) A dissertation on the nature of man, for your edification.

You realize that a tiger, following its nature, is not evil. Looking at your own species you are often less kindly, less compassionate, less understanding. It is easy to condemn your own kind.

It may be difficult for you to understand, but your species means well. You understand that the tiger exists in a certain environment, and reacts according to his nature. So does man. Even his atrocities are committed in a distorted attempt to reach what he considers good goals. He fails often to achieve the goals, or even to understand how his very methods prevent their attainment.

He is indeed as blessed as the animals, however, and his failures are the results of his lack of understanding. He is directly faced with a far more complex conscious world than the other animals are, dealing particularly with symbols and ideas that are then projected outward into reality, where they are to be tested. If they could be tested mentally in your context, there would be no need for physical human existence.

Too many complicated issues are connected here, so that I must at best simplify. It is as if man said: "Now what about this idea? What can we do with it? What will happen if we toss it out into reality, physically? How far can we go with any of the great social, scientific, religious ideas that are so peculiarly the offshoots of man's mind?"

If such issues could all be mentally worked out on some nonphysical drawing board, again, the great challenge of physical existence would be neither necessary nor meaningful. How far, say, can nationalism be carried? To what extent can the world be treated as if it were external to man, as an object? What can man learn by treating the body as if it were a machine? As if it were a mirage? As if it were driven by blind instinct? As if it were possessed by a soul?

To some extent, these are all unique and creative ponderings that on the part of the animals alone would be considered the most curious and enlightening intellectual achievements. The animals must relate to the earth, and so must man. As the animal must play, mate, hunt his prey or eat his berries within the physical context of sun, ground, trees, snow, hail and wind, so in a different way man must pursue his ideas by clothing them in the elemental realities of earth, by perceiving them as events.

(10:01.) When he is destructive, man does not seek to be destructive per se; but in a desire to achieve that which he thinks of as a particular goal that to him is good, he forgets to examine the goodness of his methods.

One animal chasing and killing its prey serves the greater purpose of preserving the balance of nature, whether or not the animal is aware of this—and again, the animal's intent is not evil. Man consumes ideas. In so doing he contributes to a different kind of balance, of which he is usually unaware. But no man truly acts out of the pure intent to do wrong, or to be vicious. Storms rend the summer sky, sending forth thunder and lightning. Earthquakes may ravage the countryside. You may deeply regret the havoc worked, knowing that neither the storm nor the earthquake is evil. Not only did they have no wrong intent, but the overall condition corrected the earth's balance.

(In this session Jane's delivery was often faster and more intent than usual, with many loud intervals, a few of which are indicated. She could have delivered material at a much more rapid rate, I'd say, had I been able to keep up with her through my notetaking.)

This requires some unique understanding. I am aware of that—and yet the destructive storms worked by mankind ultimately cannot be said to be any more evil than the earthquake. While man's works may often certainly appear destructive, you must not blame man's <u>intent</u>, nor must you ever make the error of confusing man with his works. For many well-intentioned artists, with the best of intentions, produce at times shoddy works of art, all the more disappointing and deplorable to them because of the initial goodness of their intent.

Their lack of knowledge and techniques and methods then become quite plain. By concentrating too deeply upon the world of newspapers and the negative reports of man's actions, it is truly easy to lose sight of what I tell you *(louder)* <u>is each man's and each woman's basic good intent.</u>

That intent may be confused, poorly executed, tangled amid conflicts of beliefs, strangled by the bloody hands of murders and wars—and yet no man or woman ever loses it. That represents the hope of the species, and it has ever remained lit, like a bright light within each member of the species; and that good intent is handed down through the generations. It is far more potent, that illumination, than any hates or national grudges that may also be passed along.

<u>It is imperative, for any peace of mind, that you believe in that existence of man's innate good intent.</u>

It is shared by all of the other animals. Each animal knows that under certain conditions the other may fight or posture aggressively, or defend its nest. Each animal knows that in time of hunger it might be hunted by another. Except for those situations, however, the animals are not afraid of each other. They know that each other animal is of good intent.

(Louder:) <u>Grant your own species the same.</u>

(10:20.) Now: Make a distinction in your mind between man and man's works. Argue all you want against his works, as you read in your newspapers of errors, stupidities, treachery or war. Collect pages and reams of such material if it suits your fancy—and I am speaking not only to you, or to Ruburt, but to anyone who hopes to find a hint of truth, peace of mind, or creativity.

Collect books of man's failures. I do not personally know why anyone would collect the worst works of any artist, and get pleasure in ripping them apart. Man has produced some fine works: The high level of verbal communication, the multitudinous varieties of emotional interactions and of cultural exchange, the facility with exteriorization of ideas and concepts, the reaches of the imagination—all of these, and many others, are unique in the universe.

To identify man with his poorest works is to purposefully seek out the mars, the mistakes, of a fine artist, and then to condemn him. To do this is to condemn yourselves personally. If a scientist says consciousness is the result of chance, or Darwin's theories say that basically man is a triumphant son of murderers, many people object. If you say, however, that men are idiots, or that they are not worth the ground they walk upon, you are saying the same thing. For you must be concerned with this reality as you know it; in those terms, to condemn man is to condemn the species as you know it, and the practical terms of your world.

To say that people can escape to another probability is pragmatically a cop-out—this is apart from the reality of probabilities, for I am speaking from your emotional viewpoint.

Now: Physically your body has a stance in space and time. I will speak of primary and secondary experience. Let us call primary experience that which exists immediately in sense terms in your moment of time—the contact of body with environment. I am creating certain divisions here to make our discussion—or *(with a smile)* monologue—easier. Therefore, I will call secondary experience that information that comes to you through, say, reading, television, discussion with others, letters, and so forth.

The secondary kind of experience is largely symbolic. This should be clear. Reading about a war in the middle of a quiet sunny afternoon is not the same thing as being in the war, however vivid the description. Reading about the energy shortage is not the same as sitting in a cold house. Reading about the possible annihilation

of mankind through nuclear destruction or other stupidities, while
you are sitting calmly enough in your living room, is obviously far
divorced from the actuality described in an article.

At the levels with which we are concerned, the body must
primarily react to present, immediate, primary existence in space
and time. At other levels it is equipped to handle many kinds of
data, in that I have mentioned before the precognition of cells. But
the body depends on the conscious mind to give it a clear assess-
ment of precise conditions of the space and time it occupies. It
depends upon that knowledge.

Do you want a break?

(10:41. "No.")

If you are safely ensconced in a comfortable room, in no
present danger, your senses should accurately convey that information. Your conscious mind should assimilate it. It should be an
easy enough accomplishment to look around you and see that you
are in no danger.

Your conscious mind is meant to give your body an assess-
ment of what I will call cultural conditions, for there are sophis-
tications and specifications that in your terms consciousness alone
can assess. If, under conditions naturally safe in the terms of primary experience, you become overwhelmed by unsafe signals from
secondary experience—that is, from your reading or whatever—you
show a lack of discrimination. You are not able to differentiate
between the physically safe present situation, and the imagined,
which is perhaps unsafe, calling forth the alarms of danger.

The body mechanisms become highly disoriented. The
signals to the body are very contradictory, so that after a while, if
such conditions continue, you can no longer tell whether you are
in actual danger or imagined danger. Your mind then forces your
body to be in a state of constant alert—but more unfortunately,
you train yourself to ignore your direct, sensual feedback in the
present moment.

(Jane, as Seth, delivered all of this material most emphatically.)

Your body then might say you are safe, and your senses
show you that no danger is present—yet you have begun to rely so
upon secondary experience that you do not trust your creature
reactions.

Because of man's great gift of imagination, however, the
alarm signals not only invade a safe present moment, but go jangling
into the next one and the one following, and are endlessly

projected into the future. To whatever extent, and in whatever fashion, each individual is therefore robbed of his or her belief in the personal ability to act meaningfully or with purpose in the present.

The body cannot act tomorrow, today. Its sense data must be clear. This resulting feeling of powerlessness to act leads to a state of hopelessness of varying degrees—and that mood does not tie itself to specific details, but pervades emotional life if it is allowed to. To whatever degree, the condemning, critical material too often becomes self-prophesying—for those who put merit on it *(loudly)* allow it to cloud their reactions.

In your terms, while you live, and in the most pertinent terms of intimate sensation, your reality must be what you perceive in the framework of your time, and what you create within that framework as it is experienced. Therefore, I entreat you not to behave as if man will destroy himself in some future—not to behave as if man is an imbecile, doomed to extinction, a dim-witted, half-crazy animal with a brain gone amuck.

None of the prophesied destruction man so fears is a reality in your time; nor, for all of the critical prophets through the ages, and the forerunners of doom, has the creativity of man destroyed itself in those terms.

(Loudly:) There are those who make careers of condemning the faults and failings of others, or of the species itself, and because of that attitude man's great energy and good intent remain invisible. Man is in the process of becoming. His works are flawed—but they are the flawed apprentice works of a genius artist in the making, whose failures are indeed momentous and grotesque only in the light of his sensed genius, which ever leads him and directs him onward.

When you are considering the future in your terms, constructive achievements are as realistic as destructive ones. In those terms, each year of man's existence in fact justifies a more optimistic rather than pessimistic view. You cannot place man's good intent outside of the physical context, for outside of that context you do not have the creature that you know. You cannot say that nature is good, but spawned man, which is a cancer upon it, for nature would have better sense. You cannot say, either, that Nature—with a capital N—will destroy man if he offends her, or that Nature—with a capital N—has little use for its own species, but only wants to promote Life—with a capital L—for Nature is within each member of each species; and without each member of each species, Nature—with a capital or a small N—would be nonexistent.

(*Amused:*) I will let you rest your natural fingers.

(*11:09. My writing hand was tired—one of the few times this has happened in the sessions. Jane's pace had been much faster than usual, and often much louder than it usually is. I thought the material was excellent. Jane didn't really want to take a break. In fact, she was ready to resume in a few minutes, but I asked her to wait a bit until my hand rested somewhat. Resume in the same manner, then, at 11:14.*)

Because you are natural creatures, within you there is a natural state of being. That state can be an ever-present reservoir of peace, vitality, and understanding.

Whatever your scientists think, your body and your consciousness and your universe spring constantly into actualization. Therefore, through cultivating the clear experience of your own consciousness and being with time and with the moment as you feel it, you can draw upon the greater vitality and power that is available.

To do this, rely upon your immediate sense data, not secondary experience as described. That primary sense data, while pinpointed in the present, providing you with the necessary stance in time, still can open up to you the timelessness from which all time emerges, can bring you intuitive intimations, hinting at the true nature of the ever-present coming-to-be of the universe.

That kind of experience will let you glimpse the larger patterns of man's creativity, and your part in it. You have been taught to concentrate upon criticisms and faults in your society; and in your times it seems that everything will work out wrong— that left alone the world will run down, the universe will die, man will destroy himself; and these beliefs so infiltrate your behavior that they organize much of your experience and rob you of the benefits nature itself everywhere provides in direct primary experience.

Often then you ignore your senses' reality in the world—the luxurious vitality and comfort of the daily moment—by exaggerating the importance of secondary experience as defined for this discussion.

The most negative projection or prophecy seems to be the most practical one; when you are reading of the world's ills, you say in all honesty, and with no humor: "How can I ignore the reality, the destructive reality, of the present?" In the most practical, immediate, mundane terms, however, you and your world are in that moment naturally and physically safe, as your bodily senses immediately perceive. In the most basic of bodily terms you are <u>not</u> reacting to present conditions.

This would be only too clear if you <u>were</u> physically experiencing the conditions about which you <u>might</u> be reading. If the world <u>were</u> falling down about your shoulders, you would only too clearly understand that "earlier" you were reacting to an imagined and not a real situation.

I am afraid that I think some of this will still escape you—meaning Ruburt, yourself, and others. But while disasters, imagined or encountered second-handedly, may in fact later occur, they are far different from physically encountered ones. You only add to their unfortunate nature by negatively brooding upon what might happen in the future, and you destroy your own stance. Your stance in time is highly important, for it is your practical base of operations.

You must trust your sense data in that regard. Otherwise you confuse your psychological and corporal stance, for the body cannot be in a situation of safety and danger at the same time. It wastes its resources fighting imaginary battles.

(11:40.) To some people wars, poverty, murder, treachery, corruption, <u>are</u> primary experience, and must be dealt with—as requiring immediate action. The body must react. Such persons are beaten up, or robbed. Those are immediate sense data, and in one way or another they do react. However feebly, their point of power corresponds immediately with the point of danger.

You cannot react physically in the same way to projected or imagined dangers. There seems to be no possible reaction. You are frustrated. You are meant to deal with your immediate, primary experience, and in so doing you take care of your responsibility. You are able to take action in your own experience, and therefore affect others. You do not have to be ignorant of wars in other corners of the world, or close your eyes. But if you allow those experiences to overcloud your present, valid intersection with reality, then you speak and act from a position not your own, and deny the world whatever benefits your own present version of reality might allow you to give.

The natural creature-validity of your senses must remain clear, and only then can you take full advantage of those intuitions and visions that must come through your own private intersection with space and time.

In those terms, the ever-actual integrity of nature everywhere surrounds you. It represents your direct experience. It offers comfort, creativity, and inspiration that you only impede if you allow secondary experience to supersede your daily moment-to-moment encounter with the physical earth.

I am aware of your questions involving the sleeping and waking portions of life on the earth. I will answer you this evening or at our next session, as you prefer.

("Well, we might as well make it next time.")

We will begin with that, then. All of this material tonight applies to people in general, and to yourselves, and is also for Ruburt specifically.

(Pause at 11:47.) If you weren't tired, I would continue.

("Okay, you can go on for a little while if you want to."

(Now Seth came through with some personal material for Jane, then ended the session at 11:59 P.M. Jane was ready for still more work, and even thought of using our recorder. I told her I was willing to take more notes, also, but she finally decided against prolonging the session.)

SESSION 800, APRIL 4, 1977
9:43 P.M. MONDAY

(We waited over 20 minutes for the session to start. Several times Jane remarked: "The delay seems real odd. . . ." But Seth continued with his material on the behavior of our species, even while bringing Psyche *to a close.)*

Dictation. *(Long pause.)* You form your own reality. That reality contributes to the experience of others, but each of you possesses a unique, original stance in space and time that is yours alone in quite practical terms, regardless of time's relative existence.

Only when you operate from your own stance can you help others to the best of your ability. To anticipate danger, or to imaginatively take on the troubles of others robs you of the very energy with which you could help them. I am not saying, therefore, to turn your eyes from the unfortunate conditions of the world. Practical help is needed in all areas of the human life. Yet it is far better, and more practical ultimately, to concentrate upon the beneficial elements of civilization—far better to organize your thoughts in areas of accomplishment than to make mental lists of man's deficiencies and lacks.

Such a practice leads to feelings of helplessness and hope-lessness, in which effective action seems impossible. Life possesses an exuberance. If this is cherished, nurtured, encouraged, then additional energy is generated that is not needed for the purposes of daily private life—a superabundance, that can be effectively directed in those areas of the world where help is most needed.

The strength, vitality, and effectiveness of thought is seldom considered. Thought, you may say, will not stop a war—yet what do you think started such a war? Throughout history the down-trodden have often risen into power, using force, rebelling against their oppressors; and yet, learning little from that experience, they turn and become the new elite, the new power-holders. Their physical conditions may be completely changed. Now theirs, the offices of government, the wealth. Gone are the conditions that, it would seem, caused the uprising. Yet in retaliation they strike out, forming a new class of downtrodden who must in their turn rise and retaliate.

Despite all appearances, conditions of an exterior nature do not cause wars, or poverty, or disease, or any of the unfortunate circumstances apparent in the world. Your beliefs form your reality. Your thoughts generate practical experience. When these change, conditions will change. To add your own energy, focus, and concentration to dire circumstances in other portions of the world does not help, but adds to, such situations.

To close your eyes to them in an ignorant fashion, to wash your hands of them, so to speak, is equally shortsighted. To pretend such situations do not exist, out of fear of them, will only bring the feared reality closer. It is far better to situate yourself firmly in your own reality, acknowledge it as your own, encourage your strength and creativity, and from that vantage point view those areas of the world or of your own society that need constructive help. Purposefully in your own life, in your daily dialogues with others, in your relationships through your groups or clubs, rein-force as well as you can the strength and abilities of others.

That reinforcement will add to the personal power of all other individuals with whom those people come in contact. Find the beliefs responsible for the unfortunate conditions. If the ideas in this book were thoroughly understood, then each individual would be able to assess his or her own reality realistically. There would be no need to arm a nation in advance against another nation's anticipated—but imaginary—attack.

(10:10.) Personal grudges would not build up, so that men or

women so fear further hurts that they attempt to hide from life or relationships, or shy away from contact with others. It is not virtuous to count your failings. Self-conscious righteousness can be a very narrow road. If each of you understood and perceived the graceful integrity of your own individuality, just as you try to perceive the beauty of all other natural creatures, then you would allow your own creativity greater reign. There is order in <u>all</u> elements of nature, and you are a part of it.

The greater sweep of the seasons represents the reaches of your soul. You will not attain spirituality by turning your eyes away from nature, or by trying to disentangle yourself from it. You will not "glimpse eternal life" by attempting to deny the life that you have now—for that life is your own unique <u>path</u>, and provides its own clues for you to follow.

All That Is vibrates with desire. *(Louder:)* The denial of desire will bring you only listlessness. Those who deny desire are the most smitten by it. Each of your lives are miniature and yet gigantic episodes, mortal and immortal at once, providing experiences that you form meaningfully, opening up dimensions of reality available to no one else, for no one can view existence from your standpoint. No one can be <u>you</u> but <u>you</u>. There are communications at other levels, but your experience of existence is completely original, to be treasured.

No one from any psychological threshhold, however vast, can write a book that defines the psyche, but only present hints and clues, words and symbols. The words and ideas in this book all stand for other inner realities—that is, they are like piano keys striking other chords; chords that, hopefully, will be activated within the psyche of each reader.

Each of you is couched now in the natural world, and that world is couched in a reality from which nature emerges. The psyche's roots are secure, nourishing it like a tree from the ground of being. The source of the psyche's strength is within each individual, the invisible fabric of the person's existence.

(Long pause.) Nature is luxurious and abundant in its expressions. The greater reality from which nature springs is even more abundant, and within that multidimensional experience no individual is ignored, forgotten, dismissed, lost, or forsaken. A tree does not have to ask for nourishment from the ground or the sun, and so everything that you need is available to you in your practical experience. If you believe you are not worthy of nourishment, if you believe that life itself is dangerous, then your own beliefs make

it impossible for you to fully utilize that available help. In large measure, since you are still alive, you are of course nourished. You cannot close out the vitality of your own being that easily, and the vitality "squandered" on deeper bouts of depression is often greater than the energy used in creative pursuits. You are a portion of All That Is; therefore the universe leans in your direction. It gives. It rings with vitality. Then forsake beliefs that tell you otherwise. Seek within yourself—each of you—those feelings of exuberance that you have, even if they are only occasional, and encourage those events or thoughts that bring them about.

You cannot find your psyche by thinking of it as a separate thing, like a fine jewel in an eternal closet. You can only experience its strength and vitality by exploring the subjective reality that is your own, for it will lead you unerringly to that greater source of being that transcends both space and time.

End of session. End of book. (Pause.) For our next one will be a beauty.

("Will it?" I tried to egg Seth on a bit. The session hadn't been underway long before I'd realized he was bringing Psyche to a close. Even Jane's voice, speaking for him, had been somehow indicative of a summing-up.)

It will indeed.

(10:40.) Now, briefly: The overall stance of the species is largely maintained by the waking-sleeping patterns that you mentioned recently. In such a fashion, one large portion of the species focuses in physical reality while the other large portion holds a secure foothold in inner reality—

(Our cat, Willy Two—or Billy—had been sleeping beside me on the couch. Waking up now, he stretched, jumped down, then up into Jane's lap as she spoke for Seth. Billy sat facing her. I laid my notebook aside and picked him up. Seth spoke as I carried the cat to the cellar door.)

He is a sweet creature.

("Yes." As soon as I sat down again, Seth finished the sentence he'd begun before Billy's interruption:)

—working on the interior patterns that will form the next day's realities, and providing probable previews of future events. Waking and sleeping reality is therefore balanced in the world mind—not the world brain.

However, the sleeping portion of the species represents the brain's unconscious activities in the body—particularly when you think of the motion of all of the species' actions en masse in a given day. Those conscious motions have an unconscious basis. If you think of a mass world brain—one entity—then it must wake and sleep in patterns. If you think of mass daily action as performed by one gigantic being, then all of those conscious actions have unconscious counterparts, and a great intercommunication of an inner nervous system must take place.

Part of such a brain would have to be awake all of the time, and part engaged in unconscious activity. This is what happens.

Diverse cultures are thus able to communicate as the cultural knowledge of various parts of the world is given to the sleeping portion of the entire organism. When they sleep, the waking nations add the day's events to the world memory, and work out future probabilities.

I will give you more on this. I had forgotten it when I ended the session prematurely. Ruburt's hesitation was caused this evening by misplaced nostalgia at ending our book. You are both indeed beginning a new, more productive, surprisingly pleasant and somewhat extraordinary period of your lives. And now I bid you a fond good evening.

("Thank you very much, Seth. Good night."

(As can be seen by Seth's comments about the mass world mind-brain, he was all ready to launch into some new material. And though he mentioned a new book, Jane and I had no idea that he'd begin one within a few weeks' time—yet that's exactly what happened.

(Volume 1 of "Unknown" Reality came out in the fall of 1977— and by then Seth was well into his latest, The Individual and the Nature of Mass Events, even though this book, Psyche, hadn't yet been typed for publication. I was still working on the notes for Volume 2 of "Unknown" Reality.

(Jane's writing on William James also developed into a book: The Afterdeath Journal of an American Philosopher. So during Seth's dictation of this present manuscript, she produced on her own the Cézanne and James books. Surely all of the creativity cited in this note is the "proof of the pudding," then—evidence of the psyche's richness and abilities. Jane displays those attributes in her own way, of course, yet their equivalents are inherent in each of us, waiting to be used.)

Index

Index

221